The CHEFS compendium

Who is who among chefs working in Britain today

Edited by Roy Ackerman

ALFRESCO
LEISURE PUBLICATIONS PLC

Preface

Alfresco Leisure Publications PLC is proud to publish *The Chefs Compendium*. We aim to bring together in one volume the wealth of talent cooking in Britain today, telling you who is who in the industry.

The book provides a glimpse behind the swing doors, behind the tall toques and whites, and finds out what makes chefs want to become chefs – and then what keeps them in the kitchen!

Glossary of some terms used

The symbol ⬡ indicates that the chef is a member of the British Branch of the Académie Culinaire de France.

Antonin Carême created the kitchen system which is still in use today. He divided the kitchen into the sixteen stations which he considered necessary to run a large kitchen with a full brigade efficiently and to a high standard of excellence. They are as follows:

1 *Chef de cuisine and sous chef* Head chef and deputy	**9** *Grillardin* Grill cook
2 *Saucier* Sauce cook	**10** *Cocottier* Egg cook
3 *Poissonnier* Fish cook	**11** *Friturer* Fryer
4 *Potager or entremetier* Vegetable cook	**12** *Fournier* Oven cook
5 *Potage* Soup cook	**13** *Tourier* Dough and paste maker
6 *Rôtisseur* Roast cook	**14** *Confiseur* Confectioner
7 *Brocheur* Spit roaster	**15** *Glacier* Ice-cream cook
8 *Gardemanger* Larder cook	**16** *Pâtissier* Pastry cook

A *chef de partie* is a chef in charge of any of these sixteen stations; a *chef tournant* is a chef who 'floats' between stations; and a *commis chef* is a junior chef in any of the stations.

Introduction

by Roy Ackerman

The cooking in restaurants in Britain has been shaped largely by traditions established by the work of certain key professional chefs, whose commis and trainees have tempered the skills of their masters with inspired directions of their own. Likewise, a band of gifted amateurs in the '60s and '70s set out to establish their own identities in an industry ready for new inspiration and ideals.

Looking back in time we can see how the kitchens of Britain have progressed and developed since the days of Carême, Escoffier, Francatelli and Soyer, under the tutelage of the likes of Eugene Kaufeler of The Dorchester, Silvano Trompetto of The Savoy, and Louis Virot of the Savoy Grill – all grand hotels. They were followed by the new masters, amongst others Michel Bourdin of The Connaught, Anton Mosimann (first at The Dorchester, now of Mosimann's), Albert and Michel Roux, Richard Shepherd and Francis Coulson. In the last fifteen years or so, these chefs have made an enormous impact on the restaurant trade in Britain, as indeed have Nico Ladenis and Raymond Blanc (along with their disciples), and – originally in the gifted amateur category – Kenneth Bell, George Perry-Smith and Joyce Molyneux.

Young people who have worked with the master chefs and in some cases evolved skills which equal those of their teachers, include Pierre Koffmann, Paul Gayler, David Cavalier, Herbert Berger, Richard Sawyer, Michel Perraud, Rowley Leigh and Peter Chandler. And in turn many of these have sent out their own trainees, who are

4

working to establish a position in the industry and will doubtless continue to revolutionise the restaurant trade in the future. It is a constant process of evolution and progress.

One of the difficulties facing chefs of all ages today is the lack of time to learn the finer arts of cooking and presentation, and the lack of opportunity to study under a master chef. Certainly this was the case when I did my apprenticeship, yet a period of training under an established and successful chef is perhaps the best way to refine your knowledge and realise what talent you may have.

The Academy of Culinary Arts has been founded in Great Britain with the aim of improving professional cooking and raising the profile of the industry. The doors of the Academy will be open only to people currently employed within the industry and with a proven record, who wish to study under a recognised master at a higher level of expertise. The idea was conceived by the Académie Culinaire de France. The Académie's President, Michel Bourdin, has worked with a dedicated team to bring the project to fruition, and has been assisted in this by the National Advisory Catering Council, on which I am proud to sit.

The Master Classes to be given by members of the Académie Culinaire de France in no way replace or seek to undermine the valuable day-to-day training which an apprentice may receive from an individual chef at his place of work. Rather, they are designed to impart the finer arts of food production and presentation for which there may be little time in a working environment. It is, in a sense, a post-graduate college, which numbers among its tutors some of the most impressive talents working in the industry today.

Hopefully, many people working in the restaurant, catering and hotel industry will have the opportunity of attending the Academy of Culinary Arts and thereby helping with new-found knowledge and skills to improve further the style, perception and taste of Britain's food in the coming decade.

Competitions for young chefs
American Express are sponsors of Young Chef Young Waiter of the Year Competition with the Restaurateurs' Association of Great Britain, now in its eighth year, and this has produced a whole string of successful young chefs over the years and has helped highlight the industry. Likewise Diners Club has sponsored the Roux Brothers' scholarships for the seventh successive year and an equally impressive list of young people have been encouraged to enter. Among past winners of these competitions, now well known in their own right, are Chris Suter, David Cavalier, Roger Narbett and Idris Caldora.

Sadly, whilst every endeavour has been made to include in this book as many chefs as possible, the space available does not permit an exhaustive list. Also, some chefs were unfortunately too busy to assist with our research. Hopefully, each edition of *The Chefs Compendium* will be longer than the last, thereby reflecting the continuing improvement of interest in good food in Great Britain.

David *Adlard*

Michael *Aldridge*

David Adlard is one of British cooking's late developers. Armed with a degree in Chemistry, he worked in industry for ten years before deciding it wasn't really for him and enrolling on a TOPS course in catering at Kilburn Polytechnic. Even after the course, David still had only the haziest notion of what he wanted to do, and drifted through a number of indifferent establishments before joining Michel Bourdin's kitchens at The Connaught, a turning point in his career. Not only did David enjoy the classical discipline of Bourdin's cuisine, but grew in confidence as Bourdin sensed the potential in his new recruit.

Continuing *wanderlust* took him to Le Talbooth in Essex, and stints in France and the USA, where he met his wife, Mary. Together they returned to England and set about looking for their own restaurant. An old butcher's shop was eventually found in Wymondham, not far from David's native Norwich. Here, with Connaught-instilled precision, he offered a short, three-choice per course menu adapting classical techniques to strictly seasonal and, where possible, local produce.

Early in 1989, the couple traded the rustic simplicity of Wymondham for the soft, green padded walls of Upper St Giles Street in Norwich. Here, the tenets are unchanged: overall simplicity, good ingredients and strong tastes, with an emphasis on meticulously prepared stocks as the base for the sauces.

DAVID ADLARD
Adlard's
79 Upper St Giles Street
Norwich
Norfolk
(0603) 633522

Michael Aldridge was born in South Africa of British parents. His family frequently entertained, both for business and pleasure. Michael's nanny was also the cook, and often she would allow him an opportunity to stir the pot – which must, as he says, have stirred his mind! In addition, his grandmother and mother were both excellent cooks. As if by magic his mother could make a meal from practically nothing. However, she hated making pastry which, fortunately, Michael enjoyed doing. The decisive moment was when at the age of thirteen he modelled the coat-of-arms of the local church in sugar.

He went to school in South Africa and England, and in 1973 took a three-year course at Westminster College, gaining his Diploma with Distinction. He began his career as a commis at The Connaught, where Michel Bourdin was already chef de cuisine. Leaving The Connaught in 1979, he

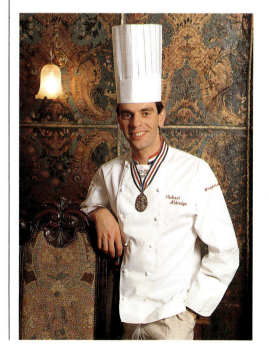

worked as a commis in both the kitchens and the pâtisserie of Roger Vergé at Le Moulin des Mougins in the South of France. Michael returned to South Africa in 1980 and spent a year as sous chef at the Royal Hotel in Durban. Then from 1981 to 1983 he became assistant manager to the Director of the Ranch Hotel in Pietersburg; returning in 1984, to the Royal as both sous chef and hotel training manager. He worked briefly at the Cape Sun in Cape Town, before returning to London in 1986 and The Connaught, this time to become premier sous chef to Michel Bourdin, supervising a brigade of around fifty.

Michael holds a number of distinctions in cookery, but his most significant achievement is the Académie Culinaire's Meilleur Ouvrier de Grande Bretagne. On receiving this award he said, 'It was an accolade I never expected. . .and I am proud to have been given the chance to enter, and to have been awarded this title. It represents my professionalism and it is recognised by my colleagues, so I must carry this title by example every day – for as long as I am a member of my profession.'

Although Michael's style is traditionally classical, he has a catholic taste in the food he chooses to eat, and believes there is always something to learn from other people's cooking. He enjoys the simplicity of true brasserie food.

MICHAEL ALDRIDGE
The Connaught Hotel
Carlos Place
London W1Y 6AL
01-499 7070

Thomas *Alf*

Thomas Alf undertook a traditional apprenticeship in his native West Germany in a small, family-run hotel, moving on from trainee to commis only being interrupted by military service. On his 'release', he took seasonal jobs around Bavaria and the Black Forest, as chef de partie and as sous chef, before leaving for the Far East.

During this time he exercised his belief – the main reason for his entering the restaurant business in the first place – that he would always be able to find work anywhere in the world, and put into practice the peripatetic existence that had always appealed to him. He revelled in new experi-

ences and widely varying styles of cooking, and made good use of them when, in 1984, he came to England and joined Leith's restaurant as sous chef, before being promoted to head chef in 1986.

Here, he has adapted his traditional ideas to be more in tune with new wave thoughts, and describes his style as modern eclectic with a traditional background. He enjoys using the best possible raw ingredients to produce food that is pleasing both to the eye and to the palate.

Perhaps not surprisingly – given the extent of his travels – his favourite food when eating out is Indian or Chinese – or steak and chips!

THOMAS ALF
Leith's Restaurant
92 Kensington Park Road
London W11 2PN
01-229 4481

Betty *Allen*

Betty Allen has won herself a place in Scottish cooking history over her ten years at the Airds Hotel. Having had no formal training, but enjoying cooking and having a husband who enjoyed eating, it seemed a natural extension for the Allen family to move to The Airds.

One of Betty's first principles is to start off with good quality ingredients. She uses herbs to simple effect and berries such as rowan for jelly with venison, or crab apples. Like others on this coast of Scotland, Betty has quietly improved the quality of supplies over the years, by painstakingly educating the people who grow, farm or deliver the vegetables, game and fish.

Whilst cooking with a homely approach, the many influences that Betty draws on come from the Allens' travels through most of the rated restaurants in France. Her philosophy is simple; and her daily four-course menu is honest in its presentation and quality, aiming to show off the produce at its best.

BETTY ALLEN
The Airds Hotel
Port Appin
Argyll PA38 4DF
(063 173) 236

Chris *Amor*

Chris Amor is a young man who developed a passionate love of food at an early age. As a lad, he spent more time in the vegetable garden and the kitchen than out on the football field, and deciding that cooking was definitely what he wanted to do, he chose the appropriate courses at Cheltenham Catering College. After college Chris spent three years with the Hilton group of hotels before moving to The Close at Tetbury in 1984, where he became head chef in 1986.

By virtue of his training, Chris's style was originally classical French, but as he progressed and was able to experiment more and more for himself, his style de-

veloped. Using a few fresh ingredients for each dish he could let the ingredients do their work and note how certain flavours and textures combined naturally in a pleasing way. This produced all kinds of delightful and unusual results, such as lamb with lavender. In his opinion, there is no need to be exotic, with such good produce available within our own shores.

For relaxation Chris enjoys very good Chinese restaurants, as they too create wonderful tastes from simple yet subtle ingredients, but enjoys any food, cooked well and served in a pleasant environment, from three-star haute cuisine to a top-class steak and kidney pie at the pub.

CHRIS AMOR
The Close Hotel
Tetbury
Gloucestershire GL8 8AQ
(0666) 52272

Susan Andrews

Susan Andrews was inspired to cook after watching *The Duchess of Duke Street* on television, so she took the appropriate City & Guilds and OND courses. She worked her way up through the brigades at the Bracken Hill Restaurant, Greenriggs Country House, Rothley Court, Mallory Court, and The Starr at Great Dunmow, before taking up her present position at Stapleford Park.

But being a girl she found it difficult to progress to chef saucier, her initial ambition. So to gain experience she started entering competitions, regularly doing well in the Michel & Albert Roux/Diners Club Scholarship and the RAGB Young Chef of the Year competition. She came second in the National Finals in 1987 and reached the semi-finals of the British Chef of the Year competition in the same year. Her advice to young female chefs is to persevere against the odds, and while acknowledging that she has received a lot of publicity as the only girl in competition finals, reckons that this can only benefit the cause in the long run.

Susan describes her cooking as English Country House style, currently with an American influence, and still finds her greatest challenges to be the sauces. Her most enjoyable meals to date have been at the Waterside Inn and Hambleton Hall.

SUSAN ANDREWS
Stapleford Park
Melton Mowbray
Leicestershire LE14 2EF
(57 284) 522

ROBERT AITKEN
Meldrum House
Old Meldrum
Aberdeen
Grampian AB5 0AE
(065 12) 2294

RICHARD ALDRIDGE
Pollyanna's Restaurant
2 Battersea Rise
London SW11 1ED
01-228 0316

JOHN AMALDI
Peter's Restaurant
65 Fairfax Road
London NW6 4EE
01-624 5804

LUCIANO AMATO
Ziani
45/47 Radnor Walk
London SW3 4BT
01-352 2698

KENNETH AMBLER
Mortimer's on the Quay
Wherry Quay
Ipswich
Suffolk IP4 1AS
(0473) 230225

ERIC ARMITAGE
L'Artiste Assoiffé
122 Kensington Park Road
London W11 2EP
01-727 4714

9

Myrtle Allen

Maybe it's all down to there being fewer hotels or maybe it's due to greater pride in those they've got, but roadside hotel signs in Ireland start a good few miles before you reach the driveway, let alone the house itself. It's at the small town of Middleton in East Cork that you'll first see one directing you to Ballymaloe House. Wind southwards through some rich farmland, on through the village of Cloyne and then, suddenly, at a small crossroads, you'll find the main gate. Drive through it and you'll eventually find yourself outside the front porch of Ballymaloe, a rambling half-Jacobean, half-Georgian building, draped languidly in lush wisteria. To the right, a cluster of outbuildings are washed a vivid Mediterranean pink. And, to the left, there's a swimming pool from where, in high season, come the yelps and shrieks of children of all ages.

Ballymaloe House is first and foremost the home of Ivan and Myrtle Allen. They set up house here well over forty years ago when Ivan – a horticultural farmer by trade – bought the house and the 400 acres that went with it. Raising their six children here, Myrtle was in effect an early practitioner of real food, buying fresh ingredients and dreaming up inventive ways of using up some of the things grown on the farm. Indeed, one of her daughters claims that it was only when she finally left home that she first tasted commercially sliced bread.

The evolution of the house into one of Ireland's foremost hotels and restaurants has been a long one, and is closely tied to Myrtle's own development. Apart from attending a local technical school as a young girl she is virtually self-taught. She's always devoured cookery books, turning in the early years to Philip Harben's *Way to Cook* and also to Constance Spry, whom she loved for her section on puddings and ice-creams. In the post-war period, she was aware of Elizabeth David but never really latched on until later, as much of the Mediterranean produce failed to materialise in East Cork.

Apart from looking after her growing family and giving friends dinner, her first move was a column in the Irish *Farmer's Journal*. Myrtle had sent in a letter regarding an article and was subsequently offered a column on, of all things, art and architecture. With typical modesty, she turned it down, feeling ill-qualified, but did suggest doing cookery from the viewpoint of a farmer's wife.

Finally, in 1964, Myrtle opened her restaurant in Ballymaloe House and called it the Yeats Room. With her children growing up and moving away, she had time on her hands and could put the big house to good use. Also, there was a complete dearth of country house establishments at a time when Robert Carrier was boldly extolling the virtues of such enterprises in France via the *Sunday Times*. So the time seemed right. Myrtle recalls that the deciding factor was that they had a tenant with more-than-suspected criminal leanings under the same roof, and this appeared to be a good way of getting rid of him! Business was terribly quiet to begin with; and publicity was limited to an 'ad' in the local paper and a notice on the gate.

With her ever-expanding library of cookery books, Myrtle's philosophy has always been that dining in a country house deserves sound country-house cooking. To do justice to the produce, not to destroy its properties, flavours and textures, remains of paramount importance. Simultaneously, a desire to re-establish and re-interpret her own native Irish cooking has expressed itself throughout her professional life, for instance her modern versions of cabbage and bacon! Myrtle was also a prime mover behind the Association of Irish Farmhouse Cheesemakers and was greatly impressed by Veronica Steele and her Milleens cheese, which soon became a staple commodity at Ballymaloe. Likewise, much of the fish used is landed just a few miles away at Ballycotton.

This pride in local goods coupled with a rare honesty and intelligence, also extends to the hotel side of things. Myrtle quickly realised that the introduction of accommodation would be a natural progression. In the same way that the pottery for the restaurant is of a speckled, low-key earthy pattern made in the village by friends of the family, so too were the furnishings an attempt to reflect an Irish tradition. The stair carpet has an early Gaelic motif hand-woven through it, and there are local watercolours, and wild flowers dotted around the public rooms. They steer well clear of today's current crop of interior design infatuations. There is even a Dame Laura Knight painting hung with understated elegance over the mantle in the drawing room.

Myrtle has always adopted a very egalitarian approach, treating staff and family alike, avoiding hierarchies. The house is no hushed shrine to gastronomy but a living, thriving, healthy family enterprise where you're just as likely to be served at table by one of Myrtle and Ivan's grandchildren as by anyone else. Perhaps the Quaker tradition of the family keeps drawing the young ones back. Single diners are often invited to join the family at their table – it's that sort of place.

Gentle-mannered Ivan and son-in-law Jim run Ballymaloe's own wine-importing business while daughter-in-law Darina takes care of the Ballymaloe Cookery School, passing on many of Myrtle's tenaciously-held principles. Salmon is poached in a minimum of salted water with no hint of wine or bouillon; vegetables are never blanched and lobsters are never split open from the back but always from the front – a technique Myrtle taught herself early on and from which she has never deviated.

All this industry and generosity somehow takes place in an environment so unselfishly civilised that it is easy to see why people get so hooked on it. Myrtle who for years always said her roots were firmly embedded in the Irish Country House tradition, recently took on a young French chef in the kitchen and was amazed at the intuitive way he worked, sensing great parallels with her own approach. 'It was so perfect for me,' she remarked. 'He completely understood. Perhaps my own principles are, after all, based on French cuisine more than I ever dared, or cared, to admit.'

Myrtle Allen
Ballymaloe House
Shanagarry
Co Cork
Republic of Ireland
010-353-21 652531

11

Jacques Astic

Jacques Astic is a quiet, self-effacing man, who went into the restaurant business because of family connections in his birthplace, Lyon. He liked the way of life, and simply could not contemplate any other possible career. So he went to hotel school for three years in Thonon-les-Bains, getting what he describes as a proper training, and fitted in his first job as commis for a year before national service.

Upon its completion he spent a year as chef saucier, still in France, before coming to England in 1966, working in various good restaurants, and settling at The Old Woolhouse in Northleach, to the delight of those in the 'know'.

Jacques says he learned cooking the right and proper way from good old-fashioned chefs in France, and, despite all new concepts and fashions, he feels he has not changed. He shuns media attention himself, and does not seem to have suffered for it one iota. All he asks is 'to be left alone to do his job as well as he can'.

Customers flock to his door, and as far as he is concerned, knowing that his customers are happy is all Jacques needs – no fuss, no false compliments. But it is no false compliment to say that he is a very good chef indeed.

Jacques Astic
The Old Woolhouse
The Square
Northleach
Gloucestershire GL54 3EE
(0451) 60366

Ernst Bachmann was born in Zürich. He recalls cooking at home as a boy of twelve, but became apprenticed to a family friend's Confiserie-Café only when he couldn't make up his mind which path of academic study to follow. His training was based on the most modern style of confiserie-pâtisserie-glacerie at the time: the best ingredients starkly presented using clean, simple lines. Although he hated the first year, he seemed more capable and artistic than his colleagues, which encouraged him to keep going, and he eventually became chief confectioner.

After his military service, Ernst came to England in 1982 to work for John Huber at Lyons Corner House, and then in the spring of 1963 he joined the London Hilton exclusively to make chocolates and petits fours for its opening. In the winter of the same year, he left for twelve months' work on a luxury Caribbean cruise liner sailing from New York. Thereafter followed a number of contracts, still as chief confectioner, for the openings of the Casino and the Sheraton Hotel in Malta; the Five Bridges in Gateshead; and the Planter's Grove Restaurant in Syon Park. Subsequently, in the winter of 1968, Ernst accepted a lecturing post at the Polytechnic of Malta and then at the Pembrokeshire Technical College, returning to the kitchen in 1971 to join Eugene Kaufeler at London's Dorchester Hotel as chef pâtissier. This was followed by a spell as chief confectioner at the Swiss Centre in Leicester Square from 1974 to 1981. He then moved to the Inter-Continental Hotel, where he has been ever since, as executive chef pâtissier working with Peter Kromberg.

In a typical day at the Inter-Continental Ernst might oversee the production of 600 plated desserts and 2,000 petits fours for a banquet of 600, plus 400-500 portions of sweets for the Coffee Shop, and a further 100 for Le Soufflé restaurant. Then there are the afternoon teas, as well as the takeaway shop within the Coffee Shop, where gâteaux and petits fours are on sale. Taken over a year, the daily average number of covers is an astonishing 1,500!

Ernst loves surprising his customers, but he is only happy if *they* are happy. He enjoys cooking for his family at home – so that keeps the costs down! When he does venture out he will choose a restaurant where the food is cooked and presented with love and care.

ERNST BACHMANN
Inter-Continental Hotel
1 Hamilton Place
Hyde Park Corner
London W1V 0QY
01-409 3131

'I love everything to do with cooking, and enjoy preparing all food from canapés through to petits fours!' So said René Bajard when we asked him why he went into the restaurant business, and this enthusiasm shines through in everything he does.

His training took him to Switzerland, Germany and then London, where he spent an initial two months with the Roux brothers. He ended up staying at Le Gavroche for ten years, during the time when the restaurant really came into its own.

However, René's dream led him on, and in 1985 he opened Le Mazarin in Pimlico; it was an opportunity to put his own individual version of the Rouxs' original theories into practice. His cooking has been described as 'precise', and it is certainly in the modern French style. His basic evening menu is called Le Chef Propose, and for the more adventurous, he also offers a Menu Gastronomique.

When not in his own kitchen, he enjoys eating good wine bar food, which he thinks can often be better than restaurant food. When at home in Wimbledon, he can sometimes also be found in his favourite local Chinese restaurant.

RENÉ BAJARD
Le Mazarin
30 Winchester Street
London SW1V 4NE
01-828 3366

Brian *Baker*

Jean *Bellavita*

Hambleton Hall, situated by Rutland Water, though almost in the heart of England itself, has become the epitome of the English country weekend for many Londoners, and its international reputation guarantees a liberal sprinkling of overseas visitors. It is civilised, charming, elegant and yet keeps a foot firmly in the English country scene. In the beginning, as Tim and Stefa Hart created Hambleton Hall, much of its reputation was built upon the culinary talents of Nicholas Gill, and a Michelin star is among the many accolades.

Brian Baker, Nicholas's successor, is probably the least known Michelin-starred chef in Britain, and it is to his credit that a change of chef at the Hall did not result in the loss of that star. Quietly, almost anonymously, he maintained the standards he inherited, but has now put his own imprint firmly upon the menu. Tim Hart may have strong opinions about food, but Brian is certainly master in the kitchen.

Unusually among chefs today, Brian is a local boy. Born at Uppingham, he came straight from school to the Hall where he trained under Nicholas Gill. He does not see his lack of college training as a drawback, having been lucky enough to work from the beginning under a single-minded chef and with an owner who keeps a keen eye on quality. He describes his technique as the simple treatment of the finest and freshest ingredients on the market, and sees himself

as a chef working within modern English and French styles while correctly pointing out that any true chef will create his own style as he develops.

Residents eat side-by-side with locals whose need for variety he fulfils with imagination, creativity, technique, quality and, as he himself says, with great enjoyment. Typically, a menu will include local game, perhaps simply treated but with a perfectly reduced sauce; the freshest fish, treated in a multitude of skilled, interesting ways; and dishes that echo our English heritage, like kedgeree. Equally, you will find that he offers vegetarians an array of provençale style vegetables treated with thick, luscious green olive oil that would be an outstanding dish in the heat and dust of south east France, but somehow seems equally in tune with the dark of a winter's day in Rutland.

BRIAN BAKER
Hambleton Hall
Hambleton
Oakham
Rutland
Leicestershire LE15 8TH
(0572) 756991

Jean Bellavita was born in Saint Raphael, France. At an early age his godfather, who was a chef, introduced him to Monsieur Lagente, chef des cuisines at the Hotel Beau Séjour in Saint Raphael. It was here, in 1939, that Jean started his apprenticeship, in the days when the apprentice was the servant of the chef de partie. His training was firmly rooted in the cuisine classique.

From 1945 until 1947 Jean served with the French Army, and then in 1952 he became chef at the Maison Bourgeoise in Paris. In 1955, out of curiosity and to learn the language, he came to England as chef tournant at The Savoy, at the time when everybody worked at The Savoy for the prestige, not for the cash!

Jean moved to the Waldorf in 1959 as sous chef, and in 1960 to the Café Royal as chef de cuisine, where he remained until 1965 when he started the catering at the Royal Festival Hall. In 1966 he joined Rank as executive chef at the Royal Lancaster, which officially opened in 1967. In 1968 he opened the Kennedy Hotel in Euston for Grand Metropolitan, and then moved to Nairobi where he became executive chef for Nairobi Airport Catering for a short time. He returned to London to take over the kitchens at the Talk of the Town, where he stayed from 1969 to 1982.

Since 1982 he has been senior executive chef for Trusthouse Forte, working in the Chef Development section (which includes the deployment of young chefs to Bocuse, Vergé, Guérard and Lenôtre).

Jean holds the Cordon Culinaire, and is a Chevalier de l'Ordre du Mérite Agricole.

JEAN BELLAVITA
Trusthouse Forte Group Catering Development
166 High Holborn
London WC1
01-836 9993

Herbert *Berger*

Herbert Berger was born in Gmunden, Austria, and began his career with a three-year apprenticeship at the Grand Hotel at Zell-am-See, which included three study courses at Salzburg's Catering College each lasting eight weeks. Between 1971 and 1977 he worked in Europe before becoming head chef at the Connoisseur in Golder's Green, during which time he and the restaurant were awarded a Michelin star. He left in 1979 to join Keats as head chef for a year before moving to The Connaught Hotel in 1980, working his way up through Michel Bourdin's brigade as chef saucier, garde-manger, poissonnier, and finally sous chef.

Later Herbert transferred to Claridge's as premier sous chef, leaving after a year to become, in 1986, head chef at one of London's oldest restaurants, the Mirabelle in Curzon Street, Mayfair. The Mirabelle was sold in 1988, and Herbert joined forces with Richard Sawyer, a friend since his Connaught days, to return to Keats as chef/partner in 1989.

HERBERT BERGER
Keats Restaurant
3A Downshire Hill
London NW3 1NR
01-435 3544

SANTOSH BAKSHI
Eatons Restaurant
49 Elizabeth Street London SW1W 9PP
01-730 0074

NEIL A BANNISTER
Tullich Lodge
Ballater Aberdeenshire AB3 5SB
(033 97) 55406

ANDREW BARRASS
The Swan
High Street
Lavenham
Sudbury Suffolk CO10 9QA
(0787) 247477

AMANDO BARRIO
Nineteen Restaurant
19 Mossop Street London SW3 2LY
01-589 4971

CHARLES BARTLETT
Seaview Hotel
High Street
Seaview Isle of Wight PO34 5EX
(0983) 612711

STEWART BASSETT
The Old Rectory
Campsea Ashe
Woodbridge Suffolk IP13 0PU
(0728) 746524

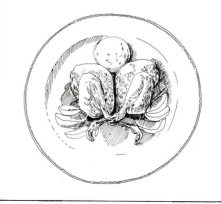

Guiseppe Bertoli

Galton Blackinston

Guiseppe Bertoli trained for four years in his native Italy, seven in Switzerland, one in Holland, and for six months in Germany before coming to England in 1962. He worked in several places for the next five years, until finally, in 1967, he found what he was looking for. It was a small, 17th-century cottage in the pretty Sussex village of Herstmonceux, and with his wife and just a couple of helpers, he turned the cottage into the Sundial Restaurant.

In those early days, Guiseppe's style was really classic French cooking, but over the years it has become more inventive, and he is constantly improving and studying new dishes. He uses local, seasonal ingredients whenever possible and combines them with great enthusiasm. Guiseppe's greatest satisfaction comes from his customers leaving his restaurant, happily replete, and saying, 'Thank you, I had a nice meal.'

With its pretty dining room, terrace, gardens, and views over the surrounding countryside, The Sundial is a very popular spot. Guiseppe's wife, Laurette, is an indispensible part of the restaurant's success, for it is she who runs the front of house with her own style and flair.

Guiseppe doesn't go out very often because his job is so time consuming, but when he does, he likes simple food, plainly cooked, and claims to be easily satisfied – not so in his own kitchen, however, where his success is due to a painstaking insistence upon the very highest standards.

GUISEPPE BERTOLI
The Sundial Restaurant
Gardner Street
Herstmonceux
East Sussex BN27 4lA
(0323) 832217

Galton Blackinston obtained a post at Miller Howe as a trainee, straight from school. Even before then, though, he had been making cakes for a market stall in his spare time, for he never wanted to do anything else but cook. He worked his way up through the brigade, and was made head chef in 1988.

Galton has now developed his style of country house cooking in the Miller Howe tradition into a fine art. But he's still learning as he goes. Each winter, when the hotel is closed, the brigade tours the world in search of new ideas. He loves eating in the top restaurants of Europe and he checks out the local competition in the Lake District during the summer. He enjoys eating any food that is fresh, well cooked and well presented. After all, this is the standard he applies to his own work at Miller Howe, as would be expected of a disciple of John Tovey.

GALTON BLACKINSTON
Miller Howe
Rayrigg Road
Windermere
Cumbria LA23 1EY
(096 62) 2536

Nicholas Blacklock

Nicholas Blacklock says that it was a distinct lack of foresight that allowed him to go into the restaurant business, and with a BSc degree in Physiology and Psychology, perhaps he should have known better! From 'basic' French beginnings he now cooks 'real' French food, and enjoys seeing a creation through from original concept to eventual fruition. He tries to produce balanced food, and flavour is much more important to him than presentation. He likes eating family food in France, or ethnic food, or anything that is different to that what he himself cooks, which is basically bistro-style French – from a different region each month.

NICHOLAS BLACKLOCK
La Bastide
20 Greek Street
London W1V 5LQ
01-734 3300

Anthony Blake

Anthony Blake's family has always been involved in the food industry and he's been cooking since his schooldays, but his main culinary training was with British Transport Hotels. From under their umbrella, he moved to The Elms at Abberley, Billesley Manor, The Castle Hotel at Taunton, and then to Eastwell Manor in Kent as Head Chef. He took up his current post as head chef at Lucknam Park, Colerne, when it opened in May 1988. He works alongside his brigade all the time – he's happiest when at his stove – and turns out his own version of modern English cooking, a distillation of all his experiences to date.

ANTHONY BLAKE
Lucknam Park
Colerne
Wiltshire SN14 8AZ
(0225) 742777

Steven Blake

Steven Blake started his apprenticeship with Trusthouse Forte, at the Hotel Russell then at Grosvenor House. He moved to The Piccadilly Hotel when it was bought and refurbished by Gleneagles. It was here that he met Louis Outhier and Michel Lorrain. Together with Anton Edelmann of The Savoy, they were his inspiration, and helped him to develop the style he now practises as head chef at Le Talbooth, in Essex. I use the word 'style' with reservation because Steven believes that food should not be put into categories, and that any dish, done well, is good.

STEVEN BLAKE
Le Talbooth
Gun Hill
Dedham
Colchester
Essex CO7 6HP
(0206) 322367

NEIL BATES
The New Mill Restaurant
New Mill Road
Eversley
Hampshire RG27 ORA
(0734) 732277

GRAHAM BEAUCHAMP
Rules Restaurant
35 Maiden Lane
London WC2E 7LB
01-836 5314

JOHN BEAUMONT
The Left Bank
88 Ifield Road
London SW10 9AD
01-352 0970

HELEN BENSON
Le Rustique
283 Putney Bridge Road
London SW15 2PT
01-788 0223

JOHN BERTRAM
Scott's Restaurant
20 Mount Street
London W1Y 5RB
01-629 5248

SUE BLOCKLEY
Tiroran House
Isle of Mull
Argyll PA69 6ES
(068 15) 232

17

Raymond Blanc

Raymond Blanc is earning a reputation of being one the finest chefs in Europe. He is driven by a burning desire to understand every aspect of the whole operation, and produces dishes of brilliance and artistic integrity. It is his combination of colours, flavours, and textures that sets him apart.

Coming to England from France to work in restaurants, he soon chose the kitchen as his domain. His first restaurant in Oxford, where he created culinary master-

pieces in a street full of launderettes and TV rental shops, revealed a major talent. Food lovers from all over Britain came to eat dazzling dishes in surroundings that typically made the best use of available space and materials. His next move was to Le Manoir aux Quat 'Saisons in a picturesque village just outside Oxford.

Le Manoir is a beautiful house set in its own grounds. Its proximity to London ensures a sophisticated audience for Raymond's talents.

The gardens of Le Manoir further enunciate the intellect and characteristic individualism of Blanc. He needs to understand the irrigation, the soil types, the weather conditions that will suit what he wants to grow. Different strains of vegetables and herbs appear in defiance of con-

ventional British farming wisdom, their cropping seasons cleverly extended by careful choice of species and staggered planting. Most are grown without resorting to artificial fertilisers. Blanc will have the best. He will grow it. He will employ experts to help him, but he himself must understand the whole process from seed to table. Each dish will contain elements from the kitchen garden which, in early 1990 will expand to produce all Raymond's needs and also possibly supply some other of the country's leading chefs. Blanc can see that food may be understood on many levels. He is intent on mastering them all. The idyllic manor house with its flourishing gardens combines art, science, and the fruits of research in perfect measure.

His other raw materials are also subjected to careful scrutiny. Pigeons, suckling pig, beef, lamb – the best that money can buy. No part of the jigsaw can be less than perfect. Fish are fresh to the touch and to the eyes. Raymond has long operated his own bakery. Bread, brioches, viennoiserie, pâtisserie – all are as fine as the best that France has. Again, traditional excuses for producing anything but the best are scrutinised by Blanc himself. Difficulties with flour, water, cooking equipment – all are overcome, the results speaking for themselves. The oils, spices and elements of liaison, essential to his creations, are superbly chosen. And the small fruits from the garden are transformed with a delicacy and invention that defies limitation.

Early 1990 sees Blanc creating a new 'cuisine'. It will be double the size. Working conditions will be ideal. Already you see Blanc in the vanguard of the action, once again leaving tracks for others to follow. His brigade is loyal; they sense his presence, his need for perfection, his drive and enthusiasm. Each is aware of his part to play in creating the final dish. Blanc works patient-ly with them, eating with them and always pushing them, inspiring them and trading his knowledge by example. He is always encouraging his largely English team to try other food, to eat out, to enter competitions and consequently to deepen their understanding of the world in which they work. Chefs from Le Manoir turn up in cookery competitions all over Europe – and with great success. Blanc combines the Frenchness of his cooking with the Englishness of his home and his garden. He is still a Frenchman but fiercely loyal to England, his adopted home. He takes a zealot's pride in dealing with 'the French' whose dismissal of all English cooking he continues to dispute.

The dishes Blanc produces reflect his genius, his complexity and of course his sheer good taste. The process is one of refinement, nothing is allowed to muddle or confuse the diner. Everything is intensely flavoured, but somehow tastes more of itself than the ingredient in the raw. A 'charlotte de légumes aux saveurs de provence et mignons d'agneau au romarin, vinaigrette aux herbes' translates as charlotte of provençale vegetables and rosemary-scented lamb served with a herb vinaigrette. But this is only half the story. The whole dish is evocative of Provence, the sun, the perfume, the oils, no matter how cloudy Oxfordshire is. Equally a terrine de bouillabaisse à la vinaigrette de safran conjures up the same region in a totally different way.

Raymond Blanc is a Frenchman abroad making superlative use of experience and available produce.

RAYMOND BLANC
Le Manoir aux Quat'Saisons
Church Road
Great Milton
Oxfordshire OX9 7PD
(0844) 278881

 Jeffrey Bland  Sonia Blech

Jeff Bland comes from Bradford, and cooking was quite an important part of life at home. At the age of fifteen his school's careers officer got him an interview at the Margaret McMillan College, and he began his apprenticeship there. From then on, his training has been practical, with long stints at the Gleneagles and other British Transport Hotels. Jeff's first job as head chef was at the Round Hill Hotel at Montego Bay in Jamaica. After that came stints at the Hilton, then a post as head chef at the BTH Station Hotel in Inverness. In 1982 he took over at the Gosforth Park Hotel in Newcastle, then in 1987 became executive chef at the Caledonian Hotel in Edinburgh.

Jeff is a good organiser and runs a happy brigade. He is as concerned about the training of his staff as he is about the food he produces. The small-style banquets he puts on allow for the vegetables to be cooked at the last moment, which is important to him. Equally so is his preference for his customers not to have to do battle with their food, so everything is served withou. bone, sinew or shell: everything on the plate can be eaten.

Jeff will buy ingredients from various sources, provided they are of the best quality. His own eating revolves around his family, and also his interest in seeing what other chefs are doing.

Jeff Bland
The Caledonian Hotel
Princes Street
Edinburgh
Lothian EH1 2AB
031-225 2433

Having originally chosen a career in linguistics, Sonia Blech came to the world of cookery by accident, fed up with the academic and business worlds. She spent five years or so in South Wales, first as a restaurateur, then becoming chef/patronne when she reckoned that she could do better than the present cook. In doing so, she gained much acclaim, and she and her husband Neville decided to open Mijanou in London. Here she has been able to transform her original style, which she describes as Escoffier-influenced, into one that is much admired and has made her one of London's top lady chefs.

Sonia's philosophy is very simple: she cooks to give herself and her customers pleasure, and there are plenty of regulars at Mijanou to testify that it works. 'Cuisine artisanale' is a label that has been applied to her cooking, and she certainly is a very 'hands-on' cook, for instance – she makes her own bread and chocolates, and takes pride in their compatability with her menus. Invention and creative interpretation are the keystones to her highly individual style. She is passionately concerned about the quality of both her ingredients and the end result. Concentrating on flavour and presentation, she also aims to provide menus that are healthy as well as interesting. One of the features of Mijanou is that it always has a varied selection for vegetarians. Another is that one of its two dining rooms is exclusively for non-smokers.

Sonia Blech
Mijanou
143 Ebury Street
London SW1W 9QN
01-730 4099

Jean-Michel Bonin

Jean-Michel Bonin was born in Vichy, France, the son and grandson of hoteliers. From an early age he helped in the kitchens, and became apprenticed in pâtisserie at Varennes-sur-Allier, followed by a spell as apprentice cuisinier at the Hotel de la Paix in Roanne.

He has worked as commis de cuisine to the Automobile Club of France (1955); as first commis de cuisine to the Plaza Athenée, Paris (1956); chef poissonnier to the Savoy Hotel (1959); sous chef at Gleneagles (1962); chef de cuisine at the Rubens Hotel, London (1967); as executive chef at the Inn on the Park (1972); and finally (1985), executive chef to the Hyde Park Hotel.

Jean-Michel has learned from his hotel days to combine his classical foundations with a lighter style – classic French cuisine and cuisine naturelle. He enjoys dining out at restaurants recommended by friends and customers – as long as the food is not too spicy.

JEAN-MICHEL BONIN
The Hyde Park Hotel
Knightsbridge
London SW1Y 7LA
01-235 2000

MADDALENA BONINO
One Nine Two
192 Kensington Park Road
London W11 2JF
01-299 0482

SILVAIN BONSI
Nikita's
65 Ifield Road
London SW10
01-352 6326

VINCENZO BORGONZOLA
Al San Vincenzo
52 Upper Mulgrave Road
Cheam
Surrey SM2 7AJ
01-661 9763

WAYNE BOSWORTH
Odette's
130 Regent's Park Road
London NW1 8XL
01-586 5486

MARTIN BOTTRILL
Truffles Restaurant
95 High Street
Bruton
Somerset BA10 0AR
(0749) 812255

JEREMY BRAZELLE
Riber Hall
Matlock
Derbyshire DE4 5JU
(0629) 582795

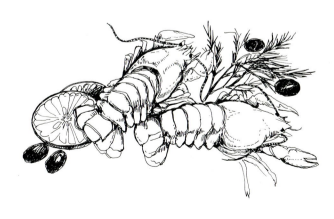

21

Michel Bourdin

Michel Bourdin was born in France and served his apprenticeship in Management, Cookery, Service, Food and Wine at the Ecole Hotelière Jean Drouant in Paris, from 1958 to 1961. He then worked at the Hotel Etoile, Avenue Victor Hugo, in Paris, followed by the Grand Hotel in Dinard, Brittany, as commis de cuisine, and during his military service was chef to the Prime Minister. Michel resumed his civilian status as commis then chef de partie at the Restaurant Ledoyen in Paris, and then as chef de partie and senior sous chef at Maxim's in Paris from 1964 to 1973. He went on to the Pavillon Royal in the Bois de Boulogne as chef de cuisine from 1973 until 1975, when he was invited to take up his rightful culinary home at the celebrated Connaught Hotel.

Today, Michel's brigade numbers over fifty chefs, catering for the hotel's residents and dinner guests in either the Grill Room or the Restaurant. The Menu Grande Carte, printed daily, offers a choice of over 100 dishes, with British and French specialities in the style of the 'Grand Hotel'. His kitchen is known as the 'Bourdin School of Cooking' – spawning a new generation of chefs around the country and abroad. Each year, one of these protégés acts as chef-host for an 'old boys' reunion over a Sunday lunch. In the past these have included Richard Sparrow at The Swan at Streatley, Richard Sawyer then at Le Talbooth in Dedham, Kevin Cape at the Bell Inn, Aston Clinton, Richard Blades at the Bird's Eye factory, and next year it is provisionally the turn of Marjan Lesnik at Claridge's.

Michel is a ceaseless campaigner, totally dedicated to maintaining the basic foundations and perpetuating the traditions of 'cuisine classique'. He never misses an opportunity to motivate others to share his ideals for the future of his profession and the art of cooking and service. The dream he has held for many years is about to be realised, with the formation of an Academy of Culinary Arts, where teaching and study will be at postgraduate level.

Sponsored for membership by Pierre Troisgros and Alex Humbert, Michel has been a member of the Académie Culinaire de France since 1968. Encouraged by the President of the Académie in France, he was one of the founder members of the Académie Culinaire de France (Filiale de Grande Bretagne). Inaugurated in London at the Connaught in 1980, he has seen the membership of the society grow from fifteen chefs to over 100 in 1989. He is also one of the original members of the chefs' Club Nine – a group of nine of London's top chefs who meet regularly to discuss their profession, and probably one of the major contributing factors to the instigation of the British branch of the Académie. A list of his other achievements and awards is formidable to read:

He was awarded a diploma of Meritant Membership by the Club des Cent, a club of 100 knowledgeable gastronomes, founded at the beginning of this century. Michel Bourdin was nominated when the Club's headquarters were based at Maxim's, when he would cater for them three times a month. He holds diplomas for the Prix Pierre Taittinger, (which he now judges), and the Prix Prosper Montagne. He is maître cuisinier de France (sponsored by Jean Delaveyne and Maurice Cazalis), and an honorary member representing Great Britain, of the Club des Chefs of the USA. He was chef/ambassador for Maxim's of Paris in Europe and the USA; and one of the first visiting lecturers invited to the Johnson and Wales Culinary University. The French Government has recognised Michel's contribution to cuisine with the honours of Chevalier du Mérite Agricole and Chevalier de l'Ordre National du Mérite. and in 1984 he received the Catey award for Chef of the Year.

When given the opportunity, Michel produces interesting insights into the cooking profession, the problems of recruitment and education, and the métier of the great and successful chefs of our time. He has an enormous number of press cuttings dating back to the days of his apprenticeship, and has featured in a number of promotional films for television, including Thames Television's *Take Six Cooks* and Roy Ackerman's *The Chef's Apprentice*. Michel is pleased that one of his sons appears to be following in his footsteps, not only by sharing his passion for the stove, but also by spending his military service cooking for President Mitterand.

With his exhausting schedule of work for The Connaught and the Académie, Michel does not have much time for hobbies. Any spare time he does find is shared with his wife, 'travelling to expand their knowledge of the world and its peoples'.

Michel Bourdin
The Connaught Hotel
Carlos Place
London W1Y 6AL
01-499 7070

23

Chris Bradley

Tessa Bramley

Chris Bradley had worked as a computer systems consultant and a hotel sales manager before buying the site on which Mr Underhill's now stands. He started converting the private house into a restaurant in November of 1980. In March 1981, he opened its doors to the public and began cooking professionally for the first time in his life. He says it's been hard work ever since, but he clearly enjoys it. And in case you were wondering, Mr Underhill is a character in Tolkien's *Lord of the Rings*.

Self-taught, Christopher offers a simplified interpretation of the great modern French chefs – Bocuse, Vergé, Guérard and Troisgros – with great emphasis on the use of fresh, seasonal ingredients, bags of flavour, and simple garnishes. He operates a no-choice menu, so he's never in the position of having to cook and serve anything that he's unhappy about. He turns out some splendid menus from his small kitchen, and uses home-grown vegetables, salads and herbs whenever possible.

For a really special occasion he would choose Le Gavroche, but otherwise he is eclectic when eating out, citing Chinese, Indian, French, Scandinavian, Italian, Californian and vegetarian as his favourites!

CHRISTOPHER BRADLEY
Mr Underhill's Restaurant
Stonham
Stowmarket
Suffolk IP14 5DW
(0449) 711206

Tessa Bramley, born and brought up in Sheffield, has never worked in a commercial kitchen other than her own but she has probably had more cookery training than most chefs in that she did a degree at a Polytechnic in London with the intention, duly fulfilled, of becoming a teacher of Home Economics. The change from teaching to cooking occurred about ten years ago, when she decided that there was nowhere in the Sheffield area that she liked to eat.

Her first venture was a small modern lunch-time bistro/smart café, in a premier shopping precinct in Sheffield. She ran it with great aplomb and success for six years. Then four years ago, and with her family's total support and backing, the Bramley home was converted to include a restaurant, and the present Old Vicarage was born.

Tessa's style has always been light, modern and eclectic, with its roots in the provincial/regional cooking of both Britain and France. To begin with the Old Vicarage opened for just a few evenings. The family found they enjoyed the slightly more formal setting that dinner rather than lunch afforded, and the restaurant has progressed from there. Tessa could now be described loosely as an exponent of modern British cooking but her great strength is to provide a modern context for traditional regional specialities. An example would be her rabbit casserole: the legs are casseroled with foie gras and the rabbit offal, while the saddle is roasted with an old English herb crust. Using the gravy from the casserole, the legs are served with the foie gras and a herb scone, and the roasted saddle is served alongside but without any gravy. The accompaniments are of typical Lancashire/Yorkshire origin, such as fried potatoes and a 'compôte' of pickled red cabbage.

Tessa is also fortunate in being able to use her own honey in her kitchen. 1989 was the best year on record for the Bramley bees (actually they belong to a solicitor friend, but the Bramleys' gardener is being trained in the art and science of the apiarist!). Two crops were collected, one from British wild flowers and herbs, and one from lime blossom.

All cooking gives Tessa Bramley satisfaction, whether it is as a job for commercial gain, or as relaxation for family and friends. She finds merely *being* in a kitchen very therapeutic, in the same way that a classical violist might play jazz at the weekends, as her son Andrew put it! Domestic cooking also gives her a chance to try out new combinations, perhaps with an oriental influence.

One of Tessa's big interests is old recipes and manuscripts, especially if handwritten. She has a collection of recipes that has been handed down through her own family and starts in the middle of the 18th Century with her great-great-grandmother's thoughts, through all subsequent generations. Family tradition is very strong for the Bramleys, and when they eat out they like to go 'en famille', choosing 'anywhere that excels', but ideally somewhere where they can stay over Sunday and Monday (when the Old Vicarage is closed) – such as Sharrow Bay, Hintlesham Hall, the Castle in Taunton, for instance. Although they like to try any style of cooking as long as the food itself is good – Japanese, Middle Eastern, modern British, classical French – the family favourite is, quite simply, Grandma's Sunday lunch! I think Tessa, in her turn, is going to be quite a hard act to follow.

TESSA BRAMLEY
The Old Vicarage
Ridgeway Moor
Ridgeway (Nr Sheffield)
Derbyshire S12 3XW
(0742) 475814

Mauro Bregoli

Philip Britten

Mauro Bregoli went straight into an apprenticeship after leaving school at fifteen, the only way to get started in Italy at that time since there were no catering colleges as such. He worked his way through the various aspects of the industry, then came to England in 1964, originally to learn the language. However, he liked this country so much he stayed to work in most of the fashionable London restaurants of the period.

In 1970 Mauro bought the beautiful 15th-century building which he turned into his well-known restaurant, The Old Manor House. It's a quintessentially English setting for some genuine Italian food, for he tries to avoid the compromises that he feels have ruined the name of Italian cooking in England. Mauro cooks the sort of food he himself likes to eat, admitting to an occasional Oriental influence. He feels that the advent of nouvelle cuisine in the 1980s, plus the poor reputation of Italian food, gave him the opportunity to really make his mark. His dedication was rewarded in 1987 by the award for the Best Lunch in Britain, sponsored by Luncheon Vouchers. This is not to say that the dinners are in any way inferior. He is also a vociferous delegate at the Chef's Conference, once entering into a famous debate with Donato Russo on the relative merits of pasta made with or without egg yolks!

When Mauro eats out, he modestly looks for somewhere with a cuisine superior to his own, or else an ethnic restaurant for a complete change of style.

MAURO BREGOLI
The Old Manor House Restaurant
21 Palmerston Street
Romsey
Hampshire SO5 8GF
(0794) 517353

Philip Britten is a young man of talent. It was spotted early by the legendary chef de cuisine at The Dorchester, Eugene Kaufeler, who was possibly the last great hotel chef of the old school. Eugene passed his mantle to that quintessential chef of the new school, Anton Mosimann, and Philip made the transition effortlessly, and still relishes those heady days at The Dorchester. A brief trip to Switzerland followed, and then a true baptism of fire for the young man: Langan's Brasserie, the fashionable London restaurant headed by Richard Shepherd. A relentless perfectionist, Richard had brought the spirit of La Coupôle to London, and Philip quickly learned that Langan's jet set clientele wanted good food, prompt service and lots of choice. Philip stayed the course. He then moved on to Chelsea and appeared at Dan's, whence former 'debs' delight', Antony Worrall-Thompson, had departed for Ménage à Trois.

Dan's had been recognised by Nico Ladenis, the arch perfectionist and hard

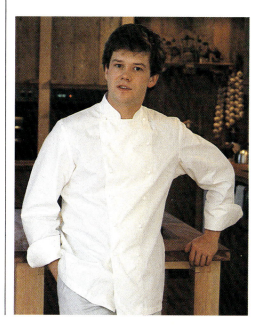

taskmaster who was on the verge of achieving his second Michelin star. Philip worked in tandem with Nico, and accolades flooded upon Chez Nico. Finally Nico departed for the Thames Valley, and Philip won his first star in his own right at Chez Nico, later leaving to pursue a career in recipe creation.

However, in 1987, David Levin – owner, architect and creator of the Capital Hotel, Knightsbridge was in search of a new chef. Ironically, his first chef had been Richard Shepherd so when Philip Britten took over it seemed as if fate itself had played a hand.

A quiet, unassuming man, Philip is no hedonist; rather a quiet technician, an artist perhaps but without the flamboyance of his former mentors. Under the direction of David Levin, he fits into the Capital as an essential part of a well-oiled machine. The result is that once again the restaurant is at the centre of the London hotel dining scene, where he enjoys a loyal following both among residents and businessmen. Philip might typically offer a consommé of crab en gelée; perhaps, a medallion of beef in a clear, perfect sauce; a rack of lamb with a herb crust; and a mousse of orange redolent with the zest of the fruit. He has created his own style. He remembers his mentors but is not a copyist. He is, quite simply, pleased to provide good food.

PHILIP BRITTEN
The Capital Hotel
22 Basil Street
London SW3 1AT
01-589 5171

Hilary Brown

Hilary Brown cooks, and her husband looks after the wine and the guests at their restaurant, La Potinière. They employ no staff and have been running it since 1975. 'October 1975', corrects Hilary, and it is in that correction that the key to her cooking lies. Accuracy, honesty and complete consistency: quality guaranteed.

Hilary trained at the Glasgow College of Domestic Science specialising in food and nutrition. This is the formal training of someone who has been described as one of

the best cooks in Scotland, with an intuitive understanding of ingredients.

With a narrow array of materials, she manages to create some good combinations and balances of flavour, colour and texture. Her influences come from yearly trips to France. The style of cooking can best be described as bourgeois: rich, creamy sauces, impeccably dressed salads, stunning dauphinoise potatoes – classical dishes cooked as they should be.

The restaurant itself is a recreation of a French country inn. Of her favourite places to eat, The Peat Inn is her nearest one.

Hilary Brown
La Potinière
Main Street
Gullane
East Lothian EH31 2AA
(0620) 843214

Nick Buckingham

Nick Buckingham was born into the catering trade and started cooking at the age of seven in his parents' restaurants – picking wild blackberries and making them into pies. At fifteen he was apprenticed to a former commis chef of the great Escoffier, going on to take City & Guilds at South Warwickshire College and continuing to extend his kitchen experience.

At twenty-one, he became the private chef to music entrepreneur Robert Stigwood, and spent three years travelling the world with his entourage. He cooked everything (from small dinner parties to banquets for 800), and everywhere (including London, New York, Morocco and Paris).

In 1975 Nick joined the Cavendish Hotel, Baslow, as executive chef, and has been there happily ever since. His basic, good family cooking has evolved through classical French cooking to his current 'spontaneous and creative' style, which uses only the best and freshest foods available. He must be one of the few chefs in the country confident enough to offer tables actually in the kitchen!

Nick takes pleasure in many aspects of cooking but he particularly likes passing on his knowledge to others, and seeing beautiful food prepared with attention to detail.

Nick Buckingham
The Cavendish Hotel
Baslow
Derbyshire DE4 1SP
(024 688) 2311

Stephen Bull

Stephen Bull was an advertising accounts manager until he was twenty-seven years old, which at least gave him a taste for good food when he travelled abroad. Having decided on a change of career, he began his training as a waiter for Peter Langan in Odin's. Having observed how to run such an establishment, he bought a restaurant in far off North Wales to practise his new-found skills! His next enterprise was called Lichfields in Richmond, Surrey. Sadly insufficient custom in Richmond failed to

justify his enthusiasm so a move to central London was made in 1989, which has proved to be a great success. As a self-taught chef, Stephen describes his style, which was influenced by good European cuisine, as 'free and easy'.

STEPHEN BULL
Stephen Bull
5-7 Blandford Street
London W1H 3AA
01-486 9696

Coming from a family with a butchery and bakery business, Roger Burdell had no formal training as a chef. After finishing a business degree, he put his initiative training into practice by knocking on the door of the Stocks Club in Melton Mowbray and asking for a job. He started on the puddings and starters, and has never looked back!

Roger worked in London for a while in the early '80s and began to catch the public eye when he went to Hambleton Hall, back in his native Midlands. He was there for two years as chef tournant and chef pâtissier, and in 1984, combined his original training with his new career, by opening the Restaurant Roger Burdell as chef/patron.

Early sources of inspiration were those doyens of the Lake District, John Tovey and Francis Coulson, but Roger admits that his style is open to any good influence that he encounters. He is constantly learning and changing, but he insists upon good ingredients, that are well prepared, simply cooked, and presented without undue fuss. As a consequence his fame has spread far beyond Loughborough, and people regularly travel long distances to enjoy his cooking. When he eats out, he will happily go anywhere that meets his own standards.

ROGER BURDELL
Restaurant Roger Burdell
11-12 Sparrow Hill
Loughborough
Leicestershire LE11 1BT
(0509) 231813

JEAN-CLAUDE BROUSELLY
Au Bois St Jean
122 St John's Wood High Street
London NW8 7SG
01-722 0400

STEVE BULLOCK
Café du Marché
22 Charterhouse Square
Charterhouse Mews
London EC1M 6AH
01-608 1609

CLARE BURGESS
The Hungry Monk Restaurant
Jevington
Polegate
East Sussex BN26 5QF
(032 12) 2178

SIMON BURNS
The Coach House Restaurant
8 North Port
Perth
Tayside PH1 5W
(0738) 27950

John
Burton-Race

John Burton-Race was born in Singapore, when his father was with the UNDP, but he went to public school in England. He was always interested in food, but went into the restaurant business because his parents did not want him to go to Art College, which was his first choice. He first attracted attention at Chewton Glen, in 1977, when Karl Wadsack was chef. From there, he went to La Sorbonne, which had employed a certain Raymond Blanc at one time. So it was that John turned up as sous chef at Le Manoir aux Quat'Saisons, later moving across to Le Petit Blanc as head chef. He had gone about as far as he could with Raymond when the premises at Shinfield came on to the market in the now-famous chef-shuffle of 1986: Nico Ladenis returned to London, John Burton-Race transformed Shinfield into L'Ortolan, and Bruno Loubet moved to Le Petit Blanc from Le Manoir.

Once installed at L'Ortolan, John was able to 'let rip' and really exploit all his ideas. He pays tribute to his classical training, using its strong flavours but lightening textures whenever possible. And the press and public have been quick to pay him the credit he deserves. He changes the menu frequently, as much for his own sake as that of his customers and suppliers, for he has a self-confessed low boredom threshold. He says that cooking is progression, and that his style changes as he goes along. The only thing that doesn't change is the natural rhythm of his cooking.

Cooking is very much his passion, and he is not often seen at front of house. More relaxed at his stove than away from it, he is nevertheless a relentless taskmaster. He expects a great deal from himself, and no less from any of his brigade or front of house staff. When he eats out he expects value for money, and he strives to offer it, too.

He acknowledges that his work is all-consuming, and for that reason would probably not encourage his children to enter the industry. You get the impression that there just aren't enough hours in the day for John, so much does he want to pack in. His emotional approach is infectious: when our researcher rang to check a few details with him, he had just lost his car keys. She desperately wanted to hot-foot it over to Shinfield and help him find them! An equal though different accolade came from another member of the team, who had been to L'Ortolan for a birthday meal: 'the best meal I've had all year' – and she had had some pretty outstanding ones in the preceding twelve months!

Reed-slim, driven and with burning eyes, John Burton-Race is very ambitious and doesn't think he has realised his potential yet.

John Burton-Race
L'Ortolan
The Old Vicarage
Church Lane
Shinfield
Nr Reading
Berkshire RG2 9BY
(0734) 888783

Idris Caldora

Kevin Cape

Idris Caldora began his working life as a waiter. Having attended cookery classes at school in Wales since the age of fourteen, he took City & Guilds and then worked his way round the kitchens of both The Savoy and The Dorchester, before being employed as commis chef pâtissier with Georges Blanc at Vonnas in France. From there, he came back to England as head chef at The Bell Inn, Belbroughton, where he worked alongside Roger Narbett, son of the owner. Between them, they monopolised the RAGB's Young Chef of the Year competition in the mid '80s, Idris winning in 1986.

The Bell Inn was then sold by its parent brewery company, and Idris moved to Bilbrough Manor in Yorkshire, again as head chef. Here he was able to develop his own style, (basically new classic French), which had begun to emerge at the Bell. He claims that it is not possible to have your own style during training, since you are duty bound to follow the regime of your employer.

Idris gains the greatest satisfaction from creating new and exciting dishes with fine ingredients. He enjoys many types of cuisine when eating out, but most of all he enjoys the kind of food that he cooks himself. That's a measure the kind of the confidence he has in his cooking.

At the time of going to press Idris moved to the Swallow Hotel in Birmingham. Lucky Birmingham!

IDRIS CALDORA
Swallow Hotel
12 Hagley Road
Five Ways
Birmingham
B16 8SJ
021-452 1144

From a boy, it was Kevin Cape's ambition to become a chef. His classically orientated apprenticeship began under Michael Gascoigne at the Wayside Manor in Reigate, followed by two years' City & Guilds course at Slough College of Further Education. He joined The Portman Hotel in 1977 as demi chef saucier and The Connaught Hotel in 1979 as chef de partie. In 1982 he left for the States and The Castle Restaurant in Massachusetts as junior sous chef. He returned to London and The Connaught after a year to become Michel Bourdin's sous chef until 1986. During this time he took part in several competitions, such as the William Hopelstein Award, the Prix Pierre Taittinger, and the first Bocuse d'Or in 1987 (in which he was a finalist). He left The Connaught in 1986 to join The Bell Inn at Aston Clinton, where he is head chef.

Despite an intensive classical background, Kevin's style has now become much more inventive and innovative, influenced by his work in Hong Kong, France and Malaysia. He likes oriental food, and eating in good restaurants in London.

KEVIN CAPE
The Bell Inn
Aston Clinton
Buckinghamshire HP22 5HP
(0296) 630252

Antonio *Carluccio*

Those who know about Antonio Carluccio's highly individual, yet very Italian food, know they will find him at the Neal Street Restaurant in Covent Garden, where he has been for a number of years. Those who would like to find out more should hurry along to meet this man with a mission.

Antonio Carluccio is a generous, passionate man – passionate about what he believes in, generous in sharing the knowledge he has acquired. For him, Italian cooking is based on the principle of obtaining the best possible end product from the best quality ingredients, ideally local but not necessarily the most expensive. His dictum of maximum returns in the minimum time can, Antonio feels, be applied equally to home cooks as to restaurant chefs. This can often result in dishes that are light, fresh, and delicious – perfectly in tune with today's busy, health-conscious world.

A great deal of damage was done to the image of Italian food in England with the upsurge of trattorias and restaurants serving food that paid more homage to the tinned tomato than to the abundance and variety of true Italian cucina. Antonio is one of the best possible advertisements for the newer wave of Italian cooking. Many will remember him for his recent forays on BBC Television's *Food and Drink Programme* where he took a young London cookery student on a tour of his homeland and succeeded – in a very short time – in winning her over to the true taste of Italy.

Half-jokingly, Antonio says that it was a challenge to go into the restaurant business, and that he started off with a combination of indomitable curiosity and greed! More seriously, however, he pays tribute to his mother's influence. From a northern Italian family of six children, he took an early interest in learning alongside his mother's stove, and being of a large family during wartime shortages, he soon became adept at spotting what might be turned into something special.

His alertness also served him well when he went for walks in the woods with his father. One day they met with an old man who taught Antonio the secrets of the truffle and other fungi. Today, Antonio is perhaps *the* authority in the food world on the fungi of this country. He has written a book on the subject, *A Passion for Mushrooms* and frequently goes mushroom and truffle hunting in the season!

ANTONIO CARLUCCIO
The Neal Street Restaurant
26 Neal Street
London WC2H 9PS
01-836 8368

30

David Cavalier

David Cavalier is on the way to establishing himself as one of England's finest young chefs. At the age of twenty-six he has established a reputation for culinary excellence that surpasses that of some older and more experienced chefs. He began his catering career when only fifteen, scrubbing pans and cooking crêpes at a family-run restaurant in Amboise, France. Then he spent two years studying culinary basics, before coming to London to serve his apprenticeship. Working his way through some of the most prestigious kitchens in London, including The Berkeley, The Royal Garden and The Grosvenor House, his training culminated in a stint in The Dorchester under Anton Mosimann.

Mosimann was extremely sympathetic to the young Cavalier and within two years he had progressed from third commis chef to junior sous chef at the tender age of twenty-one.

After a stretch in California, in 1984 he and his young wife, Susan, returned to England to buy their first restaurant, Pebbles, in Aylesbury. Susan ran front of house while David developed and perfected his own particular style of cooking.

Within two years, the Cavaliers had established themselves as serious restaurateurs with David hailed as a young man to watch, his cooking displaying a very personal style and wide range. As the couple became more successful they began to look for larger premises, and almost by default (they had been looking in the Buckinghamshire area) they ended up in Battersea in the former premises of Chez Nico.

His food is a wonderful mix of influences – classical approach interpreted in innovative ways, always perfectly executed. Anton Mosimann has been an obvious influence, and Cavaliers' menu is biased towards fish and offal. Sauces are light and concentrated in flavour, and rely little on cream and butter. David is adamant that all produce should be bought in daily in order to guarantee its freshness. He is not afraid to experiment and greatly admires the determination and imagination of Nico Ladenis.

Presentation is all-important to David but his dishes are not over-fussy. Flavours are thoughtfully combined and there is never a redundant herb or sauce. A complimentary amuse-guele, a mini-masterpiece, may precede a superb 'south coast bouillabaisse', followed by rack of lamb in a herb crust (brilliant in its simplicity), or veal sweetbreads (braised with smoked bacon and woodland mushrooms), or grilled red mullet with tomato vinaigrette. Bread is home-baked, cheeses well chosen, and the puddings are superlative. There is no skimping on quantity, no compromise on quality.

DAVID CAVALIER
Cavalier's
129 Queenstown Road
London SW8 3RH
01-720 6960

31

Sam Chalmers was born and raised in Scotland, and at an early age decided on a career in catering. He trained at the Central Hotel in Glasgow, going in at number 70, and leaving after four years, at the number 2 slot! From there he worked first in Jamaica, then at the Gleneagles, and later on a private yacht, before settling in 1976 as head chef at Le Talbooth in Essex. By 1980 he was a director.

In 1985 Sam found his next challenge, in the 16th-century timbered building in Long Melford which he transformed into Chimneys Restaurant. He added another string to his bow, by becoming more of a restaurateur than a chef. Without doubt he has great determination to succeed, a capacity for endless amounts of hard work, and maintains his high standards. He always chooses the finest raw ingredients, locally when available, and combines them into the best of British and continental cuisine.

Sam's philosophy is to encourage youngsters as much as possible, and he employs young, forward-thinking, ambitious staff. Provided they don't let his standards down they are free to contribute whatever they can to Chimneys.

SAM CHALMERS
Chimneys Restaurant
Hall Street
Long Melford
Suffolk CO10 9RJ
(0787) 79806

JEAN CALAS
Scott's
20 Mount Street London W1Y 5RB
01-629 5248

BRUCE CAMERON
Shares
12 Lime Street London EC3M 7AA
01-623 1843

ANDREW CAMPBELL
Macnab's Wine Bar
43 Balham High Road London SW12 9AN
01-675 5522

SIMON CANNER
Brinkley's Champagne Bar
17c Curzon Street London W1Y 7FE
01-493 4490

PETER CANNON
Abingworth Hall
Thakeham Road
Storrington West Sussex RH20 3EF
(079 83) 3636

ALASTAIR CARTER
Buckland-tout-Saints Hotel
Goveton
Near Kingsbridge Devon TQ7 2DS
(0548) 3055

LUCINO CELENTINO
Ma Cuisine
113 Walton Street London SW3 2HP
01-584 7585

IAN CHAMBERLAIN
Regatta Restaurant
171-173 High Street
Aldburgh Suffolk IP15 5AN
(072 845) 2011

David Chambers' mother was in the catering industry, and so from an early age David became aware of kitchens, restaurants, and the respect accorded to chefs. It was, he believes, the greatest influence on his decision to join the trade, and reading *Down and Out in Paris and London* by George Orwell inspired him to concentrate on famous, large hotels.

Recruited at school by Grand Metropolitan Hotels, David's apprenticeship began in 1969 at the Piccadilly and St Ermin's hotels, on six-week releases from Slough and Ealing Colleges. A varied career followed, starting in 1971 at St Ermin's Hotel as chef tournant. He then worked his way up through the kitchen hierarchy at the East Indian Sports Club, Claridge's, Mullard House in Tottenham Court Road, The Army & Navy Club, and The Carlton Tower.

From 1978 David worked at the Inter-Continental under Felix Muntwyler. He was promoted to executive chef in 1980, and stayed until joining the opening team as executive chef at the Dolphin Square Restaurant in London's Pimlico. In 1981 he returned to the Carlton Tower, under Bernard Gaume, moving in December 1982 to Duke's Hotel, St James's, as chef de cuisine. During this time he achieved two important 'stages' in his career: at the Michelin-starred Le Relais at Mougins he worked under the tuition of maître chef André Surmain, and then joined Place de la Marie in Mougins Village. In 1985 David moved again, this time to the new Piccadilly Hotel, now known as Le Meridien, to take up his present position as executive head chef. He is proud to have contributed to the accolades heaped on the hotel's Oak Room Restaurant.

During the formative years of his training, one of his greatest mentors was undoubtedly Bernard Gaume. David attemp-

ted to emulate the great chef on his first à la carte menu, until he found that he had set himself an almost impossible task considering the equipment and staff he had available! However, it taught him a serious lesson that menus should be written for your market rather than your ego. Lunch, David believes, should be simple, well-priced and fast, while dinner allows for a little more time and elegance even if it uses the same basic ingredients.

David's style combines traditional and creative cuisine. He lets the natural flavours blend together, and presents his dishes attractively, without being overly elaborate. He designs new gourmet dishes for the Oak Room, and the opportunity to work closely with Michel Lorain throughout the year gives him an awareness of the latest ideas in France, while still creating his own individual cuisine. A typical dish might be his suprême de grouse au chou farci truffé, a traditional variation he perfected based on an idea created by Michel Lorain. Banqueting facilities at Le Meridien can accommodate 400, and David not only stamps his personal style on the menus – many of which are adaptations of Oak Room dishes – but he also supervises the brigade for a wide range of functions from lunch receptions and cocktail parties to major banquets.

Aware of the need to keep up with current trends in cooking, when David eats out he is keen to try new experiences. A personal favourite, which he reserves for special occasions, is Japanese food. But he also admires the work of contemporaries such as Stephen Bull and Christian Delteil.

DAVID CHAMBERS
Le Meridien Hotel
Piccadilly
London W1V 0BH
01-734 8000

Peter Chandler

Peter Chandler was born in Edinburgh, although most of his early childhood was spent in Singapore, where his father was one of the Admiralty's Victualling Officers – responsible for loading up the Navy's fleets with catering supplies. Peter got his taste for Chinese food here, but family influences were also strong: his mother was French and, cliché or not, he says that his grandmother was a 'bloody good cook'! He admits that a large part of his student life on the family's return to England was spent in local hostelries, which 'seemed to have a much keener influence than Molière or Beaumarchais' whose literature he was meant to be studying.

A passion for cooking prompted him to enrol on an evening course at Carshalton Technical College – which he subsidised with day work in the building trade either as brickie's mate or bending pipes! Two large catering companies to whom he had applied for work replied that he was too highly qualified to become a chef. As Peter remarks, 'hardly an encouraging attitude for an aspiring chef – nor an endorsement of the profession!' His father then noticed an advertisement in *The Evening Standard* for an apprentice at a French restaurant – which turned out to be Le Gavroche.

He was interviewed by Albert Roux and started work as soon as he had had a haircut! Peter stayed with the Rouxs for twelve years, working the practised route through the company, starting at Le Poulbot then the Brasserie Benoits (now Le Gamin), and then on to the pastry laboratory in south west London to learn the basic skills of pâtisserie and bread-making. From there, Peter moved to Le Gavroche (this was when it was still in Chelsea) under Jean Tabaillaud, and then to the Waterside Inn with Dominic Pescheux.

An 'interlude' in France at La Réserve in Beaulieu followed, from 1976 to 1978, working for Jules Picard, a chef de cuisine with very strict Victorian values. His brigade of twenty-five at this legendary grand hotel abided by the cuisine classique regime, passing sauces through fine muslins, making sauces such as espagnoles with little or no reduction. Peter recalls the enormous vats of veloutes, the set pieces and the pièces montées. Here too Peter fell under the spell of Pierre Andiran, the old pastry chef, 'an invaluable experience'. Another indelible memory is having to make cheese soufflés, on the entremetier section, by hand and in pairs – the egg whites had to be beaten so hard that you would tire and throw the whisk at your colleague to take over. According to Peter, you can always tell the boys who have worked at La Réserve – one arm is always ten times bigger than the other!

Then it was back to the Waterside as sous chef to Christian Germain (now at the Château de Montreuil). But Peter could not see himself progressing much further within the Roux empire, so, as Albert and Michel were setting up outside catering for a firm of stockbrokers, Peter was delighted to be put in charge of the kitchens there. He used to cook over fifty meals a day with the help of one assistant and one washer-up. The experience taught him about buying, menu planning and cost control. A couple of years later, Peter returned to Le Gavroche as pastry chef before the opportunity arose in 1983 to set up the kitchens at Paris House, in the beautiful grounds of Woburn Park.

It was here that Peter developed his own style, still influenced by his very classical background. He says, 'the country changes your attitude: you have to strike a balance between the perception of what the customer wants – certainly larger portions – and what you want to present. We are very lucky here. We have staggeringly lovely produce to work with. I grow most of the

fruit – there's nothing better than picking your own apple from your own tree, slicing it and eating it with a piece of cheese – and vegetables and herbs. And the local game, such as partridge, pheasant, hare, rabbit and pigeons, is phenomenal, and of course we have Woburn Abbey venison – you couldn't get any better'. Daube of venison, which is a regular seasonal dish, is an unctuous rich stew, and served with fresh horseradish sauce it is tremendously popular. So too is the salt beef – silverside and brisket – which is a derivative of a classical pot au feu. As well as heading his brigade of six, Peter still loves the pastry section, where he says you get a better sense of feeling and colour – it satisfies his artistic flair.

The kitchen is another insight into Peter's character. Paris House was not originally intended as a restaurant, and the kitchen was created to his own design. It is compact, but spacious enough to dress the plates for an average fifty covers a day. Daylight pours in from the windows surrounding the central range, creating an illusion of even greater space and allowing him almost total vision of the cooking activities. And, with the Chandler wit, the air is as heavy with humour as it is with cooking aromas.

PETER CHANDLER
Paris House
Woburn Park
Woburn
Bedfordshire MK17 9QP
(0525) 290692

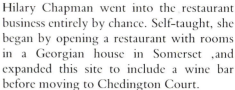

Hilary Chapman went into the restaurant business entirely by chance. Self-taught, she began by opening a restaurant with rooms in a Georgian house in Somerset ,and expanded this site to include a wine bar before moving to Chedington Court.

Hilary describes her style as good home cooking, using only the best, fresh, seasonal foods in straightforward recipes. She experiments sometimes with French classical dishes, despite lacking the formal training. Her stylistic individuality evolved slowly by trial and error, and was inspired by Jane Grigson, Robert Carrier and Elizabeth David. Hilary adapted their recipes to suit her limitations of produce and manpower.

Hilary believes that although the standard of food in Britain has improved enormously in recent years, there is still an inherent sameness in taste and presentation. She would like to see some of the leading chefs supporting her stand and refusal to use meat and poultry that has not been reared in humane conditions. Not only would this increase public awareness of the suffering of animals, but also aim at achieving healthier food for all. There are two challenges thrown down – will anyone pick them up?

HILARY CHAPMAN
Chedington Court
Chedington
Nr Beaminster
Dorset DT8 3HY
(093 589) 265

André Chavagnon

André Chavagnon is perhaps what everyone would imagine a French chef in England to be. Having been a trainee and apprentice in France, and a hospital chef in Austria during his national service, he was just twenty-four when he came to England. For the next ten years he worked at different hotels and restaurants around the country, before opening, in 1966, La Sorbonne in Oxford.

As he says of himself at that time: 'I was thirty-four years old and ambitious. I wanted to be a success, and to pass on my knowledge to younger people. I knew my job, worked hard, and had the personality to succeed.' Another of his assets was the organisational flair required to be a restaurateur as well as a chef. It should be mentioned that he only had £20 in cash in his pocket on opening day!

André has plenty to say concerning his philosophy of food. He feels that a chef should be as trustworthy as a priest, a doctor or a teacher, someone who can be relied upon to guide customers in their choice of food. It is an art to choose a well-balanced meal with no repetition of ingredients. To up and coming chefs, André gives the following advice: 'Work with your ears, nose and eyes; clench your fist in your pocket when things don't go your way; persevere and respect your teacher/chef because you'll always remember him or her in your mature years; and finally, never, never give up. If you *are* gifted, you can become a master of your trade, but it will not be easy.'

André has an ambivalent attitude about nouvelle cuisine. On the one hand, he feels that it woke up a very complaisant and dormant industry, bringing a boom in its wake. On the other, he suspects that far too many amateurs have hidden behind the tag of nouvelle cuisine. In the end it is up to the customer to decide what he or she prefers, and André sees a bright future ahead for the catering industry. More and more people have learned to appreciate an evening out with good food and wines. If they go to a professional chef, they may be given anything from classical to nouvelle cuisine, but it will be served with imagination, art and taste. As he says: 'God has given us a sense of taste, smell and appreciation. It is up to us mortals to use our senses for eating food. A pleasure we can have every day of our lives. Vive la bonne cuisine!' Let's drink to that!

ANDRÉ CHAVAGNON
La Sorbonne
130a High Street
Oxford
Oxfordshire OX1 4DH
(0865) 241320

SYLVAIN HO WING CHEONG
Chez Liline
101 Stroud Green Road London N4 3PX
01-263 6550

MARK CHRISOSTOMOU
The Seafood Restaurant
85 North Quay
Great Yarmouth Norfolk NR30 1JF
(0493) 856009

RON CLYDESDALE
Ubiquitous Chip
12 Ashton Lane
Glasgow Strathclyde G12 8SJ
041-334 5007

JEFF CONCLIFFE
Summer Lodge
Evershot
Dorchester Dorset DT2 OJR
(093 583) 424

PHILIP CORRICK
Grosvenor House Hotel
Park Lane London W1A 3AA
01-409 1290

ROBERT COUZENS
Gavver's
61 Lower Sloane Street
London SW1W 8DH
01-730 5983

JEAN COX
The Abbey
Abbey Street
Penzance Cornwall TR18 4AR
(0736) 66906

Tim Cheevers

Pierre Chevillard

I wonder how many chefs, in childhood, have managed to win a WI prize for their fruit cake? Well, Tim Cheevers did. And so began a varied career which, in the early days, ranged from the Army Catering Corps up to sous chef and, finally, head chef at Blake's Hotel in London – its trendy clientele of pop world glitterati a far cry from those of the officers' mess! His next stop, and the last before going solo, was as head chef at Thornbury Castle, replacing Kenneth Bell who, by 1984, had decided to opt out of directly running his own kitchen.

Tim Cheevers claims that his determination to have somewhere of his own emanated from a desire to reach a wider clientele - or as he puts it, 'somewhere I would be able to afford myself'. That 'somewhere' emerged in 1985 at the far end of Tunbridge Wells' High Street. His eponymous restaurant with its plain double frontage, neutral décor and uncluttered air, is simple yet convivial. Simplicity is the key-note all round. The menu is short, sharp and unpretentious – for example mussel soup and salmon poached with chervil. The cooking is imaginative but never convoluted – straightforward roasting, grilling or poaching, with a garnish never more complex than a sprig of fresh herb. Tim Cheevers has built up a network of local suppliers and remains faithful to his original intention by offering a set-price dinner menu that's excellent value by anyone's standards.

Tim Cheevers
Cheevers Restaurant
56 High Street
Tunbridge Wells
Kent TN1 1XF
(0892) 45524

Pierre Chevillard is the latest accomplished chef at Martin Skan's acclaimed hotel, Chewton Glen. The hotel has been lauded as the finest English country house hotel, and the food has played a major role in establishing this reputation.

Pierre trained under the brothers Troisgros in their famous restaurant in Roanne, having completed his apprenticeship at Le Favières and L'Hôpital. At the age of twenty-one he moved to England to work as chef de partie at Chewton Glen, and worked his way up through sheer tenacity to become the only possible replacement for Christian Delteil. He has always maintained that simplicity and freshness of ingredients are the basic rules for culinary success, and is particularly fond of French family-style cooking, the once again fashionable cuisine bourgeoise.

Although the Troisgros' influence is evident in his work, Pierre is loath to be put into any stylistic group: he says, 'Of course it is modern French cuisine, but I don't like to label my cooking as a style. I think too many chefs worry about titles on styles. I like to base my cooking around the best fresh, seasonal produce.'

He is equally at home with the most expensive ingredients and the humbler ones. Thought and creativity are evident in every dish. Starters may include home-made pasta filled with morels and served with a cèpe-flavoured sauce, or something as simple as sorrel soup. The menus change regularly according to what is in season. In July, the menu may include Dorset veal fillet with mango and lime, with autumn hailing the arrival of superbly prepared game dishes incorporating local English and imported French game. Vegetables and bread are prepared with the same attention to detail under Chevillard's watchful eye. He is still young enough to absorb new influences, and Chewton Glen has been instrumental in

allowing him to develop his strengths and to experiment with new ideas: 'My style is developing all the time – you never stop learning.'

Chevillard bears testament to the fact that hard work and culinary evangelism satisfy a single-minded desire to be happy in this job, and his approach clearly makes his customers happy too. 'I love all aspects of my work. I am as happy butchering, cleaning fish or creating a new dish. Above all, I love to cook.'

Pierre Chevillard
Chewton Glen
Christchurch Road
New Milton
Hampshire BH25 6QS
(0425) 275341

Adrian Clarke

Sally Clarke

In 1974, aged sixteen, Adrian took over the cooking for his parents' restaurant in his mother's absence. His sister had fallen ill in the USA, and so Mrs Clarke was away for a while. The Clarkes had opened the Fox & Goose in 1967 and were, in Adrian's, words like a 'torch on a dark night in Suffolk'. His mother's classical French cuisine was so sought after that she could control and develop her customers' tastes at whim.

Today, more eclectic influences have come to bear in the kitchen/restaurant world, even in more rural areas, palates have become more sophisticated.

Quick preparation of good fresh ingredients, produced in his own style of French cuisine, is Adrian's hallmark. He enjoys cooking seasonal dishes; local game in particular.

Having two small children has restricted the opportunities for Adrian to dine out, but he does try to keep in touch with new establishments as they open.

ADRIAN CLARKE
The Fox and Goose
Fressingfield
Eye
Suffolk IP21 5PB
(037 986) 247

Sally Clarke's story is one of single-minded determination to do what she believes in, and to do it to the best of her ability.

She took an OND at Croydon Technical College, learning the basic precepts that still stand her in good stead, and in particular the importance of maintaining a balance of colours, textures and flavours. She then spent a while at the Cordon Bleu institute in Paris, and worked in various Paris restaurants as an unpaid commis, just for the experience. Returning to London, she was an assistant cook at Leith's Good Food, Prue Leith's outside catering 'arm', and was then offered the job of head cook. She also went on to teach at Leith's School of Food and Wine for two years, before travelling to California where the sheer abundance, variety and freshness of produce available made her see the opportunities available for creating new, exciting dishes. This she set about realising at Michael's, in Santa Monica, where she was both chef de partie and dining room hostess.

But it was one memorable evening at the legendary Alice Waters' restaurant, Chez Panisse, that was to prove the real turning point. Sally had heard about Alice and her no-choice menus, but it was the whole concept of the restaurant that impressed her. So it was that towards the end of 1984, with the idea of a simple décor and a partially open-plan kitchen, she opened Clarke's in Kensington Church Street.

It was not long before the cognoscenti picked up on this addition to the restaurant

scene. A slow trickle turned rapidly, by word of mouth, into a steady flow, and very soon tables were at a premium. So what is the food like? Sally's style was one of the first to be described as 'eclectic', an epithet often reserved for a style that defies categorisation. That's fine by Sally, who draws her inspiration freely from everything around her. Certainly there are strong Californian influences, and modern Italian, and French of course (aided and abetted by summer family holidays spent in France, seeking out wayside 'routier' gems).

With different menus at lunch time and in the evening, and an additional lighter late supper menu, there is always plenty to do, and the care and thought she puts into the no-choice dinner menu defy those critics who say a short set menu is the easy way to operate.

SALLY CLARKE
Clarke's
124 Kensington Church Street
London W8 4BH
01-221 9225

Michael Coaker's interest in food began when eating out with his parents, so he put his interests into practice and enrolled at Slough College, where he took the City & Guilds Certificate. For immediate experience, he spent eighteen months in Paris and Switzerland.

Returning to England, he was fortunate to join The Dorchester in Anton Mosimann's brigade, and was there from 1979 to 1981 as sous chef, before taking a similar post at the Hyde Park Inter-Continental from 1981 to 1983. He has stayed with this group ever since, in 1983 moving to the Britannia and then, in 1984, to the May Fair as head chef.

Today he describes his food as modern French but with an English influence. He most enjoys cooking fish and shellfish, which he thinks are limitlessly versatile, adaptable in flavour and open to excellent presentation; but for himself he will eat out anywhere that serves good food. He is fond of ethnic food, especially Indian and Chinese, but for a special treat reckons you can't beat a Sunday roast!

MICHAEL COAKER
The May Fair Inter-Continental Hotel
Stratton Street
London W1A 2AN
01-629 7777

Michael Collom loved eating as a child, and he and his sister used to make toffee and sell it to the kids up the road! Somehow, that road led to a two-year Diploma course at Westminster College, on to The Park Lane Hotel as commis, and then to Harrods.

. Michael moved to Jamaica in 1967 and spent two years as pastry chef at the Courtleigh Manor Hotel in Kingston. He returned to England for what he intended to be a temporary stay before going back to Jamaica, taking a six-week job at Gravetye Manor. As it happened, he stayed for six years, first as chef de partie then as sous chef to Karl Löderer, whom Michael claims was his greatest inspiration. In 1980 he moved to the Priory as chef de cuisine.

Michael's menu is typically cuisine classique. As he says, 'There is no satisfaction like the satisfaction you feel when you create something new.'

Raymond Blanc provides Michael's idea of eating out, or in a simpler vein, he likes Indian food or anything oriental.

MICHAEL COLLOM
The Priory Hotel & Restaurant
Weston Road
Bath
Avon BA1 2XT
(0225) 331922

Eamonn Connolly

Francis Coulson

Eamonn Connolly is a Londoner by birth. His choice of career was a toss-up between being an electrician and a chef. Since he didn't have a clue how to change a plug, he decided on catering! He did his early training at South East London Technical College and began work at the Royal Lancaster Hotel, moving to the Churchill Hotel. It was during his thirteen years at Pollyanna's in Battersea that he really came to the public eye. In August 1988 he moved to open his own restaurant in Putney. Having been given carte blanche at Pollyanna's to cook what he liked, he developed an international style of cuisine that he took down the road to Putney, although there's a much shorter menu on offer.

A satisfied customer means a satisfied Eamonn Connolly. His own preference when eating out tends to be for the likes of Inigo Jones or Alastair Little.

EAMONN CONNOLLY
Connolly's
162 Lower Richmond Road
London SW15
01-788 3822

Many chefs achieve fame and fortune, some achieve a degree of respect, some are idolised, some become leaders. Francis Coulson fits all these categories – and yet is typical of none. The late 1940s, when it all began, saw a low point in British gastronomy. The war of course was over, but rationing still gripped the nation. Powdered eggs were within clear memory, and so was army food. Not a pretty thought for a young, aspiring restaurateur – but Sharrow Bay was. Its idyllic setting beckoned the young Francis with his suitcases, pots and pans. Legend has it that the taxi driver dropped him off saying, 'See you in three days!' Well, he was more than forty years out!

Francis Coulson was in at the beginning, and helped establish not only Sharrow Bay as a prototype for the English country house hotel, but also the Lake District itself as a mecca for gourmets from all over the world. Nowhere in England, outside London, is there a greater concentration of good eating establishments, and Sharrow Bay is the forerunner amongst them. Francis was joined in 1957 by Brian Sack, and it was from this moment that the story of Sharrow Bay began in earnest. They remain together to this day, Brian running the front of house while Francis takes care of the kitchen. Season after season, they would re-invest profits to improve standards and comfort, and work out every detail of the hotel's development with love and concern. Francis was a chef working miles away from the major wholesale markets and ports, but he broke new ground by talking to local suppliers and farmers, and making straight demands upon them.

Over the years his enterprise and insistence upon high standards have paid off – dinner at Sharrow Bay is a very special

experience. You will enjoy apéritifs with the other guests in an atmosphere of hospitality and warmth. Views across the water are spectacular, but so is the menu. Francis offers nearly two dozen starters: warm and cold mousses of chicken, duck or lobster; always several soups: carrot with coriander or basil, French onion, consommé; gravadlax; salads. Somehow Francis has absorbed the development of British food, edited it, improved it and joined it seamlessly to the values of generosity and simplicity that dictated his menu of years ago.

There is also something very 'Francis' about the pleasure he derives from everyone sitting down together – though it is Brian who has orchestrated the room so perfectly. All the wine is in place, well kept and served. The main course is a roster of twenty or so: pheasant, partridge, grouse, saddle of venison – all will appear when in season. Lamb and beef will be as sympathetically treated; vegetables will be fresh and in great abundance, perfectly complementing each dish. A short rest is now advised! For despite the richness and luxuriance of what has gone before, the legendary desserts include sticky toffee pudding, brandy snaps, crème brûlée, apple strudel, fruit pies and tarts, Pithiviers with icecream, each more wonderful than the last. Your grandmother will be as much his concern as your skinny sister. All will eat more than they thought they would, but all will be happy. And so will he.

FRANCIS COULSON
Sharrow Bay Country House Hotel
Howton Road
Ullswater
Cumbria CA10 2LZ
(085 36) 483

Beth Coventry was partly educated in France, and is a skilled linguist who turned late to cooking when working with the legendary Peter Langan during the opening days of Langan's Brasserie. Beth also has to live down the distinction of having a famous restaurant critic, Fay Maschler of *The Evening Standard*, as her sister. Beth has, however, established herself as one of the leading lady chefs at work in London today.

Green's Champagne and Oyster Bar was just that when Beth joined. Along with owner Simon Parker Bowles she has turned Greens into one of the sought after lunch venues in London. She uses only the best: Cornish crab, Scottish lobster, well butchered meat, and produces a classic English menu with hints of nursery food but also modern overtones. You will find dressed crab or potted shrimps alongside the finest smoked salmon and oysters, but you will also find a taramasalata that puts many Greeks to shame (inspired by her great friend the Marquis of Queensberry), and an amusing variation on a theme in her Scotch eggs (quails eggs given the Scotch egg treatment and served with a spicy homemade picallili. Although her clientele appears to be conservative in its tastes, Beth is never scared to lead them to new things.

Her main courses also mix the classic and the modern. Green's is a solid contemporary dining room, a perfect setting at Sunday lunch time for well-marbled roast beef with real roast potatoes, proper gravy, and horseradish with some 'bite'. Of course you will also find grilled Dover Sole, perfect lobster salads, and liver and bacon, and the plaice and chips are well worth trying.

Puddings are of course a popular item in a British restaurant. Beth proclaims a love of clean, simple tastes – the natural tastes of the good ingredients – and this is never more apparent than in her desserts. Icecreams and sorbets have clear, sharp well-

balanced flavours and silky textures. In contrast to the gooseberry fool or lemon sorbet, you have the solid old-fashioned puddings on which the Empire was built. Beth understands these well: bread and butter pudding, decadent treacle tart, apple pie, apple crumble – all these feature prominently on the menu.

The loyal clientele of Green's know that so long as Beth is in the kitchen, the legacy of British cooking is safe, and that just now and then a strange foreign dish, well conceived, will appear by its side. That too is the proper tradition of British food.

BETH COVENTRY
Green's
35-36 Duke Street
St James's London SW1Y 6DF
01-930 1376

Malcolm Cowan

Malcolm Cowan was born in Scotland, and an early love of cooking provoked a career decision when he was only fifteen. He signed up as an apprentice at the Queen's Hotel, Portsmouth, with day-release at Portsmouth Technical College. His first job was as a commis on RMS Queen Elizabeth, where he spent a year trying to conquer sea-sickness! He didn't say whether he succeeded or not, but in any event he then moved to Switzerland as a commis, and learned to ski.

He then got down to some serious cooking in London, working his way round Simpson's-in-the-Strand, The Ritz, Verry's (his first post as head chef), Walton's and Odin's; then spent six years as executive head chef at The Westbury Hotel, followed by four years as executive head chef at Maxim's de Paris in London. Then, seeking to branch out on his own, he found exactly what he was looking for at the quaintly named and located Old Plow at Speen.

His style was originally classic French, and he feels that he really developed while at Maxim's, although he also pays tribute to all the other head chefs with whom he has worked and to time spent overseas. Now, his style is French/English, robust yet eclectic, and he enjoys, especially, creating new dishes. While working within a formal brigade, his favourite sections were 'the fish' and 'the sauce'.

When he goes out to eat, he favours ethnic restaurants, either locally or in London's Chinatown.

Malcolm Cowan
The Old Plow Inn & Restaurant at Speen
Flowers Bottom
Speen
Buckinghamshire HP17 0PZ
(024 028) 300

Michael Croft

Away from their work, many chefs yearn to eat unpretentious food in straightforward surroundings. Ask them to name names and they often trot out a list that implies nothing remotely simple at all! But not so Michael Croft. The head chef of Bath's Royal Crescent Hotel likes nothing more than an honest to goodness pub meal. The Fossebridge Inn, the Three Lions at Stuckton and the Dove Inn near Warminster have all become favourite bolt-holes. This retreat to the opposite end of the spectrum probably stems from his time as an Egon Ronay inspector, when a stomach, galvanised for rich food would respond gladly out of hours to a simple poached egg on toast. Michael Croft's first job was at The Connaught. For him, Michel Bourdin was the epitome of the single-minded professional chef. Working afterwards with Michael Quinn at both Gravetye Manor and The Ritz proved a time for experimentation.

Since 1985, he's been ensconced behind the elegant Georgian sweep of The Royal Crescent, where's he's been practising the fine art of compromise, amalgamating the influences of his training grounds, blending the classic with the contemporary. He's aware that his menu must excite the taste-buds and also appeal to the simpler demands from jaded appetites caught up in the rigours of a country house trek. This balancing act is only achieved by total respect for his ingredients.

Michael Croft
The Royal Crescent Hotel
16 Royal Crescent
Bath
Avon BA1 2LS
(0225) 319090

Andrew Cussons

Andrew Cussons has wanted to cook for as long as he can remember. He took City & Guilds in Swindon and decided that the best possible start after college would be a high-class restaurant in London, so he joined Odin's where he spent a couple of years learning from the experienced chefs.

Andrew then moved to Pool Court in Yorkshire, where he was encouraged to 'do his own thing'. This period saw the emergence of his own style of cooking – traditional French and English cuisines, using the best possible ingredients to provide a wholesome meal. With added confidence, he then returned to Odin's for a while, before taking up the post of Head Chef at Langan's Bistro.

It was here that Andrew was able to think more about his future and what he wants to do. Still only twenty-two, he's decided that the way ahead lies in owner/partnerships, a lesson presumably learned under the Langan umbrella. So, with his father Peter and brother Paul, Andrew Cussons has acquired the Forresters Arms Hotel and Restaurant, which should give full rein to his creative spirit.

Andrew Cussons
The Forresters Arms
Kilburn
North Yorkshire
(034 76) 386

Brian Cutler

Brian Cutler's first cookery lessons took place when he was still at school, and were followed by a four-year apprenticeship, three at the Sheraton Skyline and one year at Fredrick's. He also took his City & Guilds qualifications by day release at Slough College.

Brian then spent about five years in top hotels around Europe gaining more experience, before returning to Fredrick's Hotel & Restaurant as head chef in 1987. It is here that his own style – a combination of nouvelle, basic, classical and continental – has evolved. As ever, he is fascinated by the different possibilities of food production. However, he is now also able to turn his attention to training youngsters.

For leisure, Brian eats out at all his local restaurants, favouring Italian and Chinese. But most of all he enjoys good old home cooking.

BRIAN CUTLER
Fredrick's Hotel & Restaurant
Shoppenhangers Road
Maidenhead SL6 2PZ
(0628) 35934

LAURENT CRÈCHE
Grill St Quentin
136 Brompton Road
London SW3 1HY
01-581 8377

REGIS CRÉPY
The Great House
Market Place
Lavenham
Suffolk CO10 9QZ
(0787) 247431

PHILIP CRIPPS
The Copper Inn
Church Road
Pangbourne
Berkshire RG8 7AR
(073 57) 2244

DENNIS CROMPTON
Greens Seafood Restaurant
82 Upper St Giles Street
Norwich
Norfolk NR13 1AQ
(0603) 623733

ANDREW CROOK
The Crown
90 High Street
Southwold
Suffolk IP18 6DP
(0502) 722275

PHILIP CROWTHER
Crowther's Restaurant
481 Upper Richmond
Road West
London SW14 7PU
01-876 6372

JOHN CURTIS
Café Rouge
2c Cherry Tree Walk
Whitecross Street
London EC1Y 2NX
01-558 0710

Jean-Yves Darcel

Clive Davidson

Martin Davies

Jean-Yves Darcel was born in Brittany. Since he lived near the sea and loved eating fish, it seemed to him perfectly logical to cook fish for a living. However, just to round off a thorough education, he also did some charcuterie training in Paris.

He cooked for a summer in his native Brittany before coming to England in 1977. Here he joined Pierre Martin's group flagship, Le Suquet.

Jean-Yves claims not to have any distinct style, and says that he simply cooks in the same way that he always has, a natural way. With such good raw ingredients available to him, both during his childhood and now in Chelsea, he has obviously found his métier.

Perhaps surprisingly for someone in a piscine environment, he even carries the theme into his private life, preferring whenever possible not to eat meat. He seeks out good vegetarian restaurants, and has an apparently limitless supply of French friends who also have restaurants in south west London, and who cook for one another on their days off. Sounds like a great idea!

JEAN-YVES DARCEL
Le Suquet
104 Draycott Avenue
London SW3 1SW
01-581 1785

Clive Davidson is a determined man with an extremely successful restaurant, and because the only way to ensure that the raw materials are the best possible is to produce them yourself, he does just that. He became a butcher a year before he bought the Champanay Inn in 1983 (he had come from the Beehive in Edinburgh), and it is 'The Steak' which is the mainstay of his business.

An Aberdeen Angus Cross, hung for at least four weeks, is then marinated to his own recipe and chargrilled – unsurprisingly Champanay's steaks have been called the best in the country. Like every good business concept it is well packaged – in this case with salads – and the comfortable surroundings match the quality of the food. But perhaps the greatest asset is the dedicated concern with consistency and high standards that is the Davidsons'.

The enterprise has been so successful that Scottish & Newcastle Breweries are jointly expanding Champanays around Scotland. The first, the Horseshoe Inn at Eddleston, has duplicated the whole design, right down to the pool for the fresh lobsters and the salvers on which the steaks are cut.

South-African born, Clive has another obsession to match meat, and that is wine. He has a list of some 1,000 bins, with at least 600 Burgundies, and he makes regular trips to the wine auctions at Beaune as well as the equivalents held in his native land.

CLIVE DAVIDSON
Champanay Inn
Linlithgow
West Lothian EH49 7LU
(050 683) 4532

Martin Davies was born and brought up in London. His mother was a catering administrator at The Mayfair Hotel and his aunt owned a pastry shop. It was here, as a child, that Martin would watch and later on be allowed to cook. He loved experimenting and thought it was all great fun. This, as well as his natural artistic flair, meant that cooking for a living seemed the obvious choice.

Through his mother's contacts Martin started his apprenticeship at The Mayfair Hotel moving on to The Empress Restaurant as chef poissonnier. Afterwards he worked at several top London establishments – The Inn on the Park, The Carlton Tower and Le Caprice – spending some time in the States and Switzerland, before joining Brown's Hotel in 1977.

In the early days, Martin went by the classical text books, but by the early 1970s his cooking was more influenced by Bernard Gaume and his accent on lightness. 'Then the new wave of French chefs changed everyone's outlooks and perception of food and cooking, giving us a chance to express ourselves. Today, I create modern English dishes from British produce, trying to be sensibly original and unfussy, sometimes surprising but hopefully never contrived, and attractive but not pretty. Taste – in all senses of the word – is paramount.'

Martin holds many awards from past competition work and he is a respected senior representative of the industry. When he is not cooking, he enjoys stocking his two large garden ponds with exotic river fish, hours playing chess, or a round of golf.

MARTIN DAVIES
Brown's Hotel
Albemarle Street
London W1A 4SW
01-493 6020

Edward Denny

Although Edward Denny was born in Scotland, he began his cooking career as a commis in a small hotel in Ireland. However, he soon found work in Ireland frustrating, so returned to Scotland, spending two years in Edinburgh working his way round and up from chef de partie to sous chef. He was briefly with Alan Hill at the Caledonian, and then came to London to work with Albert Roux at Le Gavroche. Edward pays tribute to both for helping him develop his style into a modern French cuisine. But perhaps the most important influence on his cooking came when he joined the Box Tree in Ilkley, where Michael Truelove was in charge. The two of them responded to the changing trends, bringing in more healthy, lighter dishes, and when Michael Truelove left, Edward took over.

It was a credit to the team that even with a change of restaurant ownership, regular customers did not feel any rocking to this flagship of good cooking in West Yorkshire, and critical acclaim was equally kind. The Box Tree is still considered *the* place to go for a celebration. It is customary for students of nearby Leeds University, who have obtained a First Class degree, to be taken to the restaurant by their parents after the degree ceremony.

And where does Edward Denny go to celebrate his years of hard work? He swaps with the students – his favourite is a Cantonese restaurant in Leeds!

EDWARD DENNY
Box Tree Restaurant
29 Church Street
Ilkley
West Yorkshire LS29 9DR
(0943) 608484

Among the great French restaurants in London, L'Arlequin was for a while unsung, but currently it receives accolades from all over. It is French Restaurant of the Year in the *Times*, Restaurant of the Year from Egon Ronay, holder of a black clover in *The Ackerman Martell Guide* and rated among the top four in London by *The Good Food Guide*. That such fame has taken so long for Christian Delteil is unsurprising: he is a modest and unassuming man dedicated only to producing good food.

Christian Delteil was born in the south west of France in 1954. His mother he describes as a great cook who so inspired him that he was never in any doubt as to his chosen career. At the age of fourteen he began to cook and work his way round several regions of France, cooking in highly

rated restaurants and learning techniques which still stay with him. He also learned that the badinage of the kitchen, the camaraderie, and a sense of team spirit is needed to produce excellence. Even when conscripted he continued to cook, and no doubt some particular unit of the army did a lot better than the rest!

In 1975 Christian was asked to come to England in order to continue his culinary education and at the same time improve his English. He worked at two of London's most notable restaurants, Le Gavroche and The Connaught Hotel. Here, under the wings of Albert Roux and Michel Bourdin respectively, he became a young master of his art. Martin Skan, proprietor of Chewton Glen in the New Forest, has always encouraged new talent and Christian became head chef at Chewton Glen creating some of the finest cooking outside London. His cooking was modern, always based on sound techniques and principles. He developed a kitchen

team which was strong, creative and consistent. He was able to leave Chewton Glen in the safe hands of his protégé Pierre Chevillard, who has continued in the Delteil tradition.

Christian had decided to set up his own restaurant but it is typical of him that he would not have done so without ensuring his 'succession'. While working for the Roux brothers, Christian met his wife Geneviève. Together, they created L'Arlequin, having been encouraged to come to Battersea by Nico Ladenis of Chez Nico, then next door. L'Arlequin opened to rave reviews. It was a small restaurant, dedicated to excellence, with Geneviève supervising the front of house. All that has changed is the scale, as L'Arlequin now seats about fifty.

Christian was relieved to witness the end of nouvelle cuisine. His cooking still reflects his origins in south west France: his potage faux is definitive with a clear flavour for broth and all the proper garnishes. He will roast a whole leg of a small Pyrenean lamb to perfection. Fish dishes change daily according to availability. The subtleties of Christian's techniques extend to every course.

The tone of L'Arlequin reflects the personalities of Christian and Geneviève. It is honest, at times simple, at times sophisticated, no detail is unnoticed, nothing is too much trouble. Christian is a dedicated family man whose main hobby seems unusual in one so mild-mannered: he spends Saturdays practising the martial arts, although he has never had to use any such skills on dissatisfied customers!

CHRISTIAN DELTEIL
L'Arlequin
123 Queenstown Road
London SW8 3RJ
01-622 0555

47

Ana Diment

Mark Dodson

Ana Diment was inspired by watching a very creative and talented mother at work in the kitchen, at home in Spain. As a little girl, she had her very own small pan and as soon as she could reach the stove she began making tortillas!

However, it was her husband, who is a professional chef, who encouraged her to go into the business. But she began at front of house in their early ventures together, for instance at Restaurant Diment in Kenilworth, which still bears their name.

When in the mid-1980s Phil noticed a possible gap in the London restaurant market for tapas bars – the habit in Spain of serving snacks with drinks, slightly more substantial than the ubiquitous British crisps and peanuts – it was time to swap roles. Henceforth Ana would do the cooking and Phil would look after the front of house. Tapas took off, and so popular has the habit become that the Diments now have three such establishments: the first, Meson Don Felipe in Waterloo, the second, Meson Dona Ana in Notting Hill, and the recently opened Meson Don Julien in Fulham, named after their eldest son. Watch out for Meson Don Ricardo and Meson Don Roberto!

Ana Diment
Meson Dona Ana
37 Kensington Park Road
London W11
01-243 0666

Mark Dodson comes from Derbyshire, and immediately after leaving school he worked as a catering assistant on British Rail's Sealink Ferries. But it was in 1975 that his real training began, with a three-year course at the Colchester Institute, which included industrial work release at London's Inter-Continental under Michael Nadell, then chef pâtissier, and at the Portman Inter-Continental with Felix Muntwyler, then executive chef. Mark completed his education in such illustrious company by gaining his City & Guilds qualifications and an Advanced Cookery Diploma.

His apprenticeship, however, continued with employment at the Old Court House Hotel; then he moved back to the Portman Inter-Continental with David Chambers and Anton Edelmann. He also cooked at Le Talbooth, The Savoy, and Frederick's in Camden Passage, before joining The Waterside Inn in 1983 as a commis. But with quick promotion to chef de partie in 1985 and sous chef in 1986, he succeeded Michel Perraud as chef de cuisine in 1988.

At the Waterside his food is, of course, influenced by Michel Roux. His style has a classical bias, refined by cooking to French rules, drawing upon other international influences and using ingredients from all over the world. He derives great satisfaction from a busy service, and from knowing that when the last table is served, everything he has done was how he wanted it to be. He is always curious about the cooking of other chefs and will try to find the time to eat out in good restaurants. He is also happy to eat Indian or Chinese food.

Mark Dodson
The Waterside Inn
Ferry Lane
Bray-on-Thames
Berkshire SL6 2LT
(0628) 20691

Matthew Darcy
Park Hotel Kenmare
Kenmare Co Kerry
(064) 41200

Olivier Dauvillaire
Le Gamin
32 Old Bailey London EC4M 7HS
01-236 7931

Laurent David
Lou Pescadou
241 Old Brompton Road
London SW5 9HP
01-370 1057

Laurent de la Tour
Le Marché Noir
2/4 Eyre Place
Edinburgh EH3 5EP
031-558 1608

Barbara Deane
Chinon
25 Richmond Way London W14 0AS
01-602 5968

Daniel Delagarde
Le Cadre
10 Priory Road
Crouch End London N8 7RE
01-348 0606

Raymond Desoulier
Soho Soho
11-13 Frith Street London W1
01-494 3491

Stephen *Doherty*

Iain *Donald*

Steven Doherty was born in Manchester. He thinks his interest in food was sparked off either by his grandmother's cooking or by watching Graham Kerr, television's 'galloping gourmet'. Whatever the cause, the catalyst was a friend of his father, a catering lecturer at Southport Technical College, who encouraged Steven to take a two-year cookery course. The course ended in 1976 and he applied for a job as commis chef in Silvano Trompetto's brigade at The Savoy Hotel. Much wiser for the experience, in 1978 Steven moved to Le Gavroche, which was at that time in Lower Sloane Street. He was promoted to chef de partie tournant, and in 1981 left London to broaden his experience and to learn French, spending 'two wonderful years' with Alain Chapel in Mionnay, France.

In 1983 Steven returned to Le Gavroche, now in Upper Brook Street, as sous chef, working with Albert Roux and René Bajard, succeding René as chef de cuisine in 1985. Steven stayed until the end of 1988, still working for Albert, when he moved as chef consultant to the company's new venture, Hotel Diva, in Isola 2,000, one of France's skiing resorts.

Steven returned at the beginning of 1989, and decided to accept the position as chef manager of Marlfield House in Gorey, with his wife Marjorie as manageress. Marlfield House is one of the finest country house hotels in Ireland.

One of Steven's favourite dishes to cook, and also one of Albert Roux's favourites to eat, is a light cream of shellfish soup. It's simple but extraordinarily effective, and made from an assortment of clams, Dublin Bay prawns, mussels and cockles. When he allows himself time away from the stove, he likes to get outside, swimming, playing golf, or fishing.

STEVEN DOHERTY
Marlfield House
Gorey
Co Wexford
Republic of Ireland
010-353-55 21124

Born in Aberdeen, Iain Donald began his career in the catering industry by working in a local hotel at weekends and during the school holidays.

For five years, Iain worked the summer seasons with British Transport Hotels at the Gleneagles, spending the winters in Jamaica or Switzerland. Then he joined The Dorchester in London whilst Anton Mosimann was maître chef des cuisines, and this period won him over completely to the more modern style, after his 'traditional French'

start. Iain now describes his cooking as a blend of modern and traditional, with the emphasis placed upon the balance of flavours and presentation.

Since he joined the Stanneylands in 1984, Iain has enjoyed seeing his clientele become more and more adventurous. As for himself he eats out in local restaurants which he feels are also striving for high standards, and at the top restaurants around the country in order to keep abreast of current changes of style.

IAIN DONALD
The Stanneylands Hotel
Stanneylands Road
Wilmslow
Cheshire SK9 4EY
(0625) 525225

David Dorricott

David Dorricott remembers cooking for his family as a young boy. He left Birmingham College of Food and Domestic Arts in 1959 as the star pupil of his generation. He established his career as second assistant on the HMS Edinburgh Castle, a luxury passenger liner on the Southampton-South Africa route, and then went on to gain more overseas experience in Bermuda, Abu Dhabi, Holland, and Switzerland.

In 1979 David joined Peter Kromberg at the London Inter-Continental Hotel as banqueting sous chef, later becoming executive sous chef. He was then selected to assist in the opening of the new Inter-Continental Hotel in New Orleans, after which, in 1984, he transferred to the Portman Inter-Continental, where he has been ever since.

David places great emphasis on imaginative and healthy menus, stressing the finest and freshest ingredients at all times. He is a regular judge at international competitions, and participated again at the Culinary Olympics in 1988, when his whole team won medals.

David's leisure activities include horse-riding, parachuting, and skiing.

DAVID DORRICOTT
The Portman Inter-Continental Hotel
22 Portman Square
London W1
01-486 5844

Stella Doyle

Dublin-born Stella Doyle is one of Ireland's growing band of female chefs who have made their mark on the culinary scene. She had no formal training as such and is virtually self-taught. In the years that she and husband John have owned and run Doyle's, they have always closed during the winter months, when Stella visits others' working kitchens for her own enjoyment and experience.

They found Doyle's somewhat by chance, as they were actually looking for somewhere to live. But the house already had a licence; and since at that time John was operating a trawler (having given up working for an advertising agency in Dublin), a regular daily catch of fish was ensured. Opening as a restaurant seemed the logical course of action!

Stella's original style was 'extremely simple' and it's now 'simple, but with more exciting sauces'. Although she prefers cooking and eating fish, she has no real preferences and will find a challenge in cooking anything at all.

STELLA DOYLE
Doyle's Seafood Bar
John Street
Dingle
Co Kerry
Republic of Ireland
010-353-66 51174

Alain Dubois

Alain Dubois came to Bristol from France in 1970, en route to Canada. Canada was the land of opportunity, so he thought, but a good knowledge of English would be necessary; so he arrived at the Unicorn Hotel as chef de partie. Twenty years later he's still in the West Country, his plans to go West long abandoned!

During his sojourn here he has worked at the Priory Hotel in Bath, moving with its then owners to Hunstrete House as head chef. From there he went to The Lygon Arms in Broadway, and is now back in Bristol, at Bistro 21.

Having trained in Rennes, Alain spent his period of national service catering for army officers. From a conventional style of cooking he has developed his own distinctive and unusual style. He was very unhappy when nouvelle cuisine held sway, for he felt the sometimes small portions cheated customers.

His own favourite food is fish, and he encourages his clientele to try a wide variety; and when he eats out, it is often Chinese.

ALAIN DUBOIS
Bistro 21
21 Cotham Road South
Kingsdown
Bristol
Avon BS6 5TZ
(0272) 421744

Graham Dunton

Graham Dunton was born in Buckinghamshire to a family of master bakers, which neatly decided his future for him. He enrolled at Slough College for a two-year course in Food and Service, then specialised in pastry for a further two-year advanced course with John Huber.

His career then took him to The Dorchester, where he was actually taken on by Eugene Kaufeler but went to work for his successor, Anton Mosimann. When Graham started at the hotel, he was one of twenty-two pâtissiers in a brigade which totalled some 120 chefs. Mosimann gradually pruned it down to around seventy.

In 1978, he moved to the Hyatt Carlton Tower, working with Robert Mey in 'the pastry'. In 1981, Graham joined the Hotel Baur à Lac in Zürich, returning to London for a month only when he was persuaded to consider employment at The Connaught Hotel with Michel Bourdin. He claims he was press-ganged – but he stayed for seven years! He succeeded the old chef pâtissier, Wally Ladd, who warned Graham that Monsieur Bourdin was very fond of puff pastry and used it with almost everything. And indeed Graham and his team of twelve did make a great deal of it, often more than eighty kilos a week, by hand of course, as well as The Connaught's famous sherry trifles: Genoise sponge, covered in home-made black cherry preserve and soaked in a syrup of sherry and rum, covered in a thick custard of eggs and cream, topped with whipped cream, and decorated with fresh almonds and raspberries.

But the pâtisserie was impractical, and the hotel's needs had outgrown it, so it was refurbished. It took three years to plan and two years to build a new one, at a cost of about £1 million. Still retaining mostly marble work surfaces, its retard prover, and unusually high standard of service-ware, it nevertheless became one of the most advanced in any hotel at the time. Graham considers his experience at The Connaught the most valuable and interesting he could have had, enjoying the old-fashioned standards, the marble tables, the best ingredients, the traditional recipes.

By 1988, Graham felt he needed to move into the commercial world of the Pâtisserie Honoré where they prepare 1,000 portions of entremets daily – truffle torte, various charlottes, individual pâtisseries, fruit tarts and éclairs, as well as banqueting work for 300–400.

Graham feels deeply about his work, and loves simple, good produce, and planning what to do with it. He is himself a keen gardener, and grows masses of vegetables and herbs which suit his preference for simple, uncomplicated food at home.

GRAHAM DUNTON
Pâtisserie Honoré
3 Brewery Mews Business Centre
St. John's Road
Isleworth
Middlesex
01-568 7565

ROSEMARY DICKER
Alfred's
Upgate
Louth Lincolnshire LN11 9EY
(0507) 607431

MELANIE DICKSON
Ciboure
21 Eccleston Square London SW1W 9LX
01-730 2505

PETER DIXON
White Moss House
Rydal Water
Grasmere Cumbria LA22 9SE
(096 65) 295

STEPHEN DOOLE
The Factor's House
Torlundy
Fort William Inverness-shire PH33 6NS
(0397) 5767

JOHN DOYLE
Doyle's School House Restaurant
Main Street
Castledermot Co Kildare
066-51174

MICHEL DUBARBIER
Mon Plaisir
21 Monmouth Street London WC2H 9DD
01-836 7243

OLIVIER DUCRET
Monsieur Thompson's
29 Kensington Park Road
London W11 2EU
01-727 9957

PAUL DUVALL
Hiders
755 Fulham Road London SW6 5UU
01-736 2331

51

Anton Edelmann

Anton Edelmann is of West German origin, born in Bubesheim. His was a fairly traditional route to the top of his profession; his uncle owned and ran a hotel, and it was while working there during his school holidays that Anton discovered a taste for cooking, and began to realise his vocation.

After an apprenticeship at the Ulm Bundesbahn Hotel near his home town, he came to London and worked as commis saucier at The Savoy. He stayed for a year before returning to Europe and the Hotel de la Paix in Geneva, where he was first commis saucier and gardemanger. Then he moved to Düsseldorf and the Franziskaner as chef de partie, chef gardemanger and chef de partie saucier, before undertaking a year and a half's Military Service in the Air Force. On returning to London, he spent the following four years at The Dorchester, moving from chef de partie saucier to poissonier chaud, to gardemanger, and finally to the position of senior sous chef. In 1979, he joined The Portman Inter-Continental, as premier sous and acting head chef, before taking over as chef de cuisine at the Grosvenor House, a position which lasted eighteen months, during which time he oversaw the opening of its prestigious restaurant, Ninety Park Lane.

But it was in 1982 that Anton realised his ambition to head one of the largest kitchens in one of the world's most fabled hotels: The Savoy. 'The Savoy,' it was recently written, 'is a grande dame, a dowager duchess who can still make heads turn, whose tiara sparkles as brightly as ever. Younger rivals can only look on enviously as new generations of admirers gather around her . . .'

His first 'recipe' involved the total re-design and refurbishment of the kitchen at an estimated cost of £1.5 million. Eighteen months later, during which Anton and his brigade found temporary kitchens (at a further cost of £800,000) elsewhere in the Hotel, the bill had reached £5 million ..! 'It's a cook's dream,' Anton says, 'not a penny spared nor a penny wasted. We do not have freezers, nor do we have tin openers because we do not need them. We work with only fresh produce which arrives every morning – all £20,000 worth. It is prepared, cooked

Carole Evans

and served before the kitchen is cleared of food again the same night.'

Anton has a brigade of eighty chefs and sixty ancillary workers serving an average of 1,500 covers a day to the River Room, three different banqueting rooms and eight private dining rooms, as well as providing a 24-hour room service. He estimates that it takes about four years to get a kitchen of this capacity and potential fully operational and to establish a style. 'Now there's a return to "real" food – simple, hearty and enjoyable – like oxtail or steamed fish. But true simplicity in cooking only comes from experience. It divides the men from the boys – although the number of women chefs is increasing. . . In 1989, for the first time in the Savoy's history, the sous chef is a woman, Susan Tulloch. . . And it is a sign of the times that we have more British chefs in the kitchen.'

Apart from his appearances on BBC Television's Pebble Mill, since 1985 Anton has been the LBC Christmas Cook, solving listeners' last minute seasonal panics, and is a favourite with journalists because of his good humour and patience. Apparently (according to one of his colleagues), 'He's not known for raising his voice nor appearing anything but calm – in or out of his kitchen; and he's always got a smile for you. . .'

His first publication, The Savoy Food and Wine Book was released in 1988 and has sold over 35,000 copies, and 'there is another in the pipeline. . .'

Away from the Savoy, Anton enjoys eating 'anywhere and anything – as long as it's well prepared. . .', and spending time with his family at home in North London.

Anton Edelmann
The Savoy Hotel
London WC2 OEU
01-836-4343

Carole Evans can justifiably claim to be self-taught. Apart from some basic schooling in cookery from her mother, she literally picked things up as she went along. She became a farmer's wife at the age of nineteen and remembers buying a Cordon Bleu magazine for 4/6d a week. Raising four children in an agricultural environment near Abergavenny, she was forever making junket from fresh milk, being handed buckets of sweetbreads to deal with, and other such tasks. She remarried several years later and, having a cricketing and shooting husband, invariably used to trot along behind with the food.

Today she runs her restaurant, Poppies, at Brimfield, in a delightful summery room allied to the village pub. Her husband took voluntary redundancy from the brewery and they ended up taking the Roebuck as a tenancy in 1983. Whilst he learned the trade, Carole stuck to the bar food. Everything was home-made – cottage pies, soups, baked hams, and even the pickles and chutneys for the ploughman's – this won her a slot on BBC2's Perfect Pickle programme!

As she gained confidence, so she got more adventurous and thus the pub evolved into the restaurant of today. Carole is frank on the subject of hard work and maintains

there is a complete absence of glamour in cooking. Lifting a stock pot later cost her £300 in getting treatment for her back! However, the pleasure gained from grateful customers looking in at the kitchen door makes it all worthwhile.

Carole Evans
Poppies Restaurant
The Roebuck
Brimfield
Hereford & Worcester SY8 4LN
(058 472) 230

Gunn Eriksen

Gunn Eriksen arrived in this country from Norway on a world tour. It was 1978. But she got no further than Inverness, which is where she met Fred Brown, with whom she now runs the famous Altnaharrie Inn.

Her background is completely unrelated to cooking and catering in the accepted sense: for her, cooking is an art in itself – very much as Carême felt that cooking was an extension of architecture. Her training, informal and formal, runs something like this. Her home was always teeming with people to feed and her mother would explain how things were made and always displayed great patience. The more formal training came from her Art teacher who, as well as showing the importance of colour, depth and texture in her tapestry work, also taught her how to learn from others' techniques without actually copying them. So, an artist's training developed in an enquiring mind an inner eye for colour and design: not, you would agree, a classical training for a chef, but perhaps one from which others might learn.

Today, Gunn Eriksen is considered by some to be one of the top chefs in the country, although she herself finds that hard to understand. Perhaps her personal philosophy is another key to her success. She has never sought fame, but allied to a natural modesty are these ideas have more to do with the teachings of the East than with cooking. For example, she believes that you should always look into the belly of a fish to learn what it fed on, just as you should know how it was killed, as both have a bearing on how it should be cooked and how it will taste. A frightened animal releases a chemical which alters the flavour.

Gunn's artistic training has given her the ability to match in her mind a whole store of flavours, some remembered and some perhaps just freshly tasted on one of her a country walks, from which much of

her inspiration and ingredients come. The hawthorn and cucumber soup is just one example. She nibbles on a leaf as she passes a shrub and it is blended from memory with fresh cucumber, but it takes a special kind of person to blend the resulting flavour with pigeon stock and so create the final soup. Gunn's larder is on her doorstep, and she has to stop her guests weeding the nettles and bishop's weed from time to time. As well as these, there are sorrel and bittercress, rowan and elderflower. And her kitchen garden might even be said to encompass the sea. Fishing boats drop off their catch on their way to Ullapool, and in the bay in front of the 17th-century droving inn she keeps lobster, mussels and crab.

Gunn's designs for presentation are not culled from the pages of Bocuse, Vergé and Guérard. The books on her shelves are of wild flowers, trees and artists. Her ideas come from glimpses of her surroundings, moments in the living world around her.

How did Altnaharrie begin? In 1980 she and Fred had decided to let the old Inn to an English couple to run for the season. But two weeks before the first guests were due to arrive the couple decided not to come. So Gunn had to cook. Not without reason is her name derived from a Norse word meaning 'to fight'.

The Inn may be reached in two ways, either by a long walk over the hills from Dundonnell or more directly across Loch Broom from Ullapool. Ullapool is a purpose-built town, designed in 1788 by the British Fishing Society as home for the workforce that fished the herring which then shoaled in their millions in Loch Broom. After fifty years the herring were fished out and the town went into decline, but today it is a busy port again, as the larger boats can go further afield for their catch, and the huge Russian factory ships sit for months at a time, processing the local catch. Indeed, it is easier to buy a set of Scrabble in Russian than it is to get decent fresh vegetables, and it with this problem that Gunn has had to contend. She found that she was sending back produce which a lot of bigger hotels had already rejected. The Highlands attitude was that you were lucky to get anything at all! She did not share that attitude, and along with a few other pioneers has improved the level of quality available in the whole area.

Always sensitive to the environment and culture of a place, Gunn's personal choice of food naturally varies as to where she finds herself – but wherever she is or whatever she cooks, you can be sure that the choice will be hers alone.

GUNN ERIKSEN
The Altnaharrie Inn
Ullapool
Ross-shire IV26 2SS
(085 483) 230

David Everitt-Matthias

From the age of seven, David Everitt-Matthias wanted to be a chef, and he owes his initial enthusiasm to an aunt who loved cooking. He started off at The Inn on the Park in Mayfair, under the tutelage of Jean-Michel Bonin, learning all the fundamentals of French classic cuisine. He attended Ealing College during this time to gain his City & Guilds qualifications, and did 'stages' with the likes of Pierre Koffmann, at La Tante Claire, where he realised just what could be achieved as a chef/patron.

In 1985 David helped set up a restaurant in Putney specialising in Seychellois fish, and he counts this as invaluable experience both in building up a clientele and learning about new fish. He then moved to Fingals in Fulham, bringing a more modern cuisine to that establishment.

But what David really wanted to do was to set up on his own, and he achieved this in August 1987, when he opened Le Champignon Sauvage in Gloucestershire as chef/patron. Here, he puts into practice a style that he says is constantly evolving in accordance with his experience. Each change of menu is a natural development, as he tries to achieve the best possible end result, an almost perfect combination of flavours and textures.

When eating out, David's choice ranges from the nearby Buckland Manor to his local pub on a Sunday lunchtime. In short, wherever the food is good and the true flavours fully understood.

DAVID EVERITT-MATTHIAS
Le Champignon Sauvage
24-26 Suffolk Road
Cheltenham
Gloucestershire GL50 2AQ

ANDY EASTICK
The Market Bar
240 Portobello Road
London W11
01-229 6472

EUGENE ECHOLS
Soho Brasserie
23-25 Old Compton Street
London W1V 5PJ
01-439 9301

JOHN ELLIOTT
Les Ambassadeurs
5 Hamilton Place
Hyde Park Corner
London W1V 0ED
01-499 3626

ROBERT ELSMORE
Hunstrete House Hotel
Chelwood
Near Bristol
Avon BS18 4NS
(076 18) 578

RENÉ EMIN
The French Horn Hotel
Sonning-on-Thames
Berkshire RG4 0TN
(0734) 692204

GILLIAN ENTHOVEN
Le Mesurier Restaurant
113 Old Street
London EC1V 9JR
01-251 8117

Ray Farthing

Max Fischer

Mark Fisher

As a boy Ray Farthing enjoyed cooking, so when his father encouraged him to join a trade, it seemed the obvious choice. However, he had some early obstacles to overcome: at school he had been prevented from taking 'O' level cookery and was told he would never make a chef, so it became important for Ray to prove his teacher wrong.

He began as an apprentice at the Pier, at Harwich, and came under the expert supervision of Chris Oakley, to whom he pays tribute as the man who put him on the right road. From the Pier he moved within the Milsom empire to Le Talbooth, first as commis and then as third chef. Then, in 1983, he spent the best part of a year as personal chef to the Earl and Countess Spencer at Althorp House. His next post was at the Castle Hotel in Taunton, where he was sous chef; and then in 1986 he moved to Calcot Manor as head chef.

Originally, his style was classical, but at Calcot, particularly, it has developed from its solid foundations to a more modern interpretation. He tries to use classical combinations 'with a twist', as he puts it, developing flavours in the first place, then adding an interpretative presentation.

Two things give him particular satisfaction: to see his brigade progressing and learning well; and to receive the appreciation of his customers at the end of the day. For himself, he enjoys eating out at places which have similar standards and styles to his own, but basically plain, simple food without frills.

I wonder if that school teacher has eaten her words?

RAY FARTHING
Calcot Manor
Nr Tetbury
Gloucestershire GL8 8YJ
(066 689) 355

Max Fischer served his three-year apprenticeship in Luneburg, in his native West Germany, and supplemented his training by taking outside catering jobs – local weddings, confirmations and similar events.

He worked as a commis, both in Germany and France, before venturing to England for the first time in 1974, when he began a two-year stint at The Bell at Aston Clinton. Max spent the next four years in Stockholm and in West Germany. Then, in 1980, he returned to England, and opened Fischer's Restaurant in Bakewell. He had an unfortunate experience when expanding this business and moving it to its present location: fire broke out just prior to the opening.

However, we were delighted to learn that the day was eventually saved, and that Max and Susan Fischer are now safely installed in their new home.

Max now has his own modern European style, most influenced by his time spent in Paris. He particularly enjoys buying fresh produce at the morning's market, then recommending it to his customers that evening and selling all of it.

Going out is a rare event for him, so he likes to choose somewhere special and is quite prepared to travel some distance to exercise a personal preference for variations on a classical theme.

MAX FISCHER
Fischer's at Baslow Hall
Calver Road
Baslow
Derbyshire DE4 1RR
(024 688) 3259

From being a reluctant school pupil, Mark Fisher began his working life in an engineering workshop. But realising that this was not where his interests truly lay, he served an apprenticeship at Gough Hotels. He also attended Ipswich College on day release, where he obtained his City & Guilds qualifications.

After a brief period in industrial catering, he spent two years as second chef at the Angel Hotel, Bury St Edmonds and joined the Starr as head chef in 1982.

His parents were keen gardeners and grew an abundance of vegetables. Jam and pickle-making was a regular pastime. Mark believes in using fresh and wholesome produce, and acknowledges the influence of his parents' garden on his own style of cooking.

Given a free choice, Mark prefers to eat fish and fresh vegetables – but once a year he allows himself fish and chips!

MARK FISHER
The Starr
Market Place
Great Dunmow
Essex CM6 1AX
(0371) 874321

Alan
Ford

Kevin
Francksen

Kurt
Friedli

Alan Ford began his training as a chef in his native Kent, and finished it at Westminster College in London. He gained experience at various hotels and restaurants – Grosvenor House, The Westbury, Maxim's, The Dorchester, and The Inter-Continental in Sydney – covering every section of every kitchen in the last two years of his apprenticeship.

Alan's style was originally quite classical, but his years at the top London hotels modified it considerably. He now cooks in the modern style, but with a classical basis. He likes to make food and sauces light in texture, but full of flavour, and served in adequate quantities. For Alan, there is nothing worse than a customer saying, 'Is that it?', as the plate is put before them.

Alan took up his first and present post as head chef at Hintlesham Hall, where in Robert Mabey he had a hard act to follow. However, he has risen to the challenge with great aplomb, much to Ruth and David Watson's delight, and they've seen their confidence in him amply repaid.

Alan likes to eat out as much as possible to gain experience of different styles, so eager is he to continue learning.

ALAN FORD
Hintlesham Hall
Hintlesham
Ipswich
Suffolk IP8 3NS
(047 387) 334

Kevin Francksen always wanted to wear a tall hat like the chefs he had seen in books and magazines, and an early interest in food made cooking an obvious career choice. He began by washing up and, occasionally, cooking breakfasts at a local YMCA, and then undertook some rather more formal training at Basingstoke Technical College and the Thomas Danby College in Leeds. He topped this off with some practical experience at London's West End hotels, before returning north in 1984 to Middlethorpe Hall.

Here he began work in the pastry section, becoming sous chef in 1985 to Aidan McCormack, whom he credits as his main mentor. The learning obviously paid off, for when Aidan moved on, in 1987, Kevin was well equipped to take over as head chef and began to put into practice his own variety of modern English cooking that still betrays a fundamental grounding in the classic French school.

He eats out anywhere he can, and enjoys good pub food as well as the fare in top hotels and restaurants – of any style, any country of origin. But perhaps best of all, he still enjoys his mother's cooking.

KEVIN FRANCKSEN
Middlethorpe Hall
Bishopthorpe Road
York
North Yorkshire YO12 1QB
(0904) 641241

When Kurt Friedli was six years old, his mother took him to a cookery demonstration in his native Switzerland. He instantly decided that this was what he was going to do. He studied at the Hotel School in Neuchâtel, as well as spending his apprenticeship there. After that, he cooked his way round the world – Gstaad, Lausanne, Jersey, Grand Cayman, London, Mombasa, Essex, Derbyshire, Johannesburg and Scotland.

His real hankering, however, was for a restaurant of his own. Eventually, in December 1977, he opened, Hunters Lodge Restaurant with his wife. They soon discovered that it takes more to run a good restaurant than just being a good chef. But once having learned the finer points of atmosphere and service, and with Dottie at front of house, the formula for success was set.

KURT FRIEDLI
Hunters Lodge Restaurant
High Street
Broadway
Hereford & Worcester WR12 7DT
(0386) 853247

ELIZABETH FERRISS
Maiden Newton House
Maiden Newton
Near Dorchester
Dorset DT2 0AA
(0300) 20336

PASCAL FIOUX
St Quentin
243 Brompton Road
London SW3 2EP
01-589 8005

CHRIS FIRTH-BERNARD
The Summer Isles Hotel
Achiltibuie by Ullapool
Ross-shire IV26 2YG
(085 482) 282

CHRIS FISHER
Fossebridge Inn
Fossebridge
Northleach
Gloucestershire GL54 3JS
(028 572) 721

MARY FLINT
Boscundle Manor
Tregrehan
St Austell
Cornwall PL25 3RL
(072 681) 3557

STEPHEN FORAN
The Little Angel
Remenham
Henley-on-Thames
Oxfordshire RG9 2LS
(0491) 574165

BARRY FORSTER
Longueville Manor
St Saviour
Jersey
Channel Islands
(0534) 25501

RÉMY FOUGÈRE
Royal Lancaster Hotel
Lancaster Terrace
London W2 2TY
01-262 6737

ANTONIO FRANCO
The Basil Street Hotel
Basil Street
London SW3 1AH
01-581 3311

TIM FRANKLIN
South Lodge
Brighton Road
Lower Beeding
West Sussex RH13 6PS
(0403) 891711

V FRAPPOZA
**Manzi's Hotel &
Restaurants Ltd**
1/2 Leicester Square
London WC2H 7BC
01-734 0224

CHRISTOPHER FREEMAN
Knockie Lodge
Whitebridge
Inverness-shire IV1 2UP
(045 63) 276

DEREK FULLER
Athenaeum Hotel
116 Piccadilly
London W1V 0BJ
01-499 3464

ALAN FYKIN
Bill Bentley's
Swedeland Court
202 Bishopsgate
London EC2M 4NR
01-282 1763

Allan Garth was born in Cumbria, and says that from a very young age he was interested in cooking and eating, so becoming a chef seemed like the natural thing to do. He spent three years at Kendal College before starting his career as an apprentice in a local pub/hotel from 1969 to 1971. He worked at Slaugham Manor Hotel in West Sussex from 1971 to 1974. Nearby Gravetye Manor was his next move, and he worked there from 1974 to 1987, progressing from chef tournant to sous chef to chef de cuisine. Before moving to New Hall in Sutton Coldfield, as head chef, he did a spot as guest chef at Milton Park Country House Hotel in Bowral, Australia.

Allan learned his trade according to the old masters of cooking, and he has subsequently been influenced by traditional dishes from around the world. This has led to his style being described as 'eclectic'. He says that he is happiest when working with the best produce, and when a customer leaves his restaurant a happy person. For Allan, simple well-prepared food is the best.

ALLAN GARTH
New Hall Country House Hotel
Sutton Coldfield
West Midlands B76 8QX
021-378 2442

Paul Gayler

Paul Gayler is, at thirty-three, one of the finest of the new generation of British chefs. He describes himself as an eternal apprentice, which is his way of saying that he is constantly learning, always developing and perfecting his art. Paul Gayler trained under Anton Mosimann at The Dorchester. Six years ago he joined Inigo Jones and helped build its enviable reputation.

Paul Gayler's style is unique and, although Essex born, was described by the late Jeremy Round in the *Independent* as being more central European than that of many of his peers. He certainly takes inspiration and ideas from a wide number of sources but always produces a result which is imaginative and distinctive. Many chefs will talk about Oriental influences on their cooking. These tend to come from books or from their frequent visits to Oriental res-

taurants. Paul Gayler has gone one step further. He worked in both Chinese and Indian restaurants. His understanding of the spicing and methods of cooking is thorough and the results can be an improvement on the original.

As well as running Inigo Jones, Gayler conceived and created a fish, seafood and vegetarian menu for Burt's in London's Soho, and invented a dish which crystallizes so many of his ideas. His spring roll is visually deceptive: it looks like a tiny

version of any other spring roll. The casing, however, is made from blanched celeriac, and the filling combines shellfish, spring onions, mange touts, mouli, beansprouts and carrots. The spicing is ginger from the East, the herb is chervil a favourite in modern France, the sauce is a classic reduction of langoustine shells. All the facets of Gayler's experience come together to create – no gimmick – but a genuinely original dish.

Paul's food certainly reflects modern techniques but is underpinned by classical disciplines. His salmon tartare is marinated with Eastern spices and served in an almost Hungarian manner with soured cucumber. A tournedos of salt cod is served with a provençal rouille which merges with perfect mashed potato for a superbly balanced dish. A monkfish tail will be transformed into a pastiche of Italian osso bucco, but again it is a pastiche that works. When dealing with meat, the fillet of beef will be served with a sauce of shallot and mustard, whole garlic

and lentils. Guinea fowl might be poached in a herb broth laced with vermouth.

Paul Gayler is a modern chef but one with old-fashioned values. He works, he says, to keep his family, his wife and three children. He prefers recognition from regular customers to culinary awards, although he has received plenty of the latter in his time. He claims to enjoy the variety of running his own kitchen without ever taking the credit for the fact that so much of the variety comes from his ideas and enthusiasm.

Like his own mentor Mosimann, he is a great teacher. There are several young chefs who are carrying on the Gayler tradition although he is still young himself. His consideration for customers is well-known. He says he does not mind working fourteen hours a day as long as someone has the grace to say thank you. He was one of the first chefs in London to create specifically for vegetarians with properly crafted dishes available both à la carte and on the special menu. This is something which will develop in the 1990s. He works at the highest level all week, enjoying a curry at weekends with his wife, near his home in Essex.

PAUL GAYLER
Inigo Jones
14 Garrick Street
London WC2E 9BJ
01-836 6456

As we went to press, Inigo Jones closed.

61

Chris German

Chris German enjoyed working at the Dormy Hotel, Ferndown, at weekends during his schooldays so much so that he went to work there full-time as a trainee, taking day release to do his City & Guilds. After the Dormy, he spent four years at the Grosvenor House, cooking classical French cuisine, before moving to Odin's Restaurant. He spent two years as sous-chef for two years and was then promoted to head chef in 1984.

Gradually, through eating out at quality establishments, reading as much as possible, and experimenting both at home and at work, Chris has evolved a simple, no-nonsense style of cooking that is an amalgamation of the best of English and French cuisine. He turns top quality produce into top quality dishes, and if his customer is happy, then he is happy as well.

Chris goes across to France regularly, eating at the starred establishments, and when at home enjoys good Chinese and Indian restaurants. But perhaps his favourite haunts are the pubs around London's Smithfield Market, where he can be spotted indulging in one of their famous breakfasts!

CHRIS GERMAN
Odin's Restaurant
27 Devonshire Street
London W1N 1RT
01-935 7296

Boyd Gilmour

An Irishman to the core, Boyd Gilmour says that what made him go into the restaurant business in the first place was an overwhelming desire for an early grave, combined with hereditary madness on his father's side. His career took off when he bought a frying pan, made an omelette and won a prize. He went on to combine his training at the Royal College of Music with hard work in very good restaurants. Quite an achievement, considering he played at one time with the London Symphony Orchestra.

Boyd's original style was good food, plain and simple. His style has developed in that, as he says, good food does not change, only the presentation of it. His restaurant is French in style but English in character, set in a pretty conservatory in Kensington, and consistently popular since he opened in 1986.

Boyd loves to see customers coming back time after time and he most enjoys eating out at good restaurants, of all styles and at all price ranges.

BOYD GILMOUR
Boyd's Glass Garden Restaurant
135 Kensington Church Street
London W8 7LP
01-727 5452

GERRY GALVIN
Drimcong House
Moycullen Co Galway
(091) 85115

ALEJANDRO GARCIA
Don Pepe
99 Frampton Street London NW8 8NA
01-262 3834

BERNARD GAUME
Hyatt Carlton Tower
2 Cadogan Place London SW1X 9PY
01-235 5411

KEN GOODY
The Cemlyn
High Street
Harlech Gwynedd LL46 2YA
(0766) 780425

BERTRAND GOUTELON
Yours Faithfully
14 Nightingale Lane London SW12 8XS
01-675 6771

DOUGLAS GRAY
The Old Monastery
Drybridge
Buckie Banffshire AB2 2JB
(0542) 32660

SIMON GREENLAY
Devonshire Arms Country House Hotel
Bolton Abbey
Near Skipton North Yorkshire BD23 6AJ
(075 671) 441

TONY GRINSTEAD
Café Pelican du Sud
Hays Galleria
London Bridge City
Tooley Street London SE1
01-378 0096/7

Mark Gregory

Paul Grindle

DIDIER GUÉRIN
The Victorian House
Trunnah Road
Thornton Cleveleys Lancashire FY5 4HF
(0253) 860619

RUSTICO GUERVERRO
Hoult's
20 Bellevue Road London SW17 7EB
01-767 1858

MICHEL GUIJARRO
Le Provençale
181/183 Park View
Whitley Bay Tyne & Wear NE26 3PS
091-251 3567

JEAN-LUC GUIRAL
Monsieur Frog Restaurant
31a Essex Road London N1 2SE
01-226 3495

GORDON GUNN
Cregan House
Strathyre Perthshire FK18 8ND
(087 74) 638

Mark Gregory, born in South Wales, originally wanted to be a jockey, but during his childhood travels in Spain and Portugal he developed a love of food that rapidly became incompatible with the necessary dietary restraint of such professional horsemen. Having found an enjoyment in eating, it was no surprise when he discovered that he enjoyed cooking equally. The family lived in New Zealand at this time and Mark served his apprenticeship at Trillos in Auckland, receiving a thorough, classical grounding under Gordon Roberts, whose main emphasis was often on presentation.

After the apprenticeship, his first job, which lasted a year, was in England, as first commis at Claridge's. Afterwards he returned to the antipodes, joining the Park Royal in Brisbane, Australia, as sous chef. In 1984 it was back to New Zealand as head chef to the cultural ambassador, and then to the Hotel de Brett as head chef.

In 1988 he caught the eye of the press by winning the title of Chef of the Year at Hotelympia, and found himself courted by the media and wooed by new opportunities. The lucky suitor was the Chelsea Hotel in Sloane Street. Mark's original sporting ambitions are now satisfied by a healthy attitude to his present occupation – he spent a year as a vegetarian, and now aims for a modern health-conscious style of cooking and presentation, and especially enjoys cooking fish. When eating out for his own pleasure, he goes for strong definite flavours, often ethnic.

MARK GREGORY
The Chelsea Hotel
Sloane Street
London SW1
01-235 4377

During a two-year full-time City & Guilds catering course Paul made very specific plans for his future: to work at The Savoy and at Buckingham Palace, and after his finals, he entered the Grill kitchen of The Savoy under Louis Virot, an experience that confirmed his enthusiasm and taught Paul how to work under intense pressure, and enjoy it.

The planned move to Buckingham Palace came as a shock to a system geared to the adrenalin pumping atmosphere of The Savoy kitchens. But the more peaceful, no less well-organised regime, and a brief that included Christmas at Windsor, New Year at Sandringham, holidays at Balmoral, and trips on the Royal Yacht, provided further invaluable experience.

On cue, three years later, Paul arrived at the Box Tree, where as sous chef under Michael Truelove he developed his characteristically uncomplicated cuisine – 'meat and fish juices full of flavour and agreeable to the palate'. Then, for the first time straying from his carefully laid strategy, Paul moved to a restaurant in Charlotte Street, London, a disaster which resulted in his leaving to start a small bistro/wine bar called La Petite Fleur in Boroughbridge. After only one year, he and his young wife Judy earned a Red M in the Michelin Guide. Today, Paul is looking for funding of a new enterprise – a restaurant/catering complex with a projected turnover of £2 million. On past form there seems little doubt that he will find it.

PAUL GRINDLE
La Petite Fleur
14 Fishergate
Boroughbridge
North Yorkshire YO5 9AL
(0423) 322055

63

Ruth Hadley

Peter Hauser

Ruth Hadley had no formal training as a chef before she and her husband Tony bought The Cross at Kingussie, a simple shop-fronted restaurant in the centre of a Highland village on the A9. It is run on homely lines.

The decision to start a restaurant came about as a result of disillusionment with the general standards of eating out – a feeling of 'I can cook better than that'. Armed with books, magazines and her own instincts, Ruth launched herself upon the kitchen. Her subsequent acclaim is still looked upon by Ruth with a certain amount of bewilderment.

She cites the Troisgros brothers at Roanne, in France, as being a major inspiration: their use of prime ingredients, carefully treated and simply presented, is what it's all about. Of course it is always good to see the French using Scottish smoked salmon and Aberdeen Angus beef, and it fails to surprise her – as Ruth says, 'Scottish ingredients have long been associated with quality.'

Her eye is as good as her ability to combine flavours and colours. The complete meal is full of contrasts, not just within individual dishes but also from course to course. Hers is a style that is totally intuitive and accurate, born of an innate understanding of her product.

France remains their inspiration and the Hadleys go there every year on a wine-tasting trip, specifically to augment Tony's already remarkable wine list – and of course to eat chez les frères Troisgros!

RUTH HADLEY
The Cross
25-27 High Street
Kingussie
Highland PH21 1HX
(054 02) 762

Peter began with three years' training in Linz, Austria, then cooked his way round Europe to gain experience. He says that he learned most in Switzerland, where he liked the directness of the people and also their aptitude for classical cuisine. In 1970 he met his wife, Nita, who shared his ambitions, and they settled for ten years in the Channel Islands, where they brought Sark's Aval du Creux very much to public attention. Im-

mediately after that, Peter bought Stock Hill House in Dorset and set about proving that a chef can own and run a country house without any help from anybody else.

Peter believes that food is only good when it is fresh, and not overcooked. It also needs to be treated with love. The late Hans Koppler used to tell Peter that one needs to have more love for cooking than for a woman. This, so Peter says, is quite some-

Redmond Hayward

thing – coming from an Austrian! He has never been keen on nouvelle cuisine, and is only too pleased that the fashion has passed. He thinks the future is very exciting, full of golden opportunities for anybody with the will to succeed. He is passionate in encouraging youngsters to enter the industry as a first-choice profession, rather than as a second-best to more glamorous careers.

Peter also feels that British customers would do well to change their attitude towards service. Just because someone is cooking and serving guests it does not make them a second-class citizen to be treated badly. If the next generation of diners appreciates this fact, and the next generation of chefs is still prepared to work all hours that God sends, then he thinks that this country's catering profession will be as good as any in the world.

Peter has only one ambition left: to cook as well as mother. Considering what Peter has achieved, she must be a very hard act to follow!

PETER HAUSER
Stock Hill House Hotel and Restaurant
Wyke
Gillingham
Dorset SP8 5NR
(0747) 823626

After Ealing College, Redmond found his feet initially as second chef at the Rising Sun at St Mawes. Working at Anna's Place in Islington then gave him a chance to experiment, and he still retains in his repertoire a few dishes he learned during this time, like the gravadlax.

In 1984 he became head chef at the newly-opened Calcot Manor, near Tetbury, placing it firmly on the gastronomic map before leaving two years later to open Redmond's in Cheltenham with his wife, Pippa. In true husband-and-wife tradition they did everything themselves, and this was a crucial factor in deciding the way the cooking was executed. Little time, and the fact that there was no one to whom to delegate, meant that frills and fussiness were discarded in favour of a simple, modern English approach. The philosophy was – and still is – never to compromise on quality but nor to over-complicate.

A recent move up to Cleeve Hill with its majestic views out across the Malvern Hills has meant taking on accommodation with the restaurant and hiring extra staff. Redmond's principles remain intact, but now, with three in the kitchen, he's able to try out more ideas, perfect his sauces, and make lighter, fluffier mousselines.

One of Redmond's favourite establishments is Shaun Hill's at Gidleigh Park, to his mind a perfect hotel for getting away from it all. He describes Hill's cooking as both gutsy and polished, simple and unsophisticated. Good ground rules and, indeed, an apt summary of Redmond Hayward's own cooking.

REDMOND HAYWARD
Redmond's at Malvern View
Cleeve Hill
Cheltenham
Gloucestershire GL52 3PR
(024 267) 2017

JOY HADLEY
Rumbles Cottage Restaurant
Braintree Road
Felstead Essex CM6 3DJ
(0371) 820996

JACKIE HAMILTON
Kaspia
18/18a Bruton Place London W1X 7AH
01-493 2612

CHRISTOPHER HARDING
Harding's Restaurant
2 Station Road
North Berwick East Lothian EH39 4AU
(0620) 4737

DAVID HARDING
Craigside Manor
Little Orme
Colwyn Road
Llandudno Gwynedd LL30 3AL
(0492) 45943

MARK HARRINGTON
Ston Easton Park
Ston Easton
Near Bath Avon BA3 4DF
(076 121) 631

GERALD HASLEGRAVE
Lichfield's
13 Lichfield Terrace
Sheen Road
Richmond Surrey TW9 1AS
01-940 5236

Catherine Healy

Catherine Healy is an Irish lass through and through, who describes herself as self-taught. But such is her reputation within the cookery world that she is welcomed with open arms to do 'stages' with the likes of Albert Roux, Roger Vergé and Raymond Blanc. She had only ever cooked for her family before opening Dunderry Lodge in 1977, with her husband Nicholas. In fact, it was he who had trained in catering and always wanted to run his own restaurant, so when Dunderry became available it was a heaven-sent opportunity. However, since Catherine was already cooking at home and Nicholas found he preferred working at front of house and with wines, their present roles to evolved quite naturally. And evolve they did, in such a way that Dunderry is now one of the most highly rated establishments in Ireland.

Apart from the chefs with whom she has cooked, she pays the greatest possible tribute to Elizabeth David, whose books she still refers to constantly. Although she describes both her original and present style as simple, she will add that it is no less individual for that. She loves mixtures of styles and influences – a bit of the Far East, the Middle East, France, Italy and of course Ireland. She most enjoys taking fundamental ideas from other countries and adapting them to Irish produce. And what produce she has to work with! In her vast garden in the middle of the countryside she grows nearly all the fruit, vegetables, herbs and salads that they use. They have excellent local suppliers of game, meat and poultry, and Catherine makes everything that she can on the premises.

She gets the greatest satisfaction from making a new idea work – having the original concept and seeing it through to fruition. But when pressed, she says that 'absolutely everything in cooking, from A to Z, gives me joy – it's that kind of business, isn't it?' When she eats out, she again goes for the kind of food that she prepares – simple, not over-elaborately sauced or garnished, full of pure, natural flavours.

Her tip for youngsters entering the industry is simple: be prepared to work very very hard, put in the hours – and then be prepared to really enjoy yourself. Sounds like good advice.

CATHERINE HEALY
Dunderry Lodge
Navan
Co Meath
Republic of Ireland
010-353-46 31671

Patricia Hegarty

Patricia Hegarty had always enjoyed cooking on a small scale, and on opening Hope End Country House Hotel with her husband John in 1979, she began with a just seven tables for two and a very simple fixed menu which changed daily according to what was in peak condition in their garden and in the shops and markets. Within those fixed menus, variety was the key.

Essentially, Patricia's style has not changed since she began, and some of her original dishes still feature on her menus. She likes to let the pure, clear, distinctive flavours of ingredients speak for themselves, together with the character and texture of the basic raw materials. She defines it as English country cooking that is simple and unpretentious, eclectic but not gimmicky, traditional but not formal. The presentation of her dishes has evolved and been more finely honed, but is still restrained.

At the end of the evening, Patricia is content if she knows that each course has been complementary and harmonious. With her days fully occupied, she finds it difficult to get out and about and rarely goes to London. However, she does mention two favourites: the Croque-en-Bouche in nearby Malvern Wells, and the Carved Angel in Dartmouth. Perhaps it is no coincidence that both of these are show cases for the cooking of two other English lady chefs.

PATRICIA HEGARTY
Hope End Hotel
Hope End
Ledbury
Hereford & Worcester HR8 1JQ
(0531) 3613

67

Shaun Hill

Shaun Hill is one of the most influential of modern British chefs. He is a thoughtful and independent man who draws his inspiration from the books he reads, from his extensive travels in Europe and America, and from a diverse range of experience.

Shaun's career has taken in establishments like Carrier's, when it was the foremost setting for fashionable London food and Blake's, which helped revolutionise London hotel dining.

Shaun's dishes may include the Eastern influences of grilled scallops in a sauce of lentils; classical bourgeois France in a navarin of lamb brought skilfully up to date; or the Northern Italian influence of a fillet of veal laced with white truffle oil.

Shaun Hill takes a scientific approach to cooking in that every dish has been stripped to its basic elements, has been questioned and rebuilt with every component part, fulfilling its correct function. It is not, though, classic cooking. It has the flair and passion of a chef who enjoys eating and who also has a keen interest in combining wine and food to good effect.

Raised in the city, Shaun has now become a real countryman, striding across Dartmoor in search of mushrooms, before preparing dinner and afterwards settling down with a large brandy to discuss with friends anything from food to poetry.

SHAUN HILL
Gidleigh Park
Chagford
Devon TQ13 8HH
(064 73) 2367

Baba Hine

Baba Hine and husband Denis own and run Corse Lawn, a listed Queen Anne House. Denis runs the front of house, while Baba looks after their substantial kitchen. Over the years Baba's cooking has achieved both local and nationwide acclaim, and Corse Lawn now boasts a regular and intensely loyal clientele.

Baba began her hotel career as personal secretary to Michael Harris at the famous Bell Inn, Aston Clinton, where she met Denis. Together they moved to manage The Red Lion at Weobley in Herefordshire. Baba felt that she could do better than the professional hotel chefs and took over the kitchens. She threw herself wholeheartedly into learning about food, from the culinary basics to the most complicated classical dishes. 'In the first year, I read Larousse Gastronomique from end to end. I went to bed each night with cookery books and never stopped reading.' Her perseverance paid off and The Red Lion soon became one of the best restaurants in Herefordshire. In 1970 the couple purchased The Three Cocks Hotel near Brecon in Wales and transformed it from a dilapidated old inn to a well-respected restaurant with rooms.

In 1978 the Hines bought Corse Lawn which was an established restaurant that had ceased trading. The Hines added a new bar serving simple but excellent cooking, refurbished the restaurant, and began a process of sympathetic rebuilding in order to create one of the best hotels in Gloucestershire.

Baba Hine's cooking is a glorious mixture of the traditional and dishes of her own invention. Breakfasts at Corse Lawn are thoroughly self-indulgent and might include delicious home-made yoghurt or excellent home-made sausages. The menu in the restaurant ranges from the delicate to the hearty with a generous concession to vegetarians. The freshest ingredients are combined in delightful dishes such as medallions of veal fillet with girolles and croustades of baby sweetcorn. Superb puddings make imaginative use of fresh fruit.

Baba is always trying new recipes, inventing new dishes, and prides herself on the scope of the menu. Her style is a very successful cross between the homely and the fashionable, with a bias towards pre-nouvelle-cuisine country dishes. Portions are sensibly sized and never fussily presented. She is very firm in the management of her kitchen and the result is food cooked with personal conviction and without ostentation.

Baba Hine
Corse Lawn
Tirley
Gloucestershire
GL19 4LZ
(045 278) 479

69

Colin Hingston

Colin Hingston was born in southern Rhodesia, and claims that it was 'sheer stupidity' that brought him into the restaurant business! However, he set matters aright by spending five years as a management trainee with Trusthouse Forte. He first came to the public eye when he was chef at the Penny Anthony restaurant in Ludlow from 1978-1981. From there he moved to Thornbury Castle, developing his technique under the guidance of the legendary Kenneth Bell. Colin picked up tips on the dishes of Provence, and when Kenneth moved to France, he stepped into the master's shoes. Maurice Taylor took over ownership of the Castle in 1986 and the already strong reputation of the hotel soared. Two excellent developments, from Colin's point of view, were the making of the castle's vineyard-grown grapes into Thornbury's own-label wine, and the policy of buying in as many local speciality cheese as possible.

Colin is very much aware of the Castle's Tudor origins, but has developed some original dishes for the modern palate, for instance without the heavy sauces of the originals. However, tradition remains strong. Indeed, nouvelle cuisine only lasted for three weeks at Thornbury! The final menu style – pleasing owner, chef and customers alike – falls into the category of modern British cooking and usually includes a selection for vegetarians.

A happy kitchen, working at full stretch, producing beautiful food for happy guests, is what gives Colin his satisfaction. His own preferences when eating out? He'll go anywhere that produces good value for money, whether it be for £2 or £50 a head.

COLIN HINGSTON
Thornbury Castle
Thornbury
Avon BS12 1HH
(0454) 418511

Laszlo Holecz

Garry Hollihead

Laszlo Holecz has to be *the* London Hungarian chef, for as well as being born in Hungary, he has been associated with all the Hungarian restaurants in the capital at one time or another, and has been at the Gay Hussar since 1977.

Laszlo finds immense satisfaction in what he does, and from the outset saw good prospects for someone prepared to work hard and show loyalty. He is an unashamed champion of old-fashioned cooking, and has a dedicated following to prove him right. The food on offer at the Gay Hussar has been described as honest, bistro food, huge portions of filling dishes with a unique Hungarian touch. A long-time favourite of politicians and journalists, it is to Laszlo's credit that when ownership of the restaurant changed in 1988, none of the regulars really noticed.

LASZLO HOLECZ
The Gay Hussar
2 Greek Street
London W1V 6NB
01-437 0973

Before Sutherlands, Garry Hollihead spent most of his culinary career in large hotels with big names – five years at Ninety Park Lane under Anton Edelmann and Vaughan Archer, one year with Louis Outhier at his three-star restaurant L'Oasis, and a year in Florida doing promotional work for The Savoy before returning to London as premier sous chef to Anton Edelmann. He has also entered and been successful in many competitions, achieving gold medals at the 1986 Culinary World Cup in Luxembourg, and at Stuttgart in 1986 (at Intergastra). And in 1987, he won for Sutherlands the Mouton Cadet Menu of the Year award.

Sutherlands opened to a storm of publicity that has never really died down. The décor caught the imagination, with its etched glass frontage and simple stylish graphics, and the food is very much in tune with the times. Garry combines the traditions of classic French with a lighter more modern touch. Heavy wine-based sauces are replaced by reductions which allow the natural flavours and textures of the ingredients to speak for themselves. The menu options are delightfully simple, set price but with a choice of six or seven dishes at each course, each illustrating the balance Garry achieves between simplicity and ingenuity. For example, there might be a soup of thyme and watercress with a timbale of diced white radish, or a tartlet of baby spinach, braised leeks and quails' eggs in a rosemary and chive butter sauce, studded with trompettes de mort; and then warm sautéed fillet of tuna dressed with a saffron oil served with confits of autumn vegetables, or fillet of venison in a blueberry and marc de champagne sauce with braised red cabbage and dauphinoise potatoes; and finally a hot puff envelope filled with apple and strawberries, served with lavender ice-cream and a lavender and honey crème anglaise. There is often a choice at the cheese course, too – warm glazed ash log with a salad of Belgian endive sprinkled with a chablis dressing, or a simple selection of English farmhouse cheeses served with Sutherlands' bread. And what bread! All made on the premises, there might be honey bread, lemon thyme bread, white sesame bread, wholemeal poppy seed bread, walnut brioche and black bread. Ices, sorbets and petits fours are also all made by Garry and his brigade.

GARRY HOLLIHEAD
Sutherlands
48 Lexington Street
London W1R 3LG
01-434 3401

Simon Hopkinson

Simon Hopkinson was born in Lancashire, and via a great flourish at Hilaire in Old Brompton Road, now takes his bows repeatedly at Bibendum, in the former Michelin building where he is in partnership with Sir Terence Conran.

But we're racing on a bit. How did he get this far? – by starting as an apprentice chef at the Normandie Hotel, near Manchester, in 1972/3. He still cooks fillet steak au poivre, for instance, the way that he learned at the Normandie – good and thick and full of flavour. From the Normandie he moved as chef to the Hat and Feather restaurant in Knutsford, Cheshire. Over to Dyfed in 1974 for a year as chef at the St Non's Hotel, then a year as chef/proprietor at the Shed restaurant, Fishguard. The next two years were spent as an inspector for Egon Ronay, which gave him some very interesting new perspectives. In 1982/3 he worked as a private chef before being recruited to head up Hilaire, where he stayed until 1987, gaining an Egon Ronay star – with no strings pulled! Late in that year, Bibendum opened.

Simon had nearly worked with Sir Terence once before, when the latter was looking for a chef for the Heal's restaurant. But he turned the offer down, to Lorna Wing's good fortune; but who is to say that lightening does not strike twice? When it did, Simon didn't say no the second time. They collaborated closely on the design of Bibendum, with Sir Terence having his say on some menu choices, for example, and Simon having his on – the ashtrays!

Simon's cooking is sound and clear, and he has been in the forefront of the move away from finnicky nouvelle cuisine back to more earthy, robust, bistro food. He is an ideal exponent of the genre, and his geniality is in keeping with the outsize image of the Michelin man.

Unlike some chefs who change their menus frequently, Simon Hopkinson likes being able to eat the same dish time and again, and is reassured to find that his customers do likewise! His menu is extensive and wide-ranging, but he knows his clientele well enough to be able to ensure constantly fresh produce even with a large menu.

Ironically enough, the building which now houses his restaurant was once the London home of the Michelin Guide – it seems that Simon cannot escape the attention of the various Guides!

SIMON HOPKINSON
Bibendum
The Michelin Building
81 Fulham Road
London SW3
01-581 5817

Anthony Howarth

Anthony Howarth began his training in 1969 at the Bridge Hotel in Cambridge, where he served a four-year apprenticeship, and then he alternated between France and England for several years. First he went to Rouen and spent a year as a commis patissier at De La Poste, then back to the UK, to the Uplands Hotel in the Lake District. Next he joined the Mirabelle in London and then returned to St Tropez for a while before coming back to these shores, his first port of call on this trip being Mr Garraway's in London.

Then, in 1983, he bought his own restaurant. This was called Streets, in Ashtead, Surrey; but he found that he missed the sophistication of the West End, so he returned this time to work as sous chef at Café Pelican, moving to Le Caprice in 1989.

Anthony admits to being a very fussy eater, and would rather enjoy a very occasional but excellent meal out at a first class restaurant, perhaps Bibendum or L'Arlequin, than make more frequent visits elsewhere.

ANTHONY HOWARTH
Le Caprice
Arlington House
Arlington Street
London SW1A 1RT
01-629 2239

Clive Howe

Clive Howe is yet another who was fascinated by the world of cooking as a schoolboy, and he worked in hotels during his holidays. He trained at a college in Hertfordshire and went on to The Dorchester during Mosimann's reign. Clive was there for eight years, working his way round the kitchen, concentrating particularly on sauces. During this time he also had some spells in Europe, including Mosimann's native Switzerland. He was also a regular member of the hotel's Culinary Olympics team, and has a clutch of gold and silver medals to his credit from those competitions.

Clive's originally modern French style underwent modification during his time in charge of the quintessentially English Grill Room at The Dorchester. He now describes it as traditional English but with the ingredients cooked in a modern way.

After The Dorchester Clive went first to Rookery Hall in Cheshire, where he made a big impact, and then to The Lygon Arms in Broadway, in both cases as head chef. And it is at The Lygon that you'll find him now, pleasing customers with his blend of classic and modern cuisine.

CLIVE HOWE
The Lygon Arms
Broadway
Hereford & Worcester WR12 7DU
(0386) 852255

NIGEL HAWORTH
Northcote Manor
Northcote Road
Langho
Near Blackburn Lancashire BB6 8BE
(0254) 40555

PETER HAYES
Cobbett's Restaurant
13 The Square
Botley
Southampton Hampshire SO3 2EA
(0489) 782068

ALAN HILL
The Gleneagles Hotel
Auchterarder Perthshire PH3 1NF
(0764) 62231

ROBERT HILTON
Wilson's
236 Blythe Road London W14 OHJ
01-603 7267

PAUL HODGSON
The Lindsay House
21 Romilly Street London W1V 5TG
01-439 0450

ALLAN HOLLAND
Mallory Court
Harbury Lane
Bishop's Tachbrook
Leamington Spa Warwickshire CV33 9QB
(0926) 330214

John (Hansrüdi) Huber was born and educated in Rheinau, Zürich. His father was an expert dairy farmer, specialising in high quality herds milked solely for the production of butter and cheese. It was expected that John would acquire one of the family's pâtisseries, but the auntie in whose gift it was, changed her mind, and instead John concentrated on his apprenticeship and on attaining the Swiss National Diploma in Pâtisserie, Confiserie and Glacerie, which he achieved with Merit.

He remained in Zürich for four years as pâtissier-confiseur before moving on to work in many of Switzerland's leading confiseries in St Moritz, Lausanne, Bern and Basle. He then moved further afield to Sweden, Germany, Italy and England, to Lyon's Corner House and then Fischer's Restaurant where he mastered the English language. He next spent two years in Barcelona working for a friend of the family, before returning to Lyon's Corner House and working up to chef-pâtissier in 1965, and later transferred to J Lyon's Catering Commissiary as Pastry Research and Development Manager. From 1962 to 1968, he also worked for the Royal Household at Windsor Castle and Buckingham Palace, at State occasions and other special receptions.

In 1968 John was appointed Lecturer in Catering Studies at Slough College of Higher Education, now Thames Valley College, and in 1976 was promoted to Senior Lecturer. Twelve years later he was offered the unique and newly formed position of Principal Pastry Lecturer. He is one of the instigators of the City & Guilds Advanced Pastry course, and is its chief examiner, as well as being himself a winner in international competitions for chocolate, pulled and blown sugar, marzipan, gâteaux, pâtisserie, petits fours, ice-cream and cold sweets. His 'personal best' is the Arthur Hope Trophy which he was awarded in 1976 for the Best Exhibit on Hotelympia's Table d'Honneur. The qualifications for entry to this competition are at least three gold medals. John had exhibited in 1968, 1970, 1972 and 1974, and the year he won produced a record number of entries.

John is a member and joint secretary on the Management Committee of the British Branch of the Académie Culinaire; holds the Association Française's Grand Cordon Culinaire in recognition of his contribution to the world of cooking; is a found member of Club Nine; featured in the first series of Thames Television's *Take Six Cooks*; and is currently tussling with the ultimate book on pâtisserie.

He speaks five languages fluently, and his favourite hobbies include 'playing with chocolate and sugar, travelling, opera, painting and eating well'. He also enjoys sipping champagne on Sunday mornings, preferably sitting in the garden viewing the fruits of his wife's labours as an expert gardener.

JOHN HUBER
Thames Valley College
Wellington Street
Slough
Buckinghamshire SL1 1YG
(0753) 34585

Ros Hunter

Ros Hunter was born in Aberdeen and had a strong desire to be self-employed. She thoroughly enjoyed giving dinner parties for her friends, and having lived in Southern Africa, Canada and the Caribbean, her repertoire was wide and varied.

Without having had any formal training, her first enterprise was on the Isle of Skye. However, she started to establish her reputation at the Village Restaurant in 1984.

Here, she found a number of customers who wished to eat organic foods in a non-smoking atmosphere. In 1985 she was fortunate in discovering a local market gardener all of whose superb produce was organically grown. Encouraged by this, she has sought out organic suppliers for most of her other produce as well. Wherever possible, she uses organic, hormone-free, non-intensively reared goods.

Ros describes her style as 'extended dinner party', but others have included her name under the 'modern British' umbrella.

ROS HUNTER
The Village Restaurant
16-18 Market Place
Ramsbottom
Lancashire BL0 9HT
(070 682) 5070

ROBERT HOOD
Greywalls Hotel
Muirfield
Gullane
East Lothian EH31 2EG
(0620) 842144

MARK HOUGHTON
The White Hart Hotel
Sonning-on-Thames
Berkshire RG4 0UT
(0734) 692277

CHRIS HUDSON
Ettington Park Hotel
Alderminster
Nr Stratford-upon-Avon
Warwickshire CV37 8BS
(0789) 740740

TIM HUGHES
Morton's House Hotel
45 East Street
Corfe Castle
Dorset BH20 5EE
(0929) 480988

PAUL HUNT
Old Vicarage Hotel
Worfield
Bridgnorth
Shropshire WV15 5TZ
(074 64) 497/8

EAMONN HUNTER
Brown's Restaurant & Bar
5-9 Woodstock Road
Oxford
Oxfordshire OX2 6HA
(0865) 511995

Anton *Indans*

Peter *Jackson*

Born and educated in Nottinghamshire, and now living and cooking in rural Lincolnshire, Anton Indans has developed his own style of modern English cuisine to suit the palates of his local clientele, who did not enjoy the frugalities offered by nouvelle cuisine.

After his college course at Mansfield College he set off for Switzerland to learn French, and found himself working as a commis chef at the Hotel du Lac. From there he went to Crans Montana for a busy winter season – on and off the slopes! On then to another resort for the wealthy: Lugano, this time, for a summer season. In 1982 an opportunity arose to spend eighteen months at the Sheraton Hotel in Stockholm, where he specialised in preparing hot fish dishes. One winter there was enough; and he arrived in London in the autumn of 1983 at the Inter-Continental Hotel on Park Lane, where he worked in Peter Kromberg's brigade at Le Soufflé.

In December 1985, with his wife Alison, he found the little cottage in Beckingham that he turned into both a home and a restaurant which has been gradually and quietly attracting a great deal of critical acclaim.

ANTON INDANS
The Black Swan Restaurant
Hillside
Beckingham
Lincolnshire LN5 0RF
(0636) 84474

Peter Jackson is one of those chefs who came through the classic British Transport Hotel training. Before that he took an OND at Aberdeen, then City & Guilds at Moray College, gaining a certificate in wines and spirits from Llandrillo Technical College in Wales.

Training took Peter from Nivingston House to Gleneagles, and to the Station Hotel at Inverness; then to Bodysgallen Hall Hotel as head chef, and on to Eastwell Manor, before opening his own restaurant in 1985. He is a very competitive chef, and regularly wins awards and cookery competitions. Since coming to Glasgow he has achieved third place in the Mouton Menu Award competition, and was both a prime mover behind, and member of, the first Scottish team to go to the Frankfurt Culinary Olympics in 1988.

Peter's restaurant, The Colonial, is a forty-cover restaurant in Glasgow's merchant city. He has made it his business to give Scottish food and ingredients a higher profile, and has helped over the years to encourage small growers, including organic farmers. This has been done partly by buying from the Paris markets to show the local people exactly what he wants. His own description of his cooking is 'freestyle, in the modern Scottish manner'.

PETER JACKSON
The Colonial Restaurant
25 High Street
Glasgow
Strathclyde G1 1LX
041-552 1923

CLIVE JACKSON
Congham Hall
Lynn Road
Grimston
King's Lynn Norfolk PE32 1AH
(0485) 600250

MARGARET JACKSON
Reeds
Poughill
Near Bude Cornwall EX23 9EL
(0288) 2841

MARTIN JAMES
Bodysgallen Hall
Deganwy
Llandudno Gwynedd LL30 1RS
(0492) 84466

STEPHEN JOBSON
Fisherman's Lodge
7 Jesmond Dene
Jesmond
Newcastle-on-Tyne
Tyne & Wear NE7 7BQ
091-281 3281

LEN JOHNSON
Mélange
59 Endell Street London WC2H 9AJ
01-240 8077

STEPHEN JOHNSTON
The Buttery
652 Argyle Street
Glasgow Strathclyde G3 8UF
041-221 8188

ROGER JONES
Lilly's
6 Clarendon Road
Holland Park London W11 3AA
01-727 9359

PETER JULLIVAN
Ivy Restaurant
1-5 West Street London WC2H 9NE
01-836 4751

Marion Jones

Marion Jones is a remarkable lady, and all the more so in that she is one of a select band of extremely highly rated but entirely self-taught chefs currently working in Britain, most of whom are women. She has been making her mark in a quiet but determined way since 1978, when she and her husband Robin opened the 'Croque', as it is affectionately known.

Robin had been a restaurateur in Battersea prior to this, and Marion had wanted to cook. But instead of starting a new venture in London, they decided to move out into the country, first and foremost to choose a location where they'd be happy to live. When they had found the house they could call home, they converted it into a restaurant. The house in Malvern Wells simply felt right, and they knew instantly that it was 'the one'. In fact, it had been purpose built as a baker's and grocer's in the 1870s, during the time when the town was in its heyday as a spa. Several other large houses in the area have ended up as nursing homes or schools, but at 221 Wells Road there is a sense of continuity of purpose.

Marion's style has developed, rather than changed, since the restaurant opened. Her first principles remain as they were in the early days, namely to produce food as it *used* to be found in provincial France. For instance, there was a time when a meal in a provincial restaurant always would have started with a tureen of soup on the table, and today the menu follows the pattern established twelve years ago – soup, fish, meat, cheese and dessert – a novelty when the restaurant opened, though now a convention quite frequently encountered.

Marion sets great store by the quality of her raw ingredients, of true flavours, especially in stocks. Presentation, although important to her, is not all-important. She grows all her own herbs and salad ingredients, and most enjoys making soups and salads. In fact she almost prefers gardening to cooking! She does not believe that luxury ingredients like foie gras are necessary to make a good meal; and will often simply braise game, for example. All cuts of lamb are used, not necessarily just the best end.

The essence of this modest lady's success is her determination to maintain standards, and team-work – Robin and Marion do the preparation together during the day, and in the evenings she cooks while he serves. For relaxation they like spicy food – Indian or Chinese, whilst always keeping an eye on the local competition!

MARION JONES
Restaurant Croque-en-Bouche
221 Wells Road
Malvern Wells
Hereford & Worcester WR14 4HF
(0684) 565612

Peter *Jukes*

René *Kaiser*

Kevin *Kennedy*

At twenty-four Peter applied for various cooking jobs, only to be turned down. After reading in the *Caterer* that there were 93,000 vacancies in the trade, he wrote a letter to the magazine saying that if this was the case, then why couldn't he get one? The result was an extraordinary 500 replies, and Peter chose to start training with Grand Metropolitan, completing his City & Guilds while with them. Later he went to the Gleneagles, the Imperial at Torquay, and to The Dorchester, just when Anton Mosimann was taking over. His first job as head chef was at Greywalls in Gullane, after a brief spell at Chewton Glen under Karl Wadsack and Christian Delteil.

In May 1983 Peter took over the Cellar with his wife Vivienne, and casting around for inspiration, he noticed that at that time no-one was really focusing their attention on cooking fish. So it was that Peter set to with this product. And the fish arrived at his door so fresh that at times he has been known to keep a whole halibut for a couple of days to let it mature!

Peter eschewed the flour-based sauces of his classical training, and based his ideas on the Chewton style: simplicity and an honest acknowledgement of natural flavour. Today, he has his very own refined form of fish cookery – possibly the best in Scotland. His inspiration comes from the sea, and when he talks about fish and his favourite Alsace wine, his eyes literally light up. By choice, Peter likes to eat in the houses of other chefs. 'There is no expectation there,' he says, 'just good food.'

PETER JUKES
The Cellar Restaurant
24 East Green
Anstruther
Fife KY10 3AA
(0333) 310378

René Kaiser loved his mother's home cooking in Switzerland, so at the age of fourteen he went to work in a butcher's in Neuchâtel, starting a catering apprenticeship after a year. He subsequently worked in Europe, before arriving in England in 1964.

René's first post over here was as head chef at Gravetye Manor, and he gained experience at a few other places in the South of England before opening Stane Street Hollow in November 1975. His fairly robust cooking has won him plenty of accolades, but he says that over the past fifteen years it has become lighter, with a more delicate presentation. He grows much of the soft fruit, vegetables and herbs that he uses in the restaurant. The meat and the fish is smoked on the premises as well.

RENÉ KAISER
Stane Street Hollow Restaurant
Codmore Hill
Pulborough
West Sussex RH20 1BG
(079 82) 2819

Kevin Kennedy is probably London's one of longest serving chefs, for it was more than thirty years ago that Kevin first entered The Dorchester's kitchens as a commis. Those were perhaps the last days of the grand kitchens of Europe, legendary chefs could trace their lineage back to Escoffier and tell tales of ice sculptures the size of Brighton Pavilion! Today Kevin provides a link with that world, for Boulestin, which he re-opened in 1979, remains one of London's few great restaurants in the grand traditional style.

Kevin left The Dorchester after completing his apprenticeship, and began a journey through some of London's finest kitchens – names from the past like Verry's, the Empress Club, the Café Royal sit alongside contemporary hotels which were then opening their doors: the Europa (now the Marriott) and the Royal Garden. Kevin Kennedy attributes much of his success to his beginnings – 'the hard way, the right way' – under The Dorchester's then chef de cuisine, Eugene Kaufeler. The discipline, the good habits, the mastery of technique, the patience to watch and the ability to learn from the effortless skills of experts, the journey around the kitchen, the excitement that transfixed the whole brigade on special occasions, working as a team – all these attributes and opportunities appealed to Kevin. Now at Boulestin he is always willing to take on commis chefs, to show around groups of students, to talk to young people wishing to enter the business and, notably, to be a tireless and inspiring judge for the Young Chef and Young Waiter of the Year Competition – the premier youth competition of the industry, created and run by the Restaurateurs' Association of Great Britain. After the judging is complete it is difficult to lure Kevin away, so keen is he to answer questions from the contestants, to encourage and to advise. He believes it to be a shame that few young people will have the opportunity that he had to master his art in a kitchen of a grand establishment, in the days when apprentices were the lifeblood of an industry dedicated to producing the Escoffiers of tomorrow.

In addition to the knowledge and skill necessary to underpin the creation of new dishes or to perfect existing ones, you must have an enthusiasm for food. In early life, Kevin went to France working as a 'stageur' in Rouen and Gevrey Chambertin in Burgundy. He then saved money to visit great establishments at home and abroad, to widen his knowledge of traditional and modern French cuisine as well as other types. Now Kevin is known as an inveterate eater-out on his days off. Friends include Michael Leung of Zen, with whom he swaps techniques and advice. Kevin makes an annual trip to Singapore, demonstrating in the air for Singapore Airlines and then cooking at the Mandarin for a week. He will tirelessly and with good humour deal with customs men baffled by sacks of baby turnips or slices of smoked duck. You will see far eastern influences alongside classical dishes at Boulestin: an array of five porcelain Chinese spoons, each with a spiked piece of fish or seafood, each different, always amusing.

All this apart, Kevin names Roger Vergé as his main inspiration. In 1975 he spent time working at Vergé's legendary Moulin des Mougins in the south of France. Here, they produce hundreds of meals per week to three-star Michelin standard. Kevin looked at the raw ingredients in Provence, the new techniques employed by Vergé and his peers Guérard, Bocuse and Troisgros, and decided to bring them to London for his next venture.

Kevin's brief from Sir Maxwell Joseph was to restore the pride of Boulestin and to carry the name and the restaurant into the 1980s. He has succeeded magnificently. He sees himself as the custodian of a legacy, and he collects the original works of Boulestin. But it is with influences derived from the work of the great man, rather than his actual recipes, that Kevin has created the current Boulestin menu. He has translated a menu from the Belle Epoque extravagance of tournedos Rossini into the contemporary highly smoked warm lamb on a bed of French leaves brought over from the Rongis market that morning. Châteaubriand will be there, possibly skate in black butter, or tiny ramekins of quails eggs to go with caviar.

There will be prime pink lamb, a galette of potatoes and a shimmering clear pool of dark sauce. A grand setting, with immaculately suited waiters. Boulestin is one of the great dining rooms of London. The whole place is dominated by the ideals, skills and warmth of Kevin Kennedy, a traditional chef with modern ideas.

KEVIN KENNEDY
Boulestin
Garden Entrance
1a Henrietta Street
London WC2E 8PS
01-836 7061

79

John
Kenward

Jim
Kerr

Entirely self-taught, John Kenward has only ever worked in his own restaurant, apart from a year's outside catering in London before opening Kenwards in 1980. He has, however, always had a deep interest in food and wine, and wanted to work in a way that involved his whole self – his brain *and* his hands.

Based entirely on fresh local produce, John's menu displays his determination to use English flavours. Everything, even presentation is designed to enhance flavour. The cheeses are British, and the bread is home-made. John's style has developed steadily, refined by reading the books of Troisgros and Guérard, and selective eating out. He does not like food that is fussy in either flavour or appearance, preferring a meal that is served in an unpretentious way.

John gets the greatest satisfaction from a piece of fish, correctly cooked, particularly when it's at the Carved Angel in Dartmouth.

JOHN KENWARD
Kenwards
Pipe Passage
151A High Street
Lewes
East Sussex BN7 1XU
(0273) 472343

Jim Kerr's experience has been confined to Scotland, taking City & Guilds at Telford College in Edinburgh, and then doing a spell of dietetics at Bangor Hospital, Broxburn. With today's rapidly changing food trends the latter has proved a useful training – especially so at One Devonshire Gardens. The hotel is frequented by a lot of businessmen, often with some kind of unusual dietary requirement. This allows Jim to understand his guests, and to be accurate in his suggestions as to what they might choose to eat.

At home, Jim had felt that there was more to food than his mother's cooking, which gave him the incentive to look further afield. He began working in a local hotel for £3 a week. There, he learned the basics. Over the next few years he went from Anne Smith's Town and Country Restaurant (one of the first to begin to use fresh produce again after the introduction of frozen foods) to the Howtowdie, also in Edinburgh. When he moved to Glasgow and Charlie Parker's restaurant, he met Ken McCulloch, the man responsible for the Buttery and the Rogano. It was Ken who had the foresight to instal Jim at One Devonshire.

Jim Kerr now runs the operation from the kitchen, slipping into a jacket towards the end to go out and talk to his guests. Otherwise he prefers to keep a fairly low profile, and you are as likely to find him carrying cases as working behind the stove. He leads by example, and is prepared to do any job at any level. He would never ask anyone to do a task he has not at some time also performed himself.

The opulent surroundings of One Devonshire are in strong contrast to Jim's cooking. Clear and uncluttered, it is as he says, 'honest food, with as few ingredients as possible, keeping dishes uncomplicated and flavours unspoiled'. He is an uncompetitive chef, and this largely sets him apart from his peers in Glasgow. He believes that the industry depends on its youth, and that knowledge should be shared willingly, not shrouded in mystery.

Jim's individual style is a result of what ingredients are available, and his own considerable talents. In addition there are Japanese and Cantonese influences, both of which cuisines he enjoys eating. He learns from and has respect for all those people who shun the limelight, preferring to stay in the kitchen, perfecting their craft. Jim would put the Browns at La Potinière and the Nairns at Braeval Old Mill in this category. They make him feel proud to be part of the industry.

JIM KERR
One Devonshire Gardens
1 Devonshire Gardens
Glasgow
Strathclyde G12 0UX
041-334 9494

John King

John King was born in Kent. He realised his interest in cooking during school holiday work in the kitchens of Hever Castle, then the home of the Astor family. The cook recognised this and encouraged him to apply to Westminster College. He successfully completed a three-year course in 1970, leaving with City & Guilds qualifications and the Westminster Diploma. His first job was at The Connaught Hotel for a year as second commis. He then worked at Le Caprice as first commis (1971-1972); and The Dorchester (1972-1973). After this he worked at Dukes Hotel as chef de partie (1973-1975); and at The Berkeley Hotel as banqueting sous chef (1975-1977). He moved to the Carlton Tower in 1977 to work for Bernard Gaume as first sous chef, staying until 1982, when he left to become chef de cuisine at the Ritz Club, where he is today.

John was trained in the classical French style of haute cuisine, which he modified under the influences of Bernard Gaume and The Carlton Hotel, where the dishes were lighter, more visually appealing, and with a great depth of flavour and later. He also derived inspiration from the food and conversation of the chefs of some of the greatest restaurants in France. His own cooking is now a blend of classical and modern with lighter sauces, without excessive garnishing or gimmicks. He gives his customers what they want, bearing in mind the seasons of the year, and enjoys their appreciation of his dishes. He says that a restaurant is like a theatre – you are only as good as your last performance.

Apart from his work experience, John has an impressive track record. He was Captain of the Ritz Club team at the 1988 Culinary Olympics in Frankfurt, where they scooped thirteen gold medals and won the overall Grand Prix for best regional team in the world – out of a field of ninety-four. He is holder of the Palme Culinaire medal from the Association Culinaire Française (UK); and a member of both the Toques Blanches and the Chefs and Cooks Circle. He is a committee member of the Craft Guild of Chefs' Cookery and Food Association and a committee member and judge for Hotelympia 1990. He holds awards from the culinary salons of Hotelympia, Bournemouth, Dover and Torquay.

John's greatest pleasure comes from seeing chefs in his brigade developing their own careers and achieving their own goals. He is known for his sense of humour on which the morale of his kitchen and its team depends – it is the secret of a happy restaurant.

For his own eating pleasure, John chooses restaurants such as Le Caprice, Dynasty II and La Tante Claire. Chinese and Japanese are good diversions for him, where he can find interesting ideas in food combinations and flavours. John also makes time for as many rounds of golf as his cooking will allow!

JOHN KING
The Ritz Club
Piccadilly
London W1V 3DG
01-499 7525

Pierre Koffmann was born in Tarbes, near Lourdes. He began his cookery career at sixteen as a student at the Tarbes cookery school, not for the love of cooking but in order to do something with his life, and he soon realised he had found his vocation. He moved on to Juan les Pins on the Côte d'Azur, then to Strasbourg and then to Lausanne as a commis. He read an advertisement in *L'Hotelerie* for a commis at Le Gavroche, and came to England in 1971.

From commis he soon progressed to chef de partie at Le Gavroche before finding himself transferred to Le Gamin (then still called Brasserie Benoits) in the City. He left the Rouxs to work for the Cazalets for about eight months before rejoining the Rouxs at the end of 1972 for the opening of The Waterside Inn, where he stayed as chef de cuisine until 1974, seeing its first Michelin star in 1973 and its second in 1974.

But it is every chef's dream to own his own restaurant, so with his wife he went to France to look around. Disappointed, they returned to England and, with the help of the Roux brothers in 1977, they set up La Tante Claire in Chelsea.

With its tiny dining room that resembled a railway carriage corridor, this restaurant became famous for its cuisine and endless waiting lists for tables. It was fêted by the guides, the critics and the customers, and was awarded its first Michelin star in 1978 and its second in 1980. But such success is teamwork, and the rest of Pierre's team must be his wife Annie, a lady blessed both with determination and an astute business sense, and Jean-Pierre Durantet at front of house. In 1985, La Tante Claire underwent a £500,000 refurbishment and expansion into the adjacent premises.

Pierre was, and still is, quoted as one of Europe's best chefs. Typical of his style is a red mullet mousseline starter: pounded and puréed flesh is moulded into tiny domes of mousse and cooked with a nest of salmon eggs buried in the middle, which cascade over the plate as you cut into it – the sauce which surrounds it is made from the livers of the mullet, and dotted with tiny diced carrots, chives and tomatoes. Pierre's style of cuisine has not changed: he believes in personalising classic recipes and techniques, combining the freshest ingredients with his unique skill and imagination. La Tante Claire, which is now a member of the prestigious Relais & Chateaux Group, is considered by many a gastronomic shrine.

Often referred to as the strong and silent type, Pierre tends to keep a low profile, preferring to stay around his stove, monopolising the activities rather than appearing front of house. Like most great chefs, he is fiercely proud of his work and is intent on perfection, which accounts for his reputation as a hard task master in his kitchen. But he is by no means possessive about his recipes, and his dedication and generosity are reflected in his cooking.

PIERRE KOFFMANN
La Tante Claire
68 Royal Hospital Road
London SW3 4HP
01-351 0227

Peter Kromberg

Peter Kromberg was born and brought up near Lake Constance, Baden, in south-east Germany. His father was an outstanding pâtissier and was once asked to make a celebration cake for Hitler at the Hotel Petersburg, near Bonn. What suffering might have been saved had he poisoned the mixture. Unfortunately, it would also have affected the Führer's guest – Neville Chamberlain, the British Prime Minister!

As a small boy Peter enjoyed good food, to the point where he would even criticise his mother's cooking! At fourteen he followed his father into the profession with an apprenticeship at a hotel in Buisburg from 1955 to 1958. His first job was as chef tournant at the Schweizerhof in Luzern, Switzerland, then as chef gardemanger at the Schweizerhof in Davos. In 1963 he joined the Athens Hilton for its opening and stayed for three years as entremetier. In 1966 he joined Inter-Continental Hotels, working first at the Siam Inter-Continental in Bangkok, initially as chef gardemanger, then being promoted to executive chef when he was only twenty-six, making him the youngest head chef in the history of all the Inter-Continental Hotels throughout the world.

In 1971 Peter came to England and the Portman Inter-Continental, and in 1975 he was appointed executive chef of the London Inter-Continental at Hyde Park. With a brigade of over sixty he caters for well over 1,000 meals a day, and his name has become synonymous with Le Soufflé. This is not only because he can – and regularly does – produce 500 perfect soufflés for a banquet, but also because the hotel's 'in-house' restaurant is so named and, thanks to Peter's cuisine, has been awarded a Michelin star.

Despite his genuine and endearing modesty, he has collected a tome of articles written about him by international journalists, and featured in the second series of Thames Television's *Take Six Cooks*. The *Caterer & Hotelkeeper* awarded him their Catey as Chef of the Year in 1987. Since 1987 he has been World President of the Toques Blanches Association, an international association of many hundreds of chefs.

Once specialising in ice-carving and butter sculpture, Peter's cooking is innovative and creative, based on classical foundations, which develops according to current trends. He is a chef in pursuit of perfection and the continuation of the highest standards which give him immense satisfaction. He finds great pleasure in using the new season's produce such as game and asparagus at its best. His personal preference when eating out is for simple, basic, country cooking. He believes that physical fitness is essential to his professional lifestyle, and makes time for gardening, water skiing and sailing, skiing, squash and cycling.

PETER KROMBERG
The Inter-Continental Hotel
Hamilton Place
Hyde Park Corner
London W1V 0QY
01-409 3131

Nico Ladenis

Nico Ladenis is a man with a mission, to be at the very top of his chosen profession. His restaurant Chez Nico in Great Portland Street opened to great acclaim in June 1989. Here, he has, with his wife Dinah-Jane, created a restaurant which sums up the principles that underlie everything he does. All the luxurious restaurant's lines are clean; there are stylised hints of Art Deco, mirrors gleam – as does everything on show. Staff are immaculate, reflecting Nico's obsession with getting everything exactly right, nothing less than perfect. Once again he has broken new ground by moving into this district of London – there are no other great restaurants nearby – but Nico has been proved right, and has been relentlessly busy since day one. According to regulars, the food is his finest ever, and it is interesting to look back to when Nico began.

Born in Tanzania, he was raised in colonial East Africa on an interesting selection of food prepared by his Greek mother. Nico came to England to study Economics at Hull University and eventually found himself in the world of big business. In the early 1970s he met and married Dinah-Jane and they decided to follow Nico's career with a major oil company to South America. It was then that his single-mindedness came to the fore. He was told by an interview board that he was not a good team man. He threw in his career, returned to England, jumped into his car and promptly drove to France. He and Dinah-Jane spent months eating in the finest restaurants and some of the humbler ones too, in the course of which they were jointly inspired to create a great restaurant of their own.

Nico's restaurants began with the idea of a magnificent creation being placed before the customer. This dish would combine Nico's taste, his memories, and the principles of cooking which he has taught himself. He began in 1974 in Dulwich, in South London. Ever the pioneer he used a sign to point out that there were no prawn cocktails and absolutely *no* well-done steaks. Some dishes, like his fish soup, had their origins in Dulwich and may still be enjoyed in Great Portland Street. In Dulwich Nico received critical acclaim, and first began to build the loyal following that has stayed with him ever since.

His next move, in 1979, took him further towards the centre, to an undeveloped part of Battersea, where the major guides showered yet more accolades on Nico. Chez Nico became a restaurant of national reputation, and one of the most sought after in London. Nico always stuck to his rules: meats were served pink, dishes were served as they should be, sauces were not tinkered with.

In search of his third star, however, he needed grander surroundings and departed for Shinfield, a suburb of Reading. In his book *My Gastronomy* Nico states that the customer is not always right, an attitude that sometimes brought him into conflict with the people of Reading. But his philosophy is that you would not go to Chanel and ask them to make your dress in polyester. Equally, he feels that a great chef will create a dish that is a whole, not one for the customer to modify to suit his or her pre-conceived ideas. Remaining confident in this philosophy, Nico left Reading into the more welcoming arms of his regular London audience.

He opened Simply Nico in fairly confined quarters in Pimlico, and from a relatively small kitchen produced brilliant, intensely flavoured dishes. His filet de veau farci à la sauce de romarin (stuffed fillet of veal with brown rosemary sauce) and his caille rôtie au madère et sa galette de pommes de terre (roast quail with madeira sauce and shredded crisp potato cake) are just two warmly remembered dishes. Nico now provides these and other dishes at Chez Nico. Tartare of salmon, a simple dish, is perfection. Lamb is served pink, garnished with couscous and vegetables, and flavoured oils. Nico's famous fumet de cèpes, an intense and sophisticated sauce, remains coupled with a fillet steak. The freshest sea-bass is served with a garnish of Provence-style vegetables. The flavours are perfectly balanced.

It is the balance that Nico seeks to create that sometimes encourages controversy. But his is a painstaking search for perfection. He starts the meal with a glass of champagne, never a large scotch. He is always tasting, perfecting and adapting his recipes. One nuance, a subtlety of flavour, that is what is important – hence his apparent inflexibility regarding well-done meat.

It is said that genius is the ability to take infinite pains and this is certainly true of Nico. His flair, creativity and total understanding of food must play their part too. Anyone who is frightened of Nico would be amazed to see him at Sunday lunchtime in the company of his two daughters Natasha and Isabella, and of course Dinah-Jane, eating vast quantities of Chinese or Indian food en famille.

Nico Ladenis
Chez Nico
35 Great Portland Street
London W1
01-436 8846

Martin Lam

Martin Lam's career in catering began as a fourteen-year-old washing up in a local restaurant in Bristol to earn some pocket money, and amongst the luminaries for whom he washed up was a young Keith Floyd. Martin loved food and, had a burning desire to cook well, finding the whole lifestyle of the catering world immensely appealing.

Self-taught, but inspired by Elizabeth David, Martin gained practical experience in Bath and Cheltenham, before going to London where he joined Justin de Blank's group, working in all parts of the business. In 1978 he opened the English House restaurant in Chelsea, moving on to Le Caprice in July 1980, then to L'Escargot in 1982 as chef, then chef/director.

MARTIN LAM
L'Escargot
48 Greek Street
London W1
01-437 2679

PHILLIP KANOUN
La Mascotte
54 Cricklewood Lane
London NW2 1HG
01-452 1299

PATRICK KELL
Dunadry Inn
Dunadry
Co Antrim BT41 2HA
(084 94) 32474

GEORGE KELSO
Ardsheal House
Kentallen of Appin
Argyll PA38 4BX
(063 174) 227

YVON KENT
Mr Bistro
East Quay
Mevagissey
Cornwall PL26 6QH
(0726) 842432

SONIA KIDNEY
The Feathers Hotel
Market Street
Woodstock
Oxfordshire OX7 1SX
(0993) 812291

MARIJAN KILIC
Foxtrot Oscar
79 Royal Hospital Road
London SW3 4HN
01-352 7179

ROY KILNER
Quincy's '84
675 Finchley Road
London NW2 2JP
01-794 8499

AUDREY KILPACK
Rogue's Kitchen
St Mary Church Street
Rotherhithe
London SE16 4JJ
01-237 7452

ALAN KING
Le Chef
41 Connaught Street
London W2 2BB
01-262 5945

DEREK KNIGHT
La Giralda
66/68 Pinner Green
Pinner
Middlesex HA5 2AB
01-868 3429

KLAUS KUNKE
Julie's
135 Portland Road
London W11 4LW
01-229 8331

Rowley Leigh

Rowley Leigh had no formal cookery education and began his career in the most unlikely of places – a hamburger bar, as a grill chef. He describes his original style as 'primitive'. Despite so unpromising a start, he was taken on by the Roux brothers, and worked at Le Gavroche as a commis then as chef de partie. He says, modestly, that his main achievement there was 'just surviving', and indeed it must have been harder for him than for college-trained youngsters.

Survive he did, however, and he broadened his experience by working in the Roux Pâtisserie, then in their butchery, and for a while he was one of the buyers for all the Roux restaurants. In 1983 he went to Le Poulbot, where he spent a year as sous chef before being promoted to head chef, a post he held for three years during which this establishment was voted the *Times* 'Restaurant of the Year', thereby justifying the confidence that Michel and Albert Roux had vested in him.

A strong independent streak was always evident and Rowley branched out, helping to open Kensington Place in 1987. Here he is able to put into practice everything he learned with the Rouxs, and he is honest enough to say that they did indeed teach him everything he knows! He operates with a combination of the basic and the imaginative. But there is less emphasis on the saucing of ingredients than on achieving an unusual combination of the hearty with the refined.

Kensington Place is rarely empty. It's open all day, every day, a brasserie in all but name, and even though last orders are at 11.30pm, you can drive past at 1 o'clock in the morning and it's still packed and buzzing. The food is exciting and adventurous, the décor stark, noisy and bright, and it has never lost it's appeal as a fun place to meet, and eat some fun but seriously good food.

With such a trade, Rowley doesn't often get a chance to eat out, and Kensington Place is very often a favourite haunt for other chefs.

ROWLEY LEIGH
Kensington Place Restaurant
205 Kensington Church Street
London W8 7LX
01-727 3184

Prue Leith

Prue Leith started her first catering company, Leith's Good Food, in 1961 from a bedsitter in London's Earl's Court. From these humble beginnings, her company has become one of the best known in the country.

She opened her restaurant in 1969 and was an instant success. The menu offers old favourites and novel combinations.

In 1975, along came Leith's School of Food and Wine, offering both professional training for career cooks and short courses for gifted amateurs. This is also still going strong, and has a waiting list for most courses. Courses move with the times, for example among new ones is Cooking for Health, very much in tune with current tastes. Prue started a farm in the Cotswolds in 1976, to provide fresh produce for these various concerns.

Her prime concern has always been to produce stylish, unpretentious, excellent food, be it for a sandwich or a banquet. She is actively involved in all aspects of her group of companies, and can be found teaching at the school, supervising a party, testing dishes and wines at the restaurant – according to where she is most needed.

Prue is a well-known television presenter, speaker, broadcaster, journalist and author. She was on the board of British Rail for five years, and was responsible for the high quality of the food on the England section of the 1980s re-run of the legendary Orient Express.

Prue Leith is a lady who has had a great influence on both the commercial and domestic cookery scenes in this country over many years – long may it continue!

PRUE LEITH
Leith's Restaurant
92 Kensington Park Road
London W11 2PN
01-229 4481

CLIVE LAMB
Invery Hotel
Banchory
Royal Deeside
Kincardineshire
(033 02) 4782

BRUNO LAMBI
San Frediano
62 Fulham Road
London SW3 6HH
01-584 8375

ROBERT LANE
Old Bridge Hotel
1 High Street
Huntingdon
Cambridgeshire PE18 6TQ
(0480) 52681

ROBERT LANOE
La Croisette
168 Ifield Road
London SW10 9AF
01-373 3694

STEPHEN LAURENDALE
L'Aventure
3 Blenheim Terrace
London NW8 0EH
01-624 6232

PATRICK LAVERACK
Drum & Monkey
5 Montpellier Gardens
Harrogate
North Yorkshire HG1 2TF
(0423) 502650

GUILLAUME LE BRUN
**Restaurant Patrick
Guilbaud**
46 James Place
Dublin Co Dublin 2
(01) 764192

KATH LEADBEATER
Kilberry Inn
Kilberry by Tarbert
Argyll PS29 6YD
(088 03) 223

GILBERT LEFÈVRE
Midland Hotel
New Street
Birmingham West Midlands
021-642 2601

ROLAND LEHOURS
Roux Restaurants Ltd
539 Wandsworth Road
London SW8
01-751 3243

MICHAEL LE POIDEVIN
**Thatchers Hotel &
Restaurant**
29/30 Lower High Street
Thame
Oxfordshire OX9 2AA
(084 421) 2146

PIERRE LEVICKY
Pierre Victoire
10 Victoria Street
Edinburgh Lothian
031-225 1721

LORNA LEVIS
At The Sign of the Angel
6 Church Street
Lacock Nr Chippenham
Wiltshire SN15 2LA
(024 973) 230

BERNARD LIGNIER
Restaurant Bosquet
97a Warwick Road
Kenilworth
Warwickshire CV8 1HP
(0926) 52463

ELLIE LINK
Sonny's
94 Church Road
Barnes London SW13 0DQ
01-748 0393

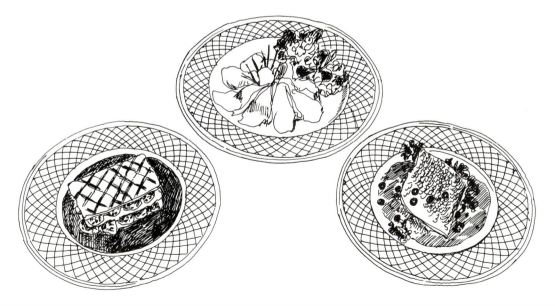

Thierry Leprêtre-Granet doesn't really know what made him want to go into the restaurant business. He probably started cooking when he was a scout, and has been hooked ever since.

He went to hotel school in St Nazaire in his native France for two years and then straight away went into a variety of different restaurants and hotels to gain experience. 1984 found him as first commis at the Hupotel Alpina, then he came to England for the first time, to Mallory Court in Warwickshire for two years as chef de partie until 1986. In 1987 he was back in France for a few months in the same grade, then came to England again, to Whitechapel Manor in Devon where he is still to be found.

Thierry has always been fond of French provincial cooking, and his own personal style has developed along those lines. He now offers nouvelle French cooking, quite light with not much cream or butter, and possibly a bit more substantial for his local clientele than that style originally implied. He loves to create an exciting dish from good raw ingredients into a delightful finished product.

Thierry does not eat out very often but expresses a marked preference for French food – and he eats at the very best places that he can afford.

Thierry Leprêtre-Granet
Whitechapel Manor
South Molton
Devon EX36 3EG
(076 95) 3377

Liz Lipmann
Café Delancey
3 Delancey Street London NW1 7NN
01-387 1985

Lindsay Little
Ardanaiseig Hotel
Kilchrenan
Loch Awe Argyll PA35 1HE
(086 63) 333

Friedrich Litty
Lainston House
Sparsholt
Winchester Hampshire SO21 2LJ
(0962) 63588

Ian Loffel
Braganza
56 Frith Street London W1V 5TA
01-437 5412

Ann Long
Long's Restaurant
Blackwater
Truro Cornwall TR4 8HH
(0872) 561111

Robert Lyons
Bay Horse Inn & Bistro
Canal Foot
Ulverston Cumbria LA12 9EL
(0229) 53972

Richard Lyth
La Noblesse
The Hospitality Inn
Kings Road
Brighton Sussex BN1 1JA
(0273) 206700

Marjan (or Mario) Lesnik was born at Ljutomer, in the Slovenia district of Yugoslavia. His mother and grandmother were in the service of the Hapsburg Royal Family and his father was a director of one of the famous Ljutomer Riesling vineyards. It seemed natural to follow in their footsteps, and a trial period working at the local restaurant during his school holidays, he enrolled for a three-year apprenticeship.

Upon its completion, he went to Vienna, to the Coq d'Or as chef de partie, then in 1973 as sous chef at a hotel in the ski resort of Badtolz in the Bavarian Alps. Later that year, after discovering that he could not get his visa extended, he came to England.

It was a convenient excuse as he had always wanted to visit this country and learn the language. He knew the manager at the Château Valeuse in the Channel Islands, who found him a position as chef de partie in the kitchens. He soon moved up to sous chef then chef de cuisine. At the end of the 1974 season, he moved to London and the Hilton in Park Lane, where his last job before moving on was as chef saucier in the Banqueting Department – experience for which he was to be grateful in later years. He worked his way up at The Connaught, from chef saucier to premier sous chef. In both 1981 and 1982 he won first prize in the UK Prix Pierre Taittinger. In 1983 he became chef de cuisine at Claridge's with a brigade of more than eighty, cooking for up to 1,000 covers a day plus room service. Recently, the kitchens have undergone a total rebuilding programme to his own design, at a cost of £4.5 million.

Although he was shaped by the regional cooking at home, and later by his Viennese experience, Marjan has blended these elements into the classical style he learned at The Connaught, and during his working visits to France with Michel Bourdin. He cooks with an open mind. He respects his classical training but desires most to be spontaneous and free. He claims his strongest influences to be Michel Bourdin and the Troisgros brothers, for their sheer professionalism and supreme dedication. Actual cooking, and finding new combinations of ingredients and flavours, gives Marjan great satisfaction. A typical dish on his menu might be pot-roasted fillet of lamb with two sauces made from a lamb stock reduction, one infused with fresh mint, and one with cream and mint added. This would be served with boiled potatoes and seasonal vegetables.

Marjan says that working at Claridge's has taught him a lot – in particular, how to be a better manager and how to listen to customers and their suggestions, several of whom can be quite demanding. It is their approval and pleasure which is not only rewarding but an inspiration to do the job even better. This is in keeping with the traditions of Claridge's. The hotel is often considered an annex to Buckingham Palace, and Marjan often finds himself planning State banquets for Her Majesty The Queen, on which occasions his brigade may cook for any number, from a few dozen to several hundred. He also caters for the many Kings, Queens and Heads of State from other countries who make Claridge's their London home.

Marjan Lesnik is often a judge for cookery competitions, and since 1985 he has been UK President of the Toques Blanche.

When eating out, Marjan prefers to go where the chef is a friend or where he knows the food tastes good, but most of all he enjoys Chinese food or home cooking.

MARJAN LESNIK
Claridge's
Brook Street
London W1A 9JQ
01-629 8860

Alastair *Little*

Everyone seems to know Alastair Little's story, how he came into cooking after an MA in Archaelogy at Cambridge, a full-time job with a film company, and then waiting at table. Subsequently, he worked in several fashionable London restaurants – Zanzibar, L'Escargot, Fingal's and 192, and it was here that he met Kirsten Pedersen and Mercedes Downend who were to become his partners in his eponymous restaurant.

The premises were found, purchased, refurbished and opened in under a year, and Alastair's concept of a restaurant, where quality is paramount and extras are unnecessary, finally came to fruition.

The simplicity seemed almost stark to begin with, but quickly caught on as both press and public realised that this was not just a quirky flash in the pan but a serious restaurant. Ironically, Alastair's so-called simplicity (regional European with Oriental influences) has now become other peoples' idea of gourmet food!

As an employer, Alastair has been held up as a shining example of 'leadership by example', and he is particularly keen to make both kitchen and front of house staff feel part of the same team. He also feeds his staff well, believing that only by appreciating good food will they be able to cook and serve properly. Another principle is never to use endangered game species, such as hare.

Alastair scores by creating his menus freshly, according to what is available in the market – you can tell what season it is by reading what he offers, for example a salad of pigeon breast, French beans, artichoke hearts and girolles; or a salad of plum tomatoes, roasted peppers and aubergine, rocket, basil, anchovies and olives. Or the menus will reflect what part of the world he is currently influenced by – you might find tataki of bonito with oshitashi (with garlic, ginger, lemon and soy dressing); or carpaccio with parmesan and truffle oil.

He has stayed happily in Soho for nearly five years now, latterly opening up the basement part of the premises as a 'grand snack bar' to serve lighter meals than in the main restaurant upstairs. He seems to have achieved his life's ambition, and is now consolidating his success, the reward of diligence.

Alastair Little
Alastair Little
49 Frith Street
London W1
01-734 5183

Karl Löderer

From an early age Karl Löderer has had a great love of cooking and took every opportunity to exercise his budding skills, first at school and then at college, in his native Vienna. He worked his way around Europe, with long spells in France and Switzerland, before coming to Britain via the Channel Islands – a route popular with middle-European chefs. With a partner, Karl opened La Frégate on Guernsey in 1960, and although he moved on after six years, he secured its reputation as one of the most popular restaurants on the island.

The next twelve years Karl spent at Gravetye Manor, in Sussex, as chef de cuisine. This was where the public and the guides really began to take notice of him. But wanting to be his own boss, he moved on in 1978, bringing his 'Midas touch' to Manleys in Storrington.

Here, Karl's originally French classic style has undergone some changes, and is now slightly more modern in presentation. However it is definitely not, as he is at pains to point out, nouvelle cuisine. As well as providing courses using local ingredients such as Romney Marsh lamb, he will produce dishes from his own heritage, such as rösti potatoes, and the wickedly delicious Salzburger nockerln for pudding.

Karl doesn't get to eat out much as all his neighbours close on Monday evenings – the same as himself. But if he manages to get up to London, then his favourite dishes will be cooked by Michel Bourdin or Nico Ladenis.

KARL LÖDERER
Manleys
Manleys Hill
Storrington
West Sussex RH20 4BT
(090 66) 2331

93

Bruno Loubet

Bruno Loubet was born in Libourne, in the south west of France, and for as long as he can remember he wanted to cook. At the age of thirteen he started working part-time in a pâtisserie, a charcuterie and a local restaurant, so that by the time he entered catering school in Bordeaux at the age of fourteen, he was already quite a old hand at many aspects of his chosen trade. Three years later he emerged, raring to go, and found his first post in Brussels, at the Hyatt Regency, where in a year he graduated from commis to demi chef de partie. With the same 'rank' he went to the Copenhague in Paris for a year, before his national service came along. He chose to serve in the navy, and finished up an officer and a head chef to the Admiral.

Presumably having acquired a taste for travel in the navy, Bruno then came to England, where his first port of call, in 1982, was Gastronome One. Here, he introduced that style of menu which was perfectly familiar to visitors to France but so hard to find in England, namely a choice of three short, set-price, frequently changing menus, usually featuring typical French bistro fare. He was an instant success in Fulham and the restaurant's passing was mourned by more than just the locals.

Having been a head chef twice, it may come as a surprise to learn that Bruno's next post was in a lower grade. But not when you hear that it was with Raymond Blanc at Le Manoir aux Quat'Saisons. He served a year with the Young Master and was rewarded with the plum appointment of head chef and manager of Le Petit Blanc in Oxford, taking over from John Burton-Race. Here, he really came into his own and his style developed into something more elaborate, and with more refinement of flavours.

It is hard to believe that Bruno was only at Le Petit Blanc for two years, but in 1988 the restaurant was sold and so he went to London, where he took over the Four Seasons Restaurant at the Inn on the Park, bringing flair and innovation to a newly refurbished dining room. Also in 1988, he won an Acorn award – being nominated by the *Caterer & Hotelkeeper* as one of their thirty bright stars under thirty years of age.

In 1988, Raymond Blanc said that Bruno Loubet would reach the top of his profession within 4 years. Some would say the prophecy has come true even sooner.

BRUNO LOUBET
The Four Seasons Restaurant
Inn on the Park
Hamilton Place
Park Lane
London W1A 1AZ
01-499 0888

George
McAlpin
Ian
McAndrew
Aidan
McCormack

George McAlpin's career choices were between cooking and Formula One motor racing, but he started cooking before he was old enough to drive, so that was that. By fifteen, he was cooking in local hotels and restaurants in his native Northern Ireland, and from early days nursed an ambition to open his own restaurant. He took City & Guilds at Catering College in Portrush, and took a circuit of several twists and turns before ending up at Ramore, his present pit-stop.

When he moved to London, he started in grand style as a commis at the House of Commons. Then, finding he preferred the sauce section, he worked as chef saucier at the Curzon House Club, Langan's Brasserie, and Le Caprice, before becoming sous chef at Walton's. His first post as head chef brought him back to Portrush where he later became a partner in the business at Ramore.

He uses local produce whenever possible, which is very often as the restaurant is quite isolated, and feels that his whole concept of cooking is different to any other in Northern Ireland. He is fascinated by the way that public taste has changed over the years, and enjoys the challenge of keeping one step ahead. His own personal favourite when eating out? Nico Ladenis.

GEORGE MCALPIN
Ramore Restaurant
The Harbour
Portrush
Co Antrim BT56 8DN
Northern Ireland
(0265) 824313

Ian McAndrew is a product of British Transport Hotels, but the experience was in his case preceded by two years at Durham College. The same period was also spent in Hamburg at The Inter-Continental, then two more years at The Dorchester, as part of Anton Mosimann's brigade. From there he moved to The Hyatt Carlton Tower (as sous chef) before taking his first post as head chef, at Eastwell Manor in Kent.

It was at Eastwell that he was really first noticed by critics, the hotel gaining a Michelin star, and the acclaim followed him when he branched out on his own, at Restaurant 74 in Canterbury, where he remained for four years. During his time at Canterbury, he published *A Feast of Fish*, a very well-received and authoritative treatise on one of his favourite foodstuffs. (*Poultry and Game* is on line, due for publication in 1990.)

Having sold Restaurant 74, largely because he sensed a lack of discerning clientele outside London (a problem which he shared at the time with Nico Ladenis), he can now be found at One Sixteen in Knightsbridge, doing what he does best – cooking the freshest first class produce simply and expertly.

IAN MCANDREW
One Sixteen
116 Knightsbridge
London SW1X 7PJ
01-823 9983

Aidan McCormack learned to cook at home with his mother, and then at the North Wales Institute where he was a full-time student. He's still learning today, or so he says, by eating out at places where he can glean a few more ideas whether French, Japanese or good home cooking.

Aidan began his career at The Savoy in London, where he received a classical grounding, and then went on to Chewton Glen. One of the highlights of his early years was a 'stage' with the Troisgros

brothers in France, which really opened his eyes to the possibilities of cooking. He came back to England and Le Talbooth in Essex, and then went back to Chewton Glen for a couple of years. After this came his first post as head chef, at Historic House Hotels' Middlethorpe Hall, where he won many accolades.

Next, Aidan decided that he could do with a spell of being his own master, so he helped set up a bistro in York, named after its address at 19 Grape Lane. However he didn't stay long and, Historic Houses welcomed him back to their new venture, Hartwell House in Buckinghamshire, where he is once again pleasing the palates of discerning diners.

AIDAN MCCORMACK
Hartwell House
Oxford Road
Aylesbury
Buckinghamshire HP17 8NL
(0296) 747444

MICHAEL MCAULEY
The Strand Restaurant
12 Stranmillis Road
Belfast
Co Down BT9 5AA
(0232) 682266

B MCCAMBRIDGE
**The Londonderry
Arms Hotel**
20 Harbour Road
Carnlough
Co Antrim BT44 OEU
(0574) 85255

JAMES MCCARTHY
Anna's Place
90 Mildmay Park
London N1 4PR
01-249 9379

JOHN MCCLEMENTS
McClements Restaurant
12 The Green
Twickenham
Middlesex TW2 5AA
01-755 0176

LADY MACDONALD
Kinloch Lodge
Sleat Isle of Skye
Highland IV43 8QY
(047 13) 214

AIDAN MCGRATH
**Brinkleys Restaurant:
Wine Gallery**
47 Hollywood Road
London SW10 9HX
01-351 1683

PAUL MCKNIGHT
Culloden Hotel
142 Bangor Road
Craigavad Holywood
Co Down BT18 0EX
(023 17) 5223

JOHN MCMANUS
Inn on the Park
Hamilton Place
Hyde Park Corner
London W1A 1AZ
01-499 0888

PAUL MAGSON
Corney & Barrow
44 Cannon Street
London EC4N 6JJ
01-248 1700

CHRISTOPHER MALCUIT
Le Bouchon
38 Queenstown Road
London SW8 3RY
01-622 2618

ANTHONY MARSHALL
Dukes Hotel
35 St James's Place
London SW1A 1NY
01-491 4840

ALISON MARTIN
Café Flo
205 Haverstock Hill
London NW3
01-435 6744

COLIN MARTIN
Ritz Club
150 Piccadilly
London W1V 9DG
01-491 4678

JUAN MARTIN
**Sharrow Bay Country
House Hotel**
Howton Road
Ullswater Cumbria CA10 2LZ
(085 36) 483

STANLEY MATTHEW
**The Mill House Hotel &
Restaurant**
Station Road Kingham
Oxfordshire OX7 6UH
(060 871) 8188

ENZO MAURO
Mauro's
88 Palmerston Street
Bollington
Nr Macclesfield
Cheshire SK10 5PW
(0625) 73898

ANTONIO MAYA
Rebato's
169 South Lambeth Road
London SW8 1XW
01-735 6388

CHARLES MERCIER
The Café Royal
68 Regent Street
London W1R 6EL
01-439 6320

ROBERT MEY
Hyatt Carlton Tower Hotel
2 Cadogan Place
London SW1X 9PY
01-235 5411

Tom McCoy

Although Tom McCoy is the chef at McCoy's, you can't write about him without mentioning his brothers, any more than you can talk about Albert Roux without mentioning Michel. Many are the tales about the McCoys and who's to say which are for real? The enigma starts with the address, which seems never to appear the same twice – McCoy's, McCoy's at the Tontine, the Cleveland Tontine, Staddlebridge, Northallerton. To be precise, the restaurant is at the busy junction of the A19 and the A172, roughly near all those places.

Coming from a family in the catering business, untrained but also uninhibited, the McCoys first venture together was a coffee bar in Middlesborough, called the Purple Onion, which, in 1968, was pretty much par for the course! The present McCoy's opened in 1978, after Tom, Eugene and Peter McCoy rather rashly wrote to the brewery who then owned the derelict coaching inn. At the time, they were running another incarnation of McCoy's at nearby Kirklevington, with elder brother John. To their horror, the brewery called their bluff. However, after much effort, the money was raised and the restaurant opened.

The next problem is the actual look of the establishment – eclectic, flamboyant and fun – decorated in a mixture of styles from the '20s, '30s and '40s, and with palms and parasols so that you feel you're eating outdoors. Then there are menus, full of wry little comments, such as 'thin, thin, ever so thin' to describe layers of puff pastry in a mille-feuille; or a densely chocolatey chocolate-and-biscuit refrigerator cake called choc-o-block Stanley, so called because Stan, who lived in the cottage up the road, still used the inn as his local, and witnessed the increasing numbers of customers. Elbowing his way to the bar, his usual opening gambit was 'choc-o-block again tonight, eh?'. When the pudding was devised, its name just sprang to mind!

But don't be misled. The food cooked by Tom McCoy is *seriously* good. He had a hard time, in the early days, getting locally the quality of produces that he required, but gradually succeeded. Now, some people supply exclusively just what he wants. McCoy's has been instrumental in introducing to Yorkshire many foods previously only available in London and the more affluent South of England. Tom enjoys giving people food that they wouldn't cook for themselves – he sees no point in simply doing what you could do at home for less.

He works on the principle that dishes his brothers enjoy, the public probably will as well. That said, he is quick to acknowledge he does not really originate, so much as introduce successful combinations.

Tom McCoy
McCoy's
The Cleveland Tontine
Staddlebridge
Nr Northallerton
North Yorkshire DL6 3JB
(060 982) 671

Tim McEntire

Dermot McEvilly

Brendan McGee

Tim McEntire is yet another chef who was inspired by a mother who had worked as a cook before starting her family. Tim took his OND at Brooklands Technical College, and then found a place as a commis at the Savoy. Here he learned the classical French repertoire that formed the basis of his early cooking technique. He worked at Drakes in Chelsea for a while, and then did a spell in Zurich to broaden his experience.

In 1978, with his partner Andrew Thomason, Tim opened his own restaurant, Partners 23. The name came from the address, the fact that Andrew and Tim were partners, and because that was their age.

Tim describes his cooking as honest and innovative. He enjoys producing a simple but perfect dish with a harmonious balance of flavours and textures. He eats out at the top restaurants when he can, and has developed a keen interest in Japanese cooking. For him it epitomizes the best principles: freshness of produce with no disguise, and good combinations of flavour and texture.

Eleven years on, even though they haven't renamed it Partners 34, the restaurant is still going strong!

TIM McENTIRE
Partners 23
23 Stonecot Hill
Sutton
Surrey SM3 9HB
01-644 7743

Dermot McEvilly saw the unfulfilled potential of the Irish market, and so embarked upon his career determined to fill the gap by serving absolutely fresh produce in a lovely setting; it wasn't long before he formed an appreciative audience. In 1958 he had enrolled at Shannon Hotel School for two years, and from there had set off to gain practical experience, firstly in Zürich for a year and then for a similar period at London's Dorchester Hotel.

Back in his homeland, Dermot first worked as manager at the Ardilaun Hotel in Galloway, and then in 1968 he and his wife, Kay, opened Cashel House where – at last – Dermot would do the cooking. His originally plain style has developed in a more modern French way. He particularly enjoys cooking seafood, and when he eats out, he'll choose fish then, too. Since the hotel has its own private beach, he is assured of a fresh and regular supply of raw materials. In Castel House, Dermot McEvilly has certainly realised his ambition.

DERMOT McEVILLY
Cashel House
Cashel
Connemara
Co Galway
Republic of Ireland
010-353-95 31001

Brendan McGee served his apprenticeship in his native Wales. He then progressed to Eastwell Manor in Kent as commis chef and then on to Leinston House as chef de partie. He then went to London to work in the Pomme d'Amour restaurant, and in 1987 arrived at Martin's as head chef.

His style of cuisine has evolved from classical French via nouvelle cuisine to its present modern derivative of the classical style. Brendan acknowledges Ian MacAndrew as his mentor in this evolution.

BRENDAN McGEE
Martin's
239 Baker Street
London NW1 6XE
01-935 3130

98

David Macrae   Murdo MacSween   Robert Mabey

David Macrae runs a very democratic kitchen. His team works a four-and-a-half day week of split shifts, and his philosophy is to get the best out of his staff by treating them properly. When one considers that his third chef was a runner-up in the Young Chef of the Year competition, then one can appreciate the formidable brigade he must have – all encouraged and appreciated by his proprietor, Martin Irons.

After an OND at Ayr Technical College, David came under the influence of Mary and Brian Chadwick at the Knife and Cleaver at Houghton Conquest, and it was there that he learned about the style of Elizabeth David. On returning north, he became chef at Mackintosh's restaurant in Edinburgh, and finally arrived at Martin Iron's restaurant in 1987 having already worked with Martin several years earlier. Together they set about producing one of the city's top restaurants.

David uses organic produce when he can, and whenever possible food is bought in on a daily basis. He uses simple ingredients, and makes exciting use of various Japanese foods. He tends to avoid the classic French restaurant when eating out, preferring vegetarian or Indian food.

David Macrae
Martin's Restaurant
70 Rose Street
North Lane
Edinburgh
Lothian EH2 3DX
031-225 3106

Murdo MacSween was born in Scotland, into a family of bakers. However, it was his aunt, Lady Compton Mackenzie who, spending most of her time in France, really inspired him to become a chef.

Murdo completed a two-year catering course at the Castle Hill School of Catering prior to starting his five-year apprenticeship, based on the French classical tradition, with British Transport Hotels. He worked his way through the Caledonian in Edinburgh, the Turnberry in Argyll, the Central in Glasgow and the Lochalsh in Kyle, before embarking on a year's work experience in Alsace.

Murdo built up a clientele at Malin Court where he was 'discovered' by the media and critics. Soon, he was persuaded to leave his beloved Scotland and head for the city lights. He became chef de cuisine at Walton's in London, staying there for six years before becoming chef de cuisine at The Elms Hotel in Abberley. His cooking won many accolades at both establishments. In 1983 he moved to Oakley Court as chef de cuisine, where he has happily remained ever since.

Murdo MacSween
The Oakley Court Hotel
Windsor Road
Windsor
Berkshire SL4 5UR
(0628) 74141

Robert Mabey used to cook for friends, but never considered it as a career until he was unable to get a job as a car mechanic! He entered one of the best apprenticeships in the world, at The Connaught, where he covered all departments of the kitchen and also did six months as a waiter. With a certain naivety, he didn't realise until afterwards how fortunate he had been.

After The Connaught, Robert spent some time at Le Gavroche, and at Adlard's when it was in Wymondham. This was followed by 'stages' with the Troisgros brothers, at Longueville Manor, and in Japan. The Japanese influence was particularly apparent in some of the dishes he created as head chef at Hintlesham Hall in Suffolk, which he joined when the Watsons took over from Robert Carrier. However, Robert's need to face new challenges arose again in 1988 when he became his own man, setting up Mabey's Brasserie, Sudbury, in his native East Anglia.

Robert reckons that the catering industry changes rapidly so with his low boredom threshold he is ideally suited to it! He also feels that it is a field with great potential for someone of a more practical than academic inclination. He has done well in competition work – Young Chef of the Year in 1981, and Chef of the Year from 1984–86, and a semi-finalist in the Prix Pierre Taittinger in 1987 and 1988.

Robert Mabey
Mabey's Brasserie
47 Gainsborough Street
Sudbury
Suffolk CO10 7SS
(0787) 74298

Ray Maddox

Jacques Marchal

Raymond Maddox went into the restaurant business in search of good food and actually began by washing pots for £3 a week! He reckoned he needed some rather more formal training, so spent two years at Manchester's Hollins College before taking his City & Guilds. Staying in the city at first, he worked at the Midland Hotel and the Piccadilly Hotel, and then moved down to London as sous chef at Durrants Hotel. He was there for five years, and during this time his classical yet natural style was finally formed.

Raymond moved to the Cavendish Club in the City as head chef, where he had total control of the kitchens. He seems happy in or near the heart of London, for he has also been head chef at the Spread Eagle in Greenwich, Café St Pierre, Bounders Restaurant, and now the City Brasserie.

His personal preferences run to plain and simple food, honestly cooked, and for relaxation he plays snooker, football, badminton and tennis.

RAYMOND MADDOX
The City Brasserie
Plantation House
Mincing Lane
London EC3
01-220 7094

Frenchman Jacques Marchal went to hotel school in Gerardmer, one of the best at the time. He cooked his way around France as a young man, and came to London on a two-year sabbatical, starting at the Café Royal in London. He went down to Plymouth in 1974 and stumbled into a partnership to create a bistro-style restaurant there called Chez Nous. There seemed to be an ideal opening for a good French restaurant in Plymouth with its excellent local resources of fish, game, meat and produce from small local growers. Although the partner left in 1980, Jacques has continued running the business, with his wife Suzanne at front of house.

Jacques describes his food as 'cuisine spontanée'. It is determined by the seasons, and improvised around the quality of basic ingredients at a given moment in time. This is particularly the case with fish, which varies in availability due to weather conditions. The new dishes are still thoroughly researched, adjustments being made at the last minute in the interests of variety and flexibility.

Each day, Jacques derives great satisfaction from selecting the fresh ingredients – he won't put dishes on the menu unless he is totally happy with the basic constituents. He also enjoys working with enthusiastic young people, some of whom come from the local catering college. He finds that through instructing them, he has started to learn new things as well. When eating out, he particularly enjoys oriental restaurants, good food of any kind, and not necessarily only that served in restaurants.

JACQUES MARCHAL
Chez Nous
13 Frankfort Gate
Plymouth
Devon PL1 1QA

ANNA MILLER
Heal's Restaurant
196 Tottenham Court Road
London W1P 9LD
01-636 1666

GIANCARLO MOERI
Eleven Park Walk
11 Park Walk London SW10 0AJ
01-352 3449

MICHAEL MONGER
The Mermaid Inn
Mermaid Street
Rye East Sussex TN31 7EU
(0797) 223065

PHILIPPE MORON
La Bouillabaisse
116 Finborough Road London SW10 9ED
01-370 4199

NICOLA & SIMON MORRIS
Grafton Manor
Grafton Lane
Bromsgrove
Hereford & Worcester B61 7HA
(0527) 579007

CHARLES MUMFORD
Launceston Place
1a Launceston Place London W8 5RL
01-937 6912

Max *Markarian*

Danilo *Minuzzo*

Max Markarian was born into an Armenian family, and played at restaurants as a child before being roped in, aged sixteen, to help out at his father's French-oriented restaurant in the Lebanon. Coming to England at the age of twenty, he was privileged to meet and be guided by the late Tony Ciorra longstanding chef at Le Caprice, before opening with him at the Knightsbridge Sporting Club in the late '60s. Max then spent two years with the Cunard group where he was in charge of a large brigade, before moving on to Leith's restaurant for six years. During this time, Prue Leith was coming to the fore as a writer and presenter of programmes, and Max was able to assist in preparation behind the scenes, as well as being given a free hand in the production of menus for the restaurant.

However, true to his family tradition he set up on his own, at Chez Max in Surbiton in 1982. Here he has combined his original Armenian and French influences into a classic style with nouvelle overtones – fresh ingredients, spices from the East, beautiful presentation – but served in generous portions. He most loves to create a new dish for appreciative customers, and for relaxation he checks out the local competition.

Max Markarian
Chez Max
85 Maple Road
Surbiton
Surrey KT6 4AW
01-399 2365

Danilo Minuzzo was born in the Veneto region of Italy, where he went to catering school from the age of fifteen. Coming to London seven years later he joined Gino Santin's group, and has remained there ever since!

Danilo had always cooked at home – in Italy, unlike England, any interest in the kitchen is fostered by Mamma, be it from son or daughter. His style was originally the traditional, regional cooking from Venice, but with the Santin group it has developed. Today he uses traditional methods of cooking but presented in a way more suited to modern tastes.

Within six months of his arrival, he had risen to second chef at Santini in Ebury Street, and in 1987, as head chef, he opened L'Incontro for the group in Pimlico Road. His favourite cooking is of pasta, which is made fresh twice daily at L'Incontro, and although he has a 'dedicated' pasta chef, Danilo still likes to keep his touch. His favourite and most popular pasta is gnocchi, and not only does he make this better than his own mother did, but also better than the restaurant manager's mother did, and that, apparently, is really saying something!

For his own relaxation, Danilo likes to eat very simple food, especially Chinese which he sees as being similar to Italian in that it is light, not over-elaborate and allows the true taste of the ingredients to shine through. An apt description of his own skills!

Danilo Minuzzo
L'Incontro
87 Pimlico Road
London SW1 8PH
01-730 3663

Heinz Nagler
Michael's Nook
Grasmere
Ambleside Cumbria LA22 9RP
(096 65) 496

Nick Nairn
Braeval Old Mill
By Aberfoyle Stirling FK8 3UY
(087 72) 711

George Ng-Yu-Tin
Beau Rivage
228 Belsize Road London NW6 4BT
01-328 9992

Joyce Molyneux

Joyce Molyneux went into cooking for the sheer love of it, but with a determination and efficiency that has been a hallmark of her career ever since: two years at Birmingham College of Domestic Science, a year with an industrial caterer, and thence to the small restaurant in Stratford-on-Avon, the Mulberry Tree, where she spent the 1950s.

In 1959 she joined George Perry-Smith at the Hole in the Wall in Bath. Joyce acknowledges the influence of George on her cooking over the next fifteen years, along with that of Elizabeth David, and now Joyce herself is a major influence on the British cookery scene. In the early 1970s

Joyce decided she wanted fresh challenges and so moved to Dartmouth, opening The Carved Angel with her business partner Tom Jaine. It's almost as if Joyce has compiled some kind of cookery bible, with The Hole in the Wall as the Old Testament and The Carved Angel as the New – each beautiful books in their own right but greatly enriching when the whole story is told.

The food at The Carved Angel is, quite simply, superb. It is an English equivalent of the French cuisine du terroir, local cooking in harmony with its surroundings. Of course in the early days Joyce experi-

enced difficulties with supplies (apart from fish) but now she is a valued customer to both butcher and fishmonger, and she has a cliff-top allotment garden in which she grows all kinds of produce which finds its way on to the menu. Neighbours grow things for her, too. What grows is what is served, so you might find a geranium-leaf ice-cream, or a peach-leaf custard, borage flowers garnishing a sorbet, lemon balm with salad leaves. She describes the food as modern English but with Mediterranean, Arab and Indian influences, while keeping as close as possible to The Angel's Devon roots.

An unusual facet of working life at The Carved Angel, but one which others would do well to imitate, is that Joyce expects staff to be able to do every job, from washing up to waiting to cooking, so that everyone has a knowledge of the product and of the service. Many people have gone on to open their own restaurants after learning from her, and she is enormously proud of their achievements – almost more so, it sometimes seems, than of her own.

Joyce Molyneux has been a major figurehead for the English cookery world for a considerable time. She has been in the forefront of a revival of the reputation of English food in the eyes of the world, and is one of just a handful of lady chefs to have reached the upper echelons of her chosen profession.

Joyce Molyneux
The Carved Angel
2 South Embankment
Dartmouth
Devon TQ6 9BH
(080 43) 2465

Jean-Yves Morel

Jean-Yves Morel began his cooking career at the age of twelve, by helping out in a local restaurant, then he took things a little more seriously by undertaking an apprenticeship in charcuterie in Lyon, France, where he also learned a lot about pâtisserie. He spent his national service in Tahiti before writing to those renowned charcutiers and pâtissiers in London, the Roux brothers, asking them for a job. To his surprise, and delight, they took him on, first at their own charcuterie and then at Le Gavroche as a commis chef. Jean-Yves pays tribute to the Roux's influence on him, not only for the development of his cooking style, but also for instilling an ethic of sheer hard work. In 1980 he found the run-down restaurant in Haslemere that he transformed into Morel's, with his wife Mary-Anne looking after the front-of-house. Without doubt, it is here that he has really blossomed.

Classical in the early days, more modern in response to current tastes today, Jean-Yves has always had his own style. He is passionate about fresh vegetables – which he sees as another of his strengths – serving vegetables and creating a perfect symbiosis by his choice of vegetables in the dish he is preparing.

Jean-Yves eats out as often as possible, for he draws great inspiration from his contemporaries. However, increasingly he looks to the East, experimenting with oriental combinations of flavours. But essentially he enjoys any kind of food, as long as it is properly cooked.

JEAN-YVES MOREL
Morel's
23-27 Lower Street
Haslemere
Surrey GU27 2NY
(0428) 51462

Anton Mosimann

Anton Mosimann's is the story of being a perfectionist. He was born in Solothurn, Switzerland, in 1947, the only son of parents who ran both a farm and a restaurant. The main influence on his boyhood was the restaurant, and by the time he was six years old he knew he wanted to be a chef. He set about achieving that ambition with a single-mindedness that characterises his every move.

Perhaps it was in recognition of this that the Hotel Baeren in Twann invited him, when he was only fifteen, to be an apprentice. He applied himself to a rigorous schedule with typical dedication, regularly working a fifteen-hour day, and cramming as much schooling as possible into his one day off a week. This resulted in the award to him, at the age of only seventeen, of the Diplôme de Cuisinier, which is not normally attained before nineteen.

He spent the next four or so years in various establishments in Europe and Canada, broadening and deepening his experience, and always learning. In 1970 he was appointed head chef at the Swiss Pavilion at Expo '70 in Osaka, leading a brigade of thirty-five chefs, all but ten of them Japanese. He won the gold medal at Expo '70 and began a lifetime's love affair with things Japanese.

No sooner had he received this accolade than he decided he could do with brushing up his pastry work, so he joined the Palace Hotel in Gstaad as a commis pâtissier. From Gstaad, he was recruited by The Dorchester in London, to become first sous chef in 1975; and in 1976, still only twenty-nine, he became the youngest ever maître chef des cuisines. He enhanced the hotel's existing high reputation to such a degree that the Terrace Restaurant earned two Michelin stars.

In 1986, the year in which he celebrated ten years at the helm of one of this country's

flagships, he took a three-month sabbatical during which, among other things, he took a bakery course in Lucerne and a restaurant and hotel management course in Lausanne, proving once again that in this world, you never stop learning.

He is an accomplished author. *Cuisine à la Carte* came out in 1981, and rapidly went into paperback; for Sainsbury's he wrote *A New Style of Cooking*; and in the autumn of 1985 came his *Cuisine Naturelle*, the result not only of years of dedicated research but also, in true Mosimann tradition, of a change of lifestyle, for here is a man who practises what he preaches. Then came *Anton Mosimann's Fish Cookery*, beautifully presented, a joy to read and to use.

Mosimann's cuisine naturelle is a form of cooking that rejects the use of butter, oil, cream and alcohol, and utilises very little salt and sugar. It came about as a response to his own needs, and the needs of those he saw around him (living stressful and unhealthy lifestyles). It was further developed under the guidance of a trained nutritionist. Combined with regular daily exercise, cuisine naturelle provides a régime for life, for living life to the full.

In 1988, Anton moved on from The Dorchester, achieving another ambition in the move – to run his own exclusive private dining club, Mosimann's in Knightsbridge. Here he has experimented even further with

new ideas, and although he still features several cuisine naturelle dishes on the menu, he has also introduced more earthy, homely flavours, such as bangers-and-mash and the famous bread-and-butter pudding. But as you would expect from Anton, these are no ordinary bangers, mash or pudding. And again, there are the Unique Selling Points at Mosimann's – the small portion of bread-and-butter pudding served to all diners as part of their dessert course, with his compliments; and the spirits all ranged in decanters, not bottles.

His style and flair can also be seen in the various dining rooms of Mosimann's, from the light Tiffany Room at the top of the former Belfry to the solid and comfortable Gucci Room below.

Anton is also a familiar face to television viewers, and the unprecedented enthusiasm brought about by the 'Anton goes to Sheffield' sequences in BBC's *Food and Drink* programme amazed him. In Autumn 1989, *Cooking with Mosimann* was shown and a book accompanied the series.

By special invitation, Anton has catered for leading public figures worldwide, including members of the British Royal family. To him, it is a privilege to have cooked for them; to most people, it is a privilege to have eaten his food! It is to his eternal credit that despite these grand associations, Anton Mosimann remains, at the heart of it all, an honest, practical and dedicated chef with a growing world-wide reputation.

ANTON MOSIMANN
Mosimann's
11b West Halkin Street
London SW1 8JW
01-235 9625

Kay Morgan

Kay Morgan had no formal training as a cook. When she gave up modelling, she started to run an antique shop. However, being an instinctive hostess, she offered tea and cakes in the shop and everything just took off from there. Her first restaurant was called Mr Midgley's, which she ran from 1981 to 1984, and then in 1985, with her husband Cliff, she opened La Chaumière in Cardiff.

Together they have eaten their way around the best establishments in France, and Kay pays due homage to the Troisgros brothers for their influence upon her, particularly in the treatment of game. But her individual style of country cooking came simply through trying out her own ideas. She calls it 'nouvelle classic', which means classic dishes, cooked and presented in the newer style, with lighter sauces that let the flavour of the main ingredients shine through.

If people are happy with her food, then Kay asks for nothing more, and blushes with pleasure on being thanked for a lovely meal. She enjoys eating out in the nearby cities of Bristol and Bath, and gets to London when she can. But it is still to France that she returns for rest and renewed inspiration.

KAY MORGAN
La Chaumière
Cardiff Road
Llandaff
Cardiff
South Glamorgan CF5 2DD
(0222) 555319

Michael Nadell was born in London's East End. He became entangled with the world of food via his uncle, who was head chef at the Leofrick Hotel in Coventry and promised to teach Michael all things culinary – apart from sugarwork. In 1963 Michael enrolled at Westminster College for a two-year course, and learned from Emile Lefebvre just how much there is to the art of pâtisserie.

In 1968, after three years as commis pâtissier at the Royal Court Hotel in Sloane Square, Michael moved to Maison Bertaux, the venerated Soho pâtisserie where at one time, he was the only Englishman. In 1969 he joined the Britannia as chef pâtissier for its opening, and later moved to Peter Kromberg's kitchen at the London Inter-Continental Hotel for its opening. He stayed until 1979, when he and his wife, Stella, decided it was time to start their own business.

At first, the Nadell Pâtisserie consisted of a brigade of three in Hackney covering just about 1,000 square feet. But it took only a year and a half for them to outgrow the original site when Michael moved to the Angel, where he has over 5,000 square feet and employs between fifty and sixty (mostly young) pâtissiers. His production of croissants (for example), using only un-salted Devonshire butter and the very best eggs sometimes exceeds 2,500 a day, not to mention the brioches, pains au chocolat and the thousand individual pâtisseries and petits fours he and his chefs bake.

Medals, cups and certificates from international shows, such as the Culinary Olympics and Hotelympia attest to an extraordinary record of achievement, but now having opted for a less anxious life on 'the other side', he prefers to judge the competitions that he used to contest. Michael is an ardent and dedicated teacher, deriving infinite pleasure from passing on his knowledge and experience to the many students whom he takes on from colleges, such as Westminster, before releasing them onto the commercial scene with the Diploma of the Nadell Apprenticeship, three years later as fully fledged chef pâtissiers.

The Nadells' enjoy eating with friends, and invariably choose Chinese and English restaurants.

MICHAEL NADELL
The Nadell Pâtisserie
1 White Lion Street London N1
01-833 2461

'Having failed to make the grade to become a professional footballer with Aston Villa, I decided to join the Navy, but my father – who at that time was a very successful caterer – persuaded me to earn a living on dry land. I was taken on by the Apollo Hotel and have never looked back.' In fact, Roger then trained at Halesowen College of Further Education and from then on he seems to have worked only with the best!

His career began with two years at The Savoy in London. He then worked with Michel Roux at The Waterside and with Albert at Le Gavroche, during which period his culinary style was firmly set. He then went to Roanne in France for a spell with the Troisgros brothers, before returning to England and The Bell Inn at Belbroughton, which was run by his father John. Here, with fellow chef Idris Caldora, the youngsters swept the board in the awards for a number of years.

When The Bell Inn reverted to its brewery owners, and with Idris Caldora installed at Bilbrough Manor, John and Roger Narbett set about finding the right showcase for Roger's talents. They settled on Sloans in Birmingham, a former fish restaurant. Sloans is now rated as one of the best restaurants in the Midlands, and Roger is quickly learning some of his father's business acumen. Although Rober might not have succeeded in his boyhood ambition to play for England, he can console himself with having cooked for the team in Rumania in 1989.

ROGER NARBETT
Sloans Restaurant
27-29 Chad Square
Hawthorne Road
Edgbaston
Birmingham
West Midlands B15 3TQ
021-455 6697

Graham Newbould has moved for a long time in a rarified atmosphere, starting with a period of two years under Michel Bourdin at The Connaught in London, where he learned the discipline required to achieve Michel's remarkable level of excellence when cooking for such large numbers. From The Connaught he moved to Buckingham Palace about which, for security reasons, little may be said. From there, he left to run the kitchens of the Prince and Princess of Wales, where of course there is equal secrecy, although judging by the television pictures of the Prince's gardens, Graham must have had some good raw materials.

Today, Graham is Head Chef at Inverlochy Castle, the bastion of Scottish culinary excellence where following, in the footsteps of fellow Connaught disciple François Huguet, he has retained the Michelin rosette. In 1989, as a member of Le Club des Chefs – exclusive to chefs who have cooked for Heads of State he cooked on Cathay Pacific's London to Hong Kong route, as part of a special promotion.

Graham's style today is very much the 'haut' version of modern British – shiny, reduced sauces and turned vegetables – and always based on sound materials.

GRAHAM NEWBOULD
Inverlochy Castle
Torlundy
Fort William
Inverness-shire PH33 6SN
(0397) 5767

MARTIN O'BRIAN
Rudland & Stubbs
35-37 Greenhill Rents London EC1M 6BN
01-253 0148

MARK ORR
Pomegranates Restaurant
94 Grosvenor Road London SW1V 3LF
01-828 6560

DAVID OSTLE
Brockencote Hall
Chaddesley Corbett
Kidderminster
Hereford & Worcester DY10 4PY
(056 283) 876

David Nicholls

David Nicholls was originally a footman at Buckingham Palace. When he left Royal service he wanted to remain in London and cooking being the only other thing he could do reasonably well, he became a chef and quickly became hooked.

That said, David has cooked in the most auspicious surroundings. From initial training at Thanet and then Westminster Technical Colleges, he started with two years at the Waldorf Hotel in the Aldwych. He then spent four years at The Dorchester with Kaufeler and Mosimann, two years at The Inter-Continental with Kromberg and then did a four-month 'stage' at the Auberge de Noues, Avignon, with Aubertine. From these influential cooks, he learned to love food, to understand it, and how to create without being contrived.

Returning to England, David progressed from The Inn on the Park as senior sous chef, to The Old Lodge at Limpsfield as chef/director, to Waltons in London as head chef for three years, and then on to The Britannia Inter-Continental in Grosvenor Square as executive chef. In 1989, he moved to The Royal Garden Hotel in Kensington, taking over from Remy Fougère. David has since brought in some of his brigade from the Britannia and made some changes, such as staff meetings at 8.30am daily, encouraging everyone to bring in new ideas to discuss. A habit which he learned from Anton Mosimann – which made a great impression on him – is to shake hands with every member of his brigade, at the beginning of each day. He is genuinely concerned for the well-being of his staff, knowing that only a happy kitchen is an efficient kitchen.

David takes the best of what food is available today and cooks purely for the pleasure of his customers. He tries to understand their tastes and to work his combinations of ingredients into presentations that they will enjoy.

As a change from chefs being inspired by their mothers, David praises his father who, told him that there are only two types of food – good and bad. Nicholls Junior comes into the former category.

DAVID NICHOLLS
The Royal Garden Hotel
Kensington High Street
London W8
01-937 8000

109

Christophe *Novelli*

Jean-Pierre *Novi*

Jean-Christophe Novelli was born and brought up near Calais. Inspired by his mother's cooking, he began working as an apprentice chef when only fifteen. Apart from the brief interruption caused by his military service – when he was a paratrooper and not a chef – he's been cooking all his life. The high spot of his time in France was probably when he was personal chef to Baron Rothschild in Paris for two years. It was after this that wave he came to England, working first at Chewton Glen in Hampshire, and then at the Parkhill Hotel.

But it was at Geddes in Southampton that Jean-Christophe really came to public attention. Within a year, the *Times* newspaper had voted the restaurant as the best outside London, and Novelli as the chef to watch in 1988. His inventive cooking, firmly based in the classic tradition but with his own very modern flair, won him many fans. No doubt many customers followed him westwards when he moved to Nansidwell Country House Hotel in Cornwall. Here, proprietors Jamie and Felicity Robertson have given him a free rein to create his own menus, and the team are confident that there's a great future ahead for the hotel.

JEAN CHRISTOPHE NOVELLI
Nansidwell Country House Hotel
Mawnan Smith
Nr Falmouth
Cornwall TR11 5HU
(0326) 250340

Jean-Pierre Novi was born and brought up at Les Baux, in Provence, and now lives and works at his own 'Provence' in Hampshire. He was encouraged to enter the profession by his father, as his parents owned and ran the highly rated La Riboto de Taven. As a youngster, Jean-Pierre worked in the restaurant, but didn't relish the prospect of a career in catering, having seen his parents work so hard all their lives. However, once he started to enjoy being a chef there was no looking back.

Jean-Pierre studied for three years at hotel school in Menton, and cooked in the officers' mess in Provence for his year's national service. Such was his dedication, that in order to learn more about foie gras,

he also studied for a year in Périgord. His first taste of England was a six-month stint as commis at Chewton Glen, after which he spent three very enjoyable years as chef at the French Embassy in Stockholm. This period also included 'stages' with Roger Vergé at Le Moulin des Mougins and with the Troisgros brothers in Roanne. Then, in 1983, Jean-Pierre set up his own restaurant, Le Provence, moving to its present site and expanding to a restaurant with rooms in 1987.

Although it was during the Embassy days that Jean-Pierre really started to enjoy cooking and to experiment, it is at Le Provence that he evolved the highly acclaimed modern French style that he employs to such effect today. Whether you prefer to regard it as a 'restaurant gastronomique français' (as it says on the brochure) or a restaurant with rooms (as it says on the door), neither does full justice to what you

will find at the Gordleton Mill.

Jean-Pierre Novi often returns to his national roots for ideas, such as bourride, a less well-known version of the famous bouillabaise. He even uses olive oil from the family's own presses, especially imported to bring him a taste of home.

Since writing, the Novis have returned to their native Provence.

JEAN-PIERRE NOVI
Provence at the Gordleton Mill
Silver Street
Hordle
Nr Lymington
Hampshire SO41 6DJ
(0590 682219

Chris Oakes

Ask Chris Oakes to describe his style of cooking and he'll invariably say, 'clean, honest and with a modern approach'. He's a modest but tenaciously strong-willed chef, never accepting compromise and always eager to improve. Despite his parents running a pub in Suffolk, Chris's school years provided few clues to his eventual career, until his final year. His headmaster, in a wildly progressive stroke, decided that girls should be taught woodwork and the boys cookery. Oakes won a Christmas cake competition and was clearly pleased with his newly acquired ability, especially as he claims cooking was the *only* thing he was any good at.

Leaving school, he drifted through a series of jobs until he was finally taken on as an apprentice at the Seckford Hall Hotel in Woodbridge. Head chef turned college lecturer Malcolm Long proved to be the first of a number of mentors, and like Gerald Milsom of Le Talbooth and Kit Chapman at The Castle Hotel in Taunton who followed subsequently, he seemed more aware of Oakes' potential than the young lad himself. Going on to work at Milsom's newly-opened fish restaurant, The Pier at Harwich, Oakes appeared to absorb readily its clear policy of serving good, plain, honest food – always of top quality but never over-elaborate.

This dictum is recognisable today in his own restaurant, simply called Oakes. Chris's approach is down to earth and unpretentious, meshing sound technique with modern principles. The results on the menu are a blend of inventiveness and tradition.

Away from cooking he enjoys simple pleasures, such as reading and walking. Not only does fresh air and exercise provide respite from the hot-plate, if the season is right, Chris is a devil for hunting out cèpes and chanterelles. These latter pursuits were developed around the Quantock Hills during his time at The Castle, which he joined after Harwich. Here, once again, Oakes had to be chivvied, this time by Kit Chapman, into taking on the role of head chef.

Oakes Restaurant was finally 'born' in November 1986, an analogy prompted by writer Laurie Lee who attended the opening party and muttered, 'Look at him. Pale, pleased and exhausted. He's just given birth.' Here, with his wife Caroline and her parents for support, Chris Oakes is able to perfect his style and to exercise complete control.

The word 'honesty' has cropped up a couple of times - unsurprisingly in fact, as it is singularly appropriate when writing about Chris. There's honesty in pricing three set menus containing no hidden extras, accompanied by wines of distinctly reasonable value. There's honest service from a knowing, well-briefed patronne. And finally, there's honesty in the kitchen where Chris Oakes' response continues to be both diligent and understated.

CHRIS OAKES
Oakes
169 Slad Road
Stroud
Gloucestershire GL5 1RG
(0453) 75995)

In the age of steam engines, Jeremy Blake O'Connor wanted to be an engine driver. Upon their demise, he decided to pursue his other love – cookery – instead. He reckons he was unique among his schoolfriends in having parents who actually took him out with them to restaurants. Indeed, cooking runs in the family. His grandmother's grandmother was Lord Byron's cook (her husband was the groundsman on his estate); and one of Jeremy's great-aunts, now eighty-four years old, provided him with a wealth of cake recipes some of which he still uses today, to her immense pride.

He began cooking during the summer after his 'O' levels, having obtained a job with his great-uncle who was manager of a now defunct steel works in Derbyshire. He was taken on in the works canteen but on his first day there, the apprentice in the directors' dining room went sick with appendicitis, which in those days meant about six weeks off work. Jeremy stepped in to help out, had his first glimpse of a commercial kitchen and that was that. He never went back to school!

When the ailing apprentice returned, Jeremy moved on to serve an apprenticeship at the five-star Grand Hotel in Birmingham until 1971 (attending college part-time, and later taking an Open University degree). He spent most of the 1970s at the Crown in Chiddingfold, under the tutelage of Angus Lamont who had been with George Perry-Smith in Bath. During this time, the Crown was awarded a Michelin star. Then came what Jeremy calls his second apprenticeship – a period of three years spent in France working at the very best places: at the Auberge de l'Ill, with the Troisgros brothers, with Michel Guérard, with Alain Raye, and at the Auberge des Templiers in the Loire Valley. He attributes all the major influences on his cooking to these years.

His early cooking was very classical, in the silver service style of the times. Swiss and Italian influences acquired whilst at the Crown started to change things, however, and he was amazed to find that the cooking at a 'mere inn' was far superior to that found at a five-star hotel, which hitherto had been his idea of the ultimate place to find good food. Three years at Thatcher's in Thame (from 1982-1985) also proved formative, bringing yet more modern influences to bear, as did the next year, at the Interlude de Tabaillaud in London, Jeremy's first post as head chef. In 1986 he became first head chef at Cannizaro House in Wimbledon, one of the first attempts to create a country house hotel close to the centre of the capital. He saw the first year through, then moved out to Aylesbury to take over Pebbles from David Cavalier.

Jeremy's present style is a cross, he says, between modern English, modern French and classical French, with French regional overtones and strong rustic tendencies. He loves to put a simple meat and a simple sauce on a plate, equal in quality and both outstanding; or to create combinations of textures and tastes conceived so as to blend or contrast with one another – something achieved par excellence by one of his heroes, John Burton-Race.

As often as possible Jeremy eats at L'Ortolan, Le Manoir aux Quat'Saisons, and La Tante Claire, for him the best three restaurants in the country. But he is equally generous in his praise for the 'often-as-you-like' places, as he calls them – Munchies and Brown's in Oxford, Chuen Cheng Ku and the New Diamond in London's Chinatown.

JEREMY BLAKE O'CONNOR
Pebbles
1 Pebble Lane
Aylesbury
Buckinghamshire HP20 2JH
(0296) 86622

James Peake went straight to The Dorchester in London as an apprentice, and did his City & Guilds by day release at Westminster College. He then spent two years at The Capital Hotel before trying his hand overseas, with The Southern Sun Hotel Company in South Africa, where he spent most of the 1970s. His first job back in England was at Dukes Hotel, and then he decided that the challenge of being head chef in a restaurant was irresistible, so he took the opportunity to join Motcomb's and Philip Lawless.

At Motcomb's his style settled into his own combination of English and French cuisine, so it's hardly surprising that when he eats out, he enjoys Langan's or the Boulestin.

JAMES PEAKE
Motcomb's Restaurant and Wine Bar
26 Motcomb Street
London SW1X 8JU
01-235 6382

Roger Pergl-Wilson sent us a cry from the heart in reply to our standard questionnaire. It was a letter which epitomised all the joys and frustrations of being a chef/patron, known to everyone who's been in the trade for twenty-five years or so. But what was apparent, above all, was the passion of someone who really cares about his work, and for whom cooking is everything.

Roger had always wanted to be a chef, and he washed up in a local restaurant in the evenings. Getting there necessitated two changes of bus, and such was his determination, that he took on a morning paper round to raise the bus fare. He did his early training at Wolverhampton College and worked locally to begin with. He did a spell in Zürich and then joined the Café Royal in Guy Mouilleron's brigade.

Roger moved to the Lake District in 1972, working at the Wild Boar at Crook, and the Royal at Bowness (where he was manager for eight years), before opening his own restaurant in 1981. When eating out, he regularly visits his neighbouring establishments in Cumbria, and when in London enjoys La Tante Claire, Chez Nico, and Rue St Jacques, to name but a few.

ROGER PERGL-WILSON
Roger's Restaurant
4 High Street
Windermere
Cumbria LA23 1AF
(096 62) 4954

Michel Perraud was born in Narmoutier, France. His parents were hoteliers, so it seemed natural to follow in the family tradition. He began his career in 1975, as an apprentice at the Dagorno Restaurant in Paris, and moved back to his parents' hotel, the St Paul, as commis chef in 1977. He spent a year in the French army, and a year at the Chez Albert in Cassis, before joining the celebrated three-star Michelin Troisgros in Roanne as chef de partie in 1979. It was Troisgros who played a significant part in developing David's perception of food and style of cuisine, which had been hitherto confined to a classical background.

Michel moved to Le Taillevent in 1980, before coming to England and The Waterside Inn, where he rose to become Michel Roux's chef de cuisine. It was while he was working at The Waterside that he won the Académie Culinaire's Meilleur Ouvrier de Grande Bretagne. Early in 1988, he left England to work as chef consultant for Georges Pralus's sous-vide empire. Homesick for Britain, he soon returned with his family, and became chef de cuisine at Les Alouettes, where he may be found today.

Michel is planning greater things for Les Alouettes this year, including 'going for a star'. He enjoys the type of food he cooks himself, but is particularly fond of Chinese. He relaxes by spending time with his young family.

MICHEL PERRAUD
Les Alouettes
7 High Street
Claygate
Esher
Surrey KT10 0SW
(024 973) 230

Nicolas Picolet was born into the restaurant trade. His grandfather owned a restaurant and his father was a pâtissier who then went into the wine business. Nicolas was very close to his grandfather and learned a great deal from him, developing his present classical technique out of these regional beginnings.

While still a youngster, he worked in the brigades of Paul Bocuse and the Troisgros brothers. He went to Lausanne for a bit more experience, and then came to London, to Au Jardin des Gourmets as second chef for two years. The next two years were spent in Los Angeles, at the 7th Street Bistrot and then at La Maison du Caviar. He then returned to Au Jardin des Gourmets as head chef at the beginning of 1988, having packed a fairly substantial amount of travel and experience under his belt.

Nicolas gains most pleasure from creating new dishes, blending several ingredients together and seeing them evolve into what he calls a perfect marriage of flavours.

NICOLAS PICOLET
Au Jardin des Gourmets
5 Greek Street
London W1V 5LA
01-437 1816

113

David Pitchford

How times have changed! David Pitchford recalls with glee working at The Dorchester in the late 1960s and attending part-time his City & Guilds course at Ealing College. He managed to develop the ingenious method of putting in extra practice on some of his weaker culinary techniques: being first commis on the night brigade, he would nip down to the fridge at around 3.00am, sneak out with a large lobster and set about bettering his lobster Newburg handywork!

David and his wife, Rona, run Read's Restaurant in the picturesque setting of Painter's Forstal, near Faversham. Not all the thatched rural idyll, Read's is housed in a post-war, single-storey, former village supermarket. Clearly a triumph of faith and determination over architecture, but it is warm and comfortable with tasteful paintings and a cosy lounge area.

Six years at The Dorchester followed by a return to Ealing College, this time as a lecturer, firmly imposed the classical principles of Escoffier on David. Read's today is very much a manifestation of that style, though David's philosophy has always been to update the classic dishes and try, where possible, to introduce a certain novelty. His personal interpretation of sole véronique, for example, has been to use salmon – contrasting medallions of farmed and wild salmon, served with a small timbale of chilled muscat grapes.

Among his peers, David looks to those with a classical base and the belief that simple is best. After his weekly trips to the London markets, he'll often try to fit in lunch at L'Arlequin.

DAVID PITCHFORD
Read's Restaurant
Painter's Forstal
Faversham
Kent ME13 0EE
(0795) 535344

Stelios Platanos

Stelios Platanos was born in Athens. His uncle had one of the best restaurants in the city, the Averof, where as a youngster Stelios used to help out. He greatly admired this uncle and simply wanted to be like him when he grew up.

Wartime saw him as a commis chef at the Café de Paris in Leicester Square, and then at the end of hostilities he moved to Les Gourmets in Lyle Street as assistant chef. Then, knowing that he wanted to have his own restaurant, he moved front of house for some experience, and was head waiter at the White Tower in Percy Street (still a bastion of Greek cooking in London), before moving to the Screenwriters' Club in Mayfair in 1949, first as head wine waiter and then as first head waiter. In 1953, on very limited capital, Stelios opened his first restaurant, La Bohème, in Queensway. At this time French was still the international language of food and so this was the style of food Stelios cooked. However, by 1965, Stelios thought the time was right for an authentic Greek restaurant in London – and he stresses the authentic. So, still in Bayswater, he opened Kalamaras and the rest, as they say, is history.

Kalamaras is now in two parts, Mega and Micro, the former the full restaurant and the latter the tiny unlicensed sister. I know it's been said before but it's worth saying again – Kalamaras is more Greek than most of the restaurants and tavernas you actually find in Greece! Long may he continue.

STELIOS PLATANOS
Kalamaras
76/78 Inverness Mews
London W2 3JQ
01-727 2564

Keith Podmore

Keith Podmore was born and educated in Birmingham. With an apparently innate desire to cook he began his apprenticeship in 1960 at the Queen's Hotel. In 1965, after a short period of work at the Turnberry Hotel, he moved to Switzerland, first to Loche-les-Bains for the summer season and then Berne for the winter, before moving to France and La Réserve at Beaulieu.

Keith came back to England in 1967 and joined British Transport Hotels as sous chef, returning to the Turnberry in 1970 for a year, before moving to The Caledonian in Edinburgh in 1971. He was promoted to chef de cuisine in 1973 and transferred to the Grand Hotel in Hartlepool, followed by the Station Hotel in Perth in 1977. He moved to London and the Charing Cross Hotel in 1981 before his appointment as chef de cuisine at Boodles in 1983.

Keith has modified his traditional classical training, describing it simply as 'modern classic'. He finds great pleasure in cooking the best ingredients properly, and this is also the style of food he enjoys eating.

When he has enough spare time and energy, he is a keen gardener, golfer and collector of antique furniture.

KEITH PODMORE
Boodles Club
28 St. James' Street
London SW1
01-930 7166

114

Pascal Pommier

David Pope

Brian Prideaux-Brune

Pascal Pommier combined practical work experience with his catering qualifications in France, and even during his national service he stayed in practice, producing about 600 meals a day for hungry soldiers – a far cry from the meals he has produced since then!

Pascal came to England in 1985, to the Mill House at Kingham, where he was first sous chef to Jeremy Blake O'Connor and then head chef of a brigade of six. During this time he did 'stages' with Raymond Blanc and Michel Roux, and realises how fortunate he was to have worked with two of the top chefs in the country.

Since the summer of 1988, Pascaie has been at the Normandie Hotel just outside Manchester. Owners Max and Gillian Moussa appreciate their lucky find, for he has brought a new vitality to the place. He pays tribute to Raymond Blanc in several dishes such as veal sweetbreads served with a hazelnut sauce with pine kernels and almonds. He even makes the croissants and brioches for breakfast in the hotel! Still only twenty-four, this is surely a young man to watch in the future.

Pascal Pommier
Normandie Hotel & Restaurant
Elbut Lane
Birtle
Nr Bury BL9 6UT
061-764 3869

David Pope was born in Bristol, and was inspired by his mother, an excellent cook, to go into cooking. He took City & Guilds at Bath Technical College, and then began a practical career that has spanned several impressive establishments.

His itinerary describes an interesting, if restless, pattern. He began at The Capital in London as a commis, staying in the city to go to Blake's Hotel as chef de partie. Then to the Cotswolds, first to the Lygon Arms as chef tournant, then as chef to Hill's restaurant in Stratford-on-Avon. Down to Devon next, to Gidleigh Park as sous chef, then back up to Cliveden as first sous chef. Finally, further down, this time to Cornwall, to the Well House at Liskeard, where he seems to have found his niche.

He most enjoys pastry work, and this is apparent in the excellent puddings he turns out. David Pope has brought to the Well House the opportunity for it to be classed with some of the very best country house hotels in Britain. We wish them both well.

David Pope
The Well House
St. Keyne
Liskeard
Cornwall PL14 4RN
(0579 42001

Brian Prideaux-Brune has been chef in his family run Plumber Manor since 1973. He trained with Geoffrey Sharp at the Grange, Covent Garden and other establishments in the Group.

His style of cooking is rooted in the classical school in which he was trained; it has developed naturally and more modern overtones are discernable. He particularly enjoys producing fish dishes, as fish is so versatile.

When eating out, Brian Prideaux-Brune would choose to visit Chinese restaurants or somewhere with a good selection of vegetarian dishes.

Brian Prideaux-Brune
Plumber Manor
Sturminster Newton
Dorset DT10 2AF
(0258) 72507

MARK PACKMAN
Chasers Brasserie
35 Store Street
London WC1E 7BS
01-631 4918

JEAN-CLAUDE PAILLARD
La Dordogne
5 Devonshire Road
London W4 2EU
01-747 1836

ALISON PARSONS
Polmaily House Hotel
Drumnadrochit
Inverness-shire IV3 6XT
(045 62) 343

TONY PARSONS
Mansion House Hotel
Thames Street
Poole
Dorset BH12 1JN
(0202) 685666

DAVID PARTRIDGE
**French Partridge
Restaurant**
Horton
Near Northampton
Northamptonshire NN7 2AP
(0604) 870033

SIMON PARTRIDGE
**Fountain House
Restaurant**
St James Square
Boroughbridge
North Yorkshire YO5 9AR
(0423) 322241

ERIC PASCHE
White Tower Restaurant
1 Percy Street
London W1P OET
01-636 8141

PAUL PASCOE
Sheekey's Restaurant
28-31 St Martin's Court
London WC2
01-240 2565

ALAIN PATRAT
Le Quai St Pierre
7 Stratford Road
London W8 6RF
01-937 6388

MARTIN J PEARN
**Buckland Manor
Restaurant**
Buckland
Near Broadway
Hereford & Worcester
WR12 7LY
(0386) 852626

JULIANO PERTUSINI
Terrazza-Est
109 Fleet Street London EC4
01-353 2680

TOM PETER
**Uplands Country
House Hotel**
Haggs Lane
Cartmel
Cumbria LA11 6HD
(053 95) 36238

BERNARD PHILIPS
The Moorings
6 Freeman Street
Wells-Next-The-Sea
Norfolk NR23 1BA
(0328) 710949

ROBERT PHILIPS
Riverside Inn
Canonbie
Dumfriesshire DG14 0UX
(038 73) 71292

BRUNO PIOTTO
Pontenuovo
126 Fulham Road
London SW3 5HU
01-370 6656

DAVID PIPER
The Dundas Arms
Station Road
Kintbury
Berkshire RG15 0UT
(0488) 58263

JEAN-LOUIS POLLET
Frederick's
Camden Passage
London N1 8EG
01-359 2888

JEAN-JACQUES PONS
Weavers Restaurant
23-27 High Street
Hadleigh
Suffolk IP7 5AG
(0473) 827247

GRAHAM POOLE
Daphne's Restaurant
110-112 Draycott Avenue
London SW3 3AE
01-589 4257

PAT PORTEUS
Breamish House Hotel
Powburn
Alnwick
Northumberland NE66 4LL
(066 578) 266

CAROLINE PRESCOTT
Combe House
Gittisham
Honiton
Devon EX14 0AD
(0404) 41938

JOHN QUIGLEY
Andrew Edmunds
46 Lexington Street
London W1R 3LH
01-437 5708

BARRY QUINION
Farlam Hall Hotel
Hallbankgate
Brampton
Cumbria CA8 2NG
(069 76) 234

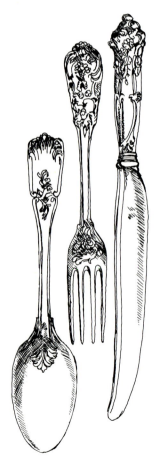

Martin Radmall studied as a full-time student at Westminster College for two years between 1973 and 1975. Having completed his studies there he spent another two years at the Grasshopper, Westerham as commis chef.

1979 saw Martin at Deane farm, Chipstead, as second chef, where he worked with Neville Goodhew who, in turn had worked with Pierre Koffmann. Neville had a tremendous influence on him and became Martin's mentor. They now work together at Honours Mill. Martin describes his style of cooking as modern French – *definitely* not nouvelle. Given a free rein and plenty of time, he most enjoys making sauces. To Martin eating out means an opportunity to seek out new ideas in good restaurants.

MARTIN RADMALL
Honours Mill Restaurant
87 High Street
Edenbridge
Kent TN8 5AU
(0732) 866757

Stephen Read had no formal training, and originally went into the restaurant business because he thought it was well paid! Presumably, he is now in the trade for the sheer love of it, having worked as waiter, washer-up, chef and manager, as well as running his own sandwich round in London's Kensington High Street.

Stephen has been chef/patron of his own restaurant, Read's in Surrey, since 1984. He cooks in bistro/brasserie modern English style, and has a dedicated local following. In true bistro fashion, he has other members of his family around helping out in the business.

STEPHEN READ
Read's Restaurant
4 The Parade
Claygate
Esher
Surrey KT10 0NU
(0372) 65105

Paul Reed has shown a fair amount of determination in his career, achieving his qualifications at Exeter College and starting off as head chef at the Buckrell Lodge Hotel in Devon!

However, Paul then went up to London and took more modest places in the brigades, first at The Hilton and then at The Dorchester, where he was fortunate to be

part of Anton Mosimann's gold medal winning team in the 1986 Culinary World Cup. From there, after a spell at the Copper Inn in Pangbourne, he went to the Chester Grosvenor, and has contributed significantly to putting this part of England on the culinary map, along with such places as Rookery Hall and the Normandie.

Paul cites Mosimann as the most powerful influence on his style, which began as fairly traditional and is now modern English.

To be a good chef, Paul believes that one of the most vital requirements is self-discipline. However, he does relax and enjoys ethnic food, finding plenty to satisfy him in his area.

PAUL REED
The Chester Grosvenor
Eastgate Street
Chester
Cheshire CH1 1LT
(0244) 324024

Derek Renouf   Gary Rhodes

Derek Renouf had four choices in the Merchant Navy: to be a deckhand, a bedroom steward, a waiter or a chef. He chose chef, found he enjoyed it, and that has been his life ever since! Some of the places that benefited from his skills on the way up include the Berners Hotel in London's West End, the Monkey Island Hotel at Bray in Berkshire, and The Castle Hotel in Taunton. He also spent four terms as a lecturer at Southend Technical college, before opening his own establishment in 1979.

From 1979 to 1986 there was only Renouf's Restaurant, but then came the Hotel Renouf, which Derek built up from scratch. He is now its Managing Director, and the hotel is actually run by his son Melvin, daughter Sarah, and son-in-law Victor.

Derek says he was inspired to run his restaurant rather more by the Belgians than by the French. In his opinion they have a more forward and open approach, making the restaurant into a theatre where the chef entertains the customer. Therefore, in the early days of his restaurant, he used to spend a fair bit of time with the customers at front of house. Nowadays, having established his reputation, he spends most of his time in the kitchen, often not venturing forth until about 10.30pm when service is virtually over. But he still gets an enormous kick from seeing a dining room full of happy customers.

Another of Derek's pleasures is to nip over to France and have lunch at Roger Vergé's, where the head waiter is also a good friend.

DEREK RENOUF
Hotel Renouf
Bradley Way
Rochford
Essex SS4 1BU
(0702) 541334

Although his hair always appears to be spiked and gelled upwards to post-punk perfection, any wayward tendencies this might imply can be quickly forgotten in the case of Gary Rhodes. He's twenty-nine and head chef of The Castle Hotel at Taunton which holds, amongst numerous awards, a Michelin star for its cooking. Gary held on to many such accolades in taking over the running of the kitchen in the wake of Chris Oakes' departure. Like many young British chefs attempting to re-establish and redefine this land's culinary traditions, he is responsible for bringing back to his menus many of the heartier dishes based around those of our mothers and grandmothers.

Rhodes was raised in Kent and, with his mother out at work, it fell to him to do most of the cooking. Instructed by Mum, he was able to do roasts and make his own stews and puddings. He enrolled at Thanet College and finished as very much the star student, grabbing both Student of the Year and Chef of the Year prizes. His first job was at the Amsterdam Hilton in 1979, a début not without incident since immediately after arriving he was involved in an accident with a van and knocked down. Moving up through the classically organised brigade, he proudly attained the post of chef saucier by his twenty-first birthday.

After such a rapid ascent of the kitchen hierarchy, Gary followed a somewhat erratic path, for instance preferring the Reform Club to a place under Michel Bourdin at The Connaught. Working at Winston's, then a new restaurant in Bloomsbury, it was his vegetable supplier who brought about an introduction to Brian Turner, then head chef at The Capital Hotel. It was during his time there that Gary resumed his upward curve, consolidating his talents and maturing under his new employer.

Sensing the need to head out on his own, Gary moved on again to the Whitehall

Hotel in Essex, making a strong impact as head chef. Despite good notices from critics, he was unhappy and returned to The Capital before finally arriving at The Castle. He came to the hotel when it was enjoying something of a renaissance due, in no small part, to Kit Chapman, its owner and driving force. Its recently renovated dining room is frequented by discerning tourists and astute local business people alike. The cooking reflects that mix, juxtaposing traditional dishes with those created firmly out of today's contemporary style.

With Kit Chapman's encouragement, Gary has begun to make full use of the Somerset area for produce. The Quantock Hills and Exmoor aren't far away, yielding game, good quality meat and farmhouse cheeses. Aware of the return in popularity sound traditional fare, he offers (particularly on the set-price lunch menu) a constantly changing range of dishes such as braised oxtail, beef stew with carrots and dumplings, and Lancashire hot pot. Less fashionable cuts of meat can, with slow cooking, be just as enjoyable. Gary feels sure that many chefs have simply forgotten how to braise or stew in order to extract maximum flavour. He is now intent on drawing as much as possible from his heritage and is clearly succeeding in restoring to centre stage a repertoire which in recent years has been given merely a supporting role.

GARY RHODES
The Castle Hotel
Castle Green
Taunton
Somerset TA1 1NF
(0823) 272671

Ferrier Richardson blazed a trail through the Glasgow culinary scene some five years ago when he brought nouvelle cuisine to both the Buttery and the Rogano. The first is a Victorian pub in a wasteland almost under the M8 flyover in Glasgow; while the Rogano, which he ran at the same time, remains a great oyster and fish restaurant, straight out of the Art Deco period when the great liners were built just down the Clyde, then the greatest shipyard in the world. On the face of it, both establishments were unlikely settings, but the names of Ken McCulloch and Alloa Breweries went hand-in-hand with Ferrier's own at the time, and he took Glasgow by storm.

Ferrier's background lies in British Transport Hotels, and this gave him a strong foundation on which to build. After leaving the Rogano, he spent some time with people of the calibre of Alain Senderens in Paris, and Guy Mouilleron in London; and then opened his own restaurant with the former restaurant manager of the Rogano, Hugh MacShannon, called simply October – as that was the month in which they opened. It sets the scene for no-nonsense simplicity. There is no room for pretension, and with Hugh's relaxed style at front of house, Ferrier can concentrate on sublimating all the styles that have influenced him – and it's all there: Japanese, French, Italian, all bound together, of course, with Scottish materials. Ferrier's energy and enthusiasm have kept him one step ahead, and that alone makes him a big attraction in this part of Scotland.

FERRIER RICHARDSON
October
128 Drymen Road
Bearsden
Glasgow
Strathclyde G61 3RB
041-942 7272

James Robins always wanted to work for himself and decided that a career in catering was most likely to provide the opportunity for him to do so.

He spent one year at the Cornwall Technical College and then went to work in France as a commis chef at Le Mas Candille in Mougins, near Cannes. On his return from France, he worked at the Riverside Restaurant at Helford, in Cornwall. From there he moved up to London and worked as commis and then demi-chef at the Capital Hotel in Knightsbridge. He then went as sous chef to Blake's Hotel in South Kensington; he progressed to head chef there and left in 1986 for the Halcyon Hotel in Holland Park, a converted town house, luxuriously and fashionably appointed. The downstairs dining room is cool and airy with a flagged floor, pastel shades and a light trellis design that is a logical extension to the patio. It provides a perfect setting for James' cooking, which he describes as 'honest, modern and English'.

JAMES ROBINS
Kingfisher Restaurant
Halcyon Hotel
81 Holland Park
London W11 3RZ
01-727 7288

Ruthie Rogers & Rose Gray's story is virtually inextricable from that of their River Café, originally opened by architect Richard Rogers as a canteen for his design practice. Now Richard's wife and her partner-in-cuisine dish up a daily changing list of Tuscan and North Italian dishes with fresh ingredients, and are at the forefront of the much-heralded new wave of Italian cooking which mostly emanates from the north of that country – clean tastes, pungent flavours, not a tin of tomatoes in sight. They rank with Antonio Carluccio at the Neal Street Restaurant and Danilo Minuzzo at L'Incontro in this respect.

As examples of their style, try the char-grilled polenta with roasted red chillies, black olives and mâche, bresaola with white truffle oil, slivers of parmesan and arugola, or marinated buffalo mozarella with fresh oregano, tapenade and bruschetta. To follow, pan-fried calves kidneys in red wine with mustard, prosciutto, garlic and blue lentils, or a bollito misto of hen, tongue and cotechino served with mostarda de Cremona, or cold poached sea-bass cooked over fennel sticks, white wine and bay, and served with salmoriglio, char-grilled aubergines and peppers with fresh basil.

Ruthie and Rose cook from an open kitchen so you see them hard at work, cutting bresaola from the slicing machine and making good use of oils, herbs and fresh vegetables. The food has excellent flavour, good texture and originality.

RUTHIE ROGERS AND ROSE GRAY
The River Café
Thames Wharf Studios
Rainville Road
London W6 9HA
01-385 3344

Philippe Roy

Restaurants came into Stephen Ross's life at a fairly early age when his family bought the Cottage in the Wood Hotel at Malvern in 1965. Stephen did an Economics degree at Bristol University, followed by a year at Thornbury Castle with Kenneth Bell. This stint as a commis really sealed his fate, and he has never looked back.

From 1973 to 1980 Stephen was chef/proprietor at Popjoy's in Bath, when it was highly rated and acclaimed by both critics and public alike. Yet more praise was heaped upon him when in 1980, with his wife Penny, he opened Homewood Park at Hinton Charterhouse, just outside the city.

Initially, Stephen cooked in a French country style, along the lines of Elizabeth David but heavily influenced by Kenneth Bell and George Perry-Smith. But starting up Homewood his style has developed a contemporary English feel, very open-minded in approach – still with strong French regional undertones but plenty of simple English salads.

Stephen has also become a hotelier by acquiring the Queensberry Hotel in Bath. It is an apartment hotel – no restaurant – from which they run a 'shuttle service' to the dining rooms at Homewood.

Stephen derives the greatest satisfaction in cooking from seeing a trainee produce dishes of a genuinely high quality without interference from the teacher/chef. When eating out he prefers restaurants that are simple or owned by his friends. Otherwise there's that great standby for off-duty British chefs – Chinese food.

STEPHEN ROSS
Homewood Park Hotel
Hinton Charterhouse
Bath
Avon BA3 6BB
(022 122) 3731

Philippe Roy grew up on a farm near Poitiers in France, where his grandmother taught him how to bake cakes. After catering school in Poitiers he went as a chef to Le Relais du Médoc in Bordeaux which had a Michelin star, and then to the Hilton hotel in Stratford-upon-Avon before returning to France and the Moulin du Vey in Normandy, specialising in old classic recipes of that region. Next he worked in Paris and Switzerland before doing his Military Service, and then spent two years at the Foie Gras restaurant in Monte Carlo. In 1982 he came to London to Ménage à Trois, before moving to Bath in 1983, to start his own restaurant, Clos du Roy. The restaurant received critical and public acclaim during its 5 years in the city, and Philippe's loyal following went with him when, in 1988, he moved to Wiltshire to open as a restaurant with rooms. His customers describe his style as 'nouvelle with enough to eat!'

PHILIPPE ROY
Clos du Roy at Box House
Box
Wiltshire SN14 9NR
(0225) 744447

Albert Roux was born at Semur-en-Brionnais, Saone et Loire, of a charcutier father and grandfather. But it was his mother, a superb cook, from whom he inherited his love of good food and cooking. Albert began his apprenticeship at fourteen with a three-year course at the Pâtisserie Leclerc, St Mande-sur-Seine in Paris. This was followed by one year as commis pâtissier at the Pâtisserie Bras in the Avenue de la République, one year as commis de cuisine with Lady Astor in London, and one year at the French Embassy in London. He then was chef de cuisine to Sir Charles Clore, before leaving England for Algeria and three years of military service. On finishing, Albert spent two years at the British Embassy in Paris, before returning to England to spend nine years as chef to Major Peter Cazelet, trainer of the Queen Mother's racehorses, at Fairlawn in Kent.

In 1967, Albert called for his younger brother Michel (who was cooking for Mlle Cécile de Rothschild in Paris at the time) to start Le Gavroche together. Initially it was in Lower Sloane Street, Chelsea. Offering the very best in haute cuisine, they took turns in the kitchen and dining room, with one aim in view: to achieve a world-wide reputation for the quality of their service and cuisine. They saw and took their chance to capitalise on the by and large bland and unexciting English taste and tradition. Over a number of years they achieved acknowledgement for their efforts – acclaim from British both and international press, as well as culinary experts and writers. The resulting volume of business compelled them to move to bigger premises. Leaving the old site to its offspring, Gavvers, Le Gavroche found a new home in Mayfair where it still reigns supreme today. It preserves its logo (a kind of establishment joke) of the untidy, wide-eyed little urchin. In 1982, Le Gavroche became the first British restaurant to win three Michelin stars.

Not only was Le Gavroche a major turning point in Albert's career but it also acted as a foundation to the brothers' now burgeoning business empire. Roux Restaurants employs over 350 people, owns three successful City restaurants (Le Gamin, Le Poulbot and Rouxl Britannia, a 300-cover restaurant specialising in the use of sous-vide dishes); the Chelsea restaurants Gavvers and Les Trois Plats and the pâtisserie in Wandsworth. The latter is also the head office, from which the contract catering service is organised (clients include Kleinwort Benson and N M Rothschild), as well as being the sous-vide factory. The Rouxs' shops include La Boucherie Lamartine in Belgravia and Baily Lamartine in Mayfair. These are 'designer meat boutiques' which also offer French cheeses and breads (including Poîlane), fruits, vegetables and salads, all of which they import. Albert also has the management contract for Fortyseven Park Street, a private hotel comprising fifty-four luxury suites above the Le Gavroche, which can provide the ultimate in luxury room service. An example of Albert's pioneering approach manifests itself in his relationship with his Gavroche suppliers. He invites them to dine with him at the restaurant in order to appreciate the standard of quality he demands.

It is recognised that the Roux brothers, with their missionary zeal, have done more for cooking in this country than virtually anyone else, raising the standards and status of food, cooking and eating. Always concerned for the future and the continuation of the traditions of the kitchens of Le Gavroche and The Waterside Inn at Bray, it has become part of the Roux philosophy to encourage and, indeed, fund some of the most talented and aspiring of their protégés. Consequently the Roux empire has expanded with initial part funding of such ventures as Pierre Koffmann at La Tante Claire, Peter Chandler (their first English apprentice) at Paris House, Jean-Louis Taillebaud, René Bajard at Le Mazarin, Steven Doherty at Marlfield House, Christian Germain at Le Château de Montreuil in France, and Michael Hutchings, their first American apprentice, at Michael's Waterside Inn in Santa Barbara. Michel Roux Junior, Albert's son, takes over frequently in the kitchens at Le Gavroche, making him the fourth generation Roux to continue the family tradition; and daughter Danielle also works in the business. Five years ago, as further encouragement to the younger generation, the Roux brothers, together with Diner's Club, began the annual British Chefs Scholarships (formerly known as Roux Scholarships).

In 1975 Albert was distinguished with the Chevalier du Mérite Agricole; in 1986 he was awarded an Honorary Doctor of Science degree for his work in sous-vide; in 1987 he was made an Officier du Mérite Agricole; and in 1988 he won the *Caterer & Hotelkeeper*'s Catey award as Restaurateur of the Year. Since 1983 he has been Vice-President of the British Branch of the Académie Culinaire de France.

In addition, Albert is a regular contributor to television and radio, and with Michel, he became a household name as a result of BBC Television's thirteen-part series *Cooking at Home with the Rouxs*.

Albert will not define his style of cooking other than by saying that 'it is the cuisine of today which, like fashion, is constantly changing, but is firmly rooted in the past.'

ALBERT ROUX
Le Gavroche
43 Upper Brook Street
London W1Y 1PF
01-408 0881

123

Michel Roux

An articulate, many-sided character with opinions and exceptional talent, Michel Roux was born in Charolles, Saone et Loire. Like his brother Albert, he inherited his mother's love of cooking and when he was fourteen he began his apprenticeship at the Pâtisserie Loyal in Paris. After three years, he worked as commis pâtissier/cuisinier at the British Embassy in Paris for two years, followed by a year as commis with Mlle Cécile de Rothschild. The next two years were taken up by military service. At the beginning of the 1960s Michel returned to Mlle de Rothschild as the youngest chef she had ever employed. This lasted six years, during which time he also worked for the Bismarcks and the Schneiders, both wealthy, aristocratic families. As he says, with no financial restraints, it was a wonderful opportunity for innovation. He once cooked a whole kilo of truffles in champagne just for a garnish!

In 1967 Michel came to England to join brother Albert in starting Le Gavroche in Lower Sloane Street. He well remembers, even in the early days, cooking for people such as Princess Margaret and Lord Snowdon, show-business personalities like the Rolling Stones, as well as the newly converted lovers of their innovative style of cooking. Their hard work, often eighteen hours a day, soon made them personalities in their own right.

In 1972 the Roux brothers invested in The Waterside Inn, a country house perched on the banks of the Thames at Bray, probably one of the most elegant and charming restaurants in the country. The Waterside was run jointly by Albert and Michel under the banner of Roux Restaurants. It achieved its first Michelin star soon after it opened in 1973, its second in 1974, and its third in 1985. In 1984 it was awarded the *Caterer & Hotelkeeper*'s Catey for Best Menu of the Year. It has been a

member of the prestigious Relais Gourmand for over ten years. Michel insists on the highest degree of perfection. He freely admits to being extremely demanding and critical, but customers expect the food and service to live up to the reputation.

Michel has many international prizes and distinctions in pâtisserie and cuisine, which he started winning as early as 1963. In 1975, along with Albert, he was distinguished by his country with the honour of Chevalier du Mérite Agricole. His own personal 'best' achievement is the Meilleur Ouvrier de France en Pâtisserie in 1976. This is France's highest award, sponsored and run by the Government in recognition of over 217 different professions – it is considered far more worthy than an Oscar! Michel is the only holder of this title to be working in Great Britain. In 1985, the *Caterer & Hotelkeeper* honoured him again as Restaurateur of the Year; and in 1987 France made him an Officier du Mérite Agricole. And later in 1987, his native country once more recognised his contribution to food and cooking with the honour of Chevalier de l'Ordre National du Mérite.

Just as Albert involves himself more and more in his own business interests, so Michel has preferred to concentrate his time at Bray. That is not to say that all of it is spent in the kitchen to the exclusion of all else. On the contrary, apart from such projects as advising British Airways on their first class in-flight menus and so forth, he has become a best-selling cookery author. Together with his brother, the first book he wrote was *New Classic Cuisine* which was published in 1983 and won the Glenfiddich Book Award in the same year. It has sold over 100,000 copies worldwide, and his second book, *The Roux Brothers on Pâtisserie*, published in 1986, has topped 150,000 copies. He wrote a book to accompany the recent BBC Television series, *Cooking at Home with the Rouxs*, for which he was responsible for preparing the food before filming, as well as starring in the programme, and *The Roux Brothers French Country Cooking* was published in the Autumn of 1989.

Michel's library of press cuttings has become so vast that it takes up an entire room at the Waterside. He finds time to support the training of young chefs and waiters. On top of this, he is still content to spend hours creating sugar masterpieces, as well as being passionate and most knowledgeable about wines, which he chooses for all the Roux restaurants.

Michel enjoys eating out with friends – particularly Chinese food, but anything is welcome, as long as it is good. He also loves to get away to his own vineyard in the South of France.

MICHEL ROUX
The Waterside Inn
Ferry Road
Bray-on-Thames
Berkshire SL6 2AT
(0628) 20691

MARK RAFFAN
Gravetye Manor
Vowels Lane
East Grinstead
West Sussex RH19 4LJ
(0342) 810567

NIGEL RAFFLES
The Pink Geranium
Melbourn
Cambridgeshire SG8 6DX
(0763) 260215

JOE RAINERT
Four Seasons
109 High Street
Wingham
Canterbury
Kent CT3 1BU
(0227) 720286

DAVID RANDOLPH
Nuthurst Grange
Nuthurst Grange Lane
Hockley Heath
Warwickshire B94 5NL
(056 43) 3972

DAVID RAYNER
Riverside Restaurant
Helford
Near Helston
Cornwall TR12 6JU
(032 623) 443

ROBERT RAYNEY
Burgh Island Hotel
Bigbury-on-Sea
Devon TQ7 4AU
(0548) 810514

NICK READE
Les Trois Plats
4 Sydney Street
London SW3 6PP
01-352 3433

NICK REED
Blostin's Restaurant
29 Waterloo Road
Shepton Mallet
Somerset BA4 5HH
(0749) 3648

STANLEY REEVE
The Old Vicarage
Witherslack
Near Grange-over-Sands
Cumbria LA11 6RS
(044 852) 381

TERRY RICH
Brookdale House
North Huish
South Brent
Devon TQ10 9NR
(054 882) 402

JASON RICHES
Ninety Park Lane
Grosvenor House Hotel
90 Park Lane
London W1A 3AA
01-409 1290

RENÉ RIEUNIER
Rieunier's Restaurant
6 Oak Street
Lechlade
Gloucestershire GL7 3AX
(0367) 52587

RUTH ROBERTS
Lynwood House Restaurant
Bishop's Tawton Road
Barnstaple Devon EX32 9DZ
(0271) 43695

PETER ROBERTSON
Ballathie House Hotel
Kinclaven By Stanley
Perthshire PH1 4QN
(025 083) 268

PATRICK ROBIN
Bubb's
329 Central Markets
London EC1A 9BN
01-236 2435

JAYNE ROBINSON
Victor's Restaurant
84 Victoria Road
Darlington
Co Durham DL1 5JW
(0325) 480818

TONY ROBSON-BURRELL
Charingworth Manor
Charingworth
Nr Chipping Camden
Gloucestershire GL55 6NS
(038 678) 555

NICK ROCHFORD
Rochford's Restaurant
96 Felsham Road
London SW15 1DQ
01-789 3323

ARMANDO RODRIGUEZ
The Stafford
16 St James's Place
London SW1A 1NJ
01-493 0111

SALVADOR RODRIGUEZ
Restaurant Elizabeth
84 St Aldate's
Oxford
Oxfordshire OX1 1RA
(0865) 242230

ANTONIO ROMANI
Kettner's Restaurant
29 Romilly Street
London W1B 6HP
01-734 6112

GUISEPPE ROSELLI
Santini
29 Ebury Street
London SW1W ONZ
01-730 4094

ROBERT ROUDESLI
Le Champenois Restaurant
Blackwater Hotel
20-22 Church Road
West Mersea
Essex CO5 8QH
(0206) 383338

ALAIN ROUSSE
La Belle Epoque
103 Great Victoria Street
Belfast
Co Down BT2 7AG
(0232) 323244

GILBERT ROUSSET
Magno's
65a Long Acre
London WC2E 9JH
01-836 6077

NICK RYAN
Crinan Hotel
Crinan
By Lochgilphead
Strathclyde PA31 8SR
(054 683) 261

DAVID RYAN
Bracewells
The Park Lane Hotel
Piccadilly
London W1Y 8BX
01-499 6321

HERVÉ SALEZ
Liaison
11 Alma Road SW18 1AA
01-870 4588

Mark Salter

Bruce Sangster

Mark Salter exemplifies the dictum 'you never stop learning'. Typically, we came upon him as he had just returned from a trip to the United States, organised by a client of Cromlix House, where he has been head chef since 1987. Mark's was a fairly classical training, starting with City & Guilds and then the Diploma of Advanced Professional Cookery at Colchester. Next, in search of experience, he travelled overseas, and it was 1986 before he reappeared in this country, as sous chef at Cromlix.

There is no doubt that travel broadens a young chef's perspectives. Mark's is a very developed style of modern French cooking, with the vegetables as part of the presentation of the main dish. But his success, like that of all the best artists, owes much to the sound training he has had.

Training for the future is a subject which concerns him a lot, and the present trend of the young looking for enormous wages before they have the necessary skills, worries him. As for eating out? He likes to experience the tables of his peers in his own cuisine, and any other, provided it is well done.

MARK SALTER
Cromlix House
Kinbuck
Dunblane
Perthshire FK15 9JT
(0786) 822125

Bruce Sangster is the archetypal competitive Scottish chef. He says that he will not leave his native Scotland for the bright city lights because of the abundance of superb produce in his own back yard. Once touched upon, it is a subject from which it is difficult to prise him: the Tay salmon, the wild chanterelles and cèpes in the woods around the hotel, game from the moors, shellfish never far away, and perhaps the finest soft fruit in the world in Perthshire, not to mention masses of herbs in the hotel's own garden – with all this, why would anyone want to move away?

After training at two local Tayside colleges and teaching at one of them for a while, Sangster is now head chef at the Murrayshall Hotel, a sumptuously refurbished house on the outskirts of Perth. His teaching experience gives him more right than most to comment on the system, and he is disappointed by the lack of interest shown by colleges in hotels such as his own. While acknowledging that his level of the industry is only the tip of the iceberg, he argues for a proper system of 'day release' – not from college to hotel but the other way around!

His competitive urge has made him Scottish Chef of the Year on no fewer than four occasions, the last being 1989. He is a tireless fan of Scottish food, and his style takes 'modern Scottish' to extremes.

For himself, Bruce likes to eat at the tables of his peers – The Peat Inn and Inverlochy Castle.

BRUCE SANGSTER
The Murrayshall Hotel
Scone
Nr Perth
Perthshire PH2 7PH
(0738) 51171

JESUS SANCHEZ
Il Passetto
230 Shaftesbury Avenue
London WC2H 8EG
01-836 9391

STEPHEN SANDERSON
Penguin Café
Princes Square
Off Buchanan Street
Glasgow Strathclyde G1 3JN
041-221 0303

KEITH SAXBY
The Greenhouse Restaurant
27a Hays Mews London W1X 7RJ
01-499 3331

HANS SCHWEITZER
Midsummer House
Midsummer Common
Cambridge Cambridgeshire CB4 1HA
(0223) 69299

LIN SCRANNAGE
Market Restaurant
104 High Street (near Edge Street)
Smithfield City Centre
Manchester Greater Manchester M4 1HQ
061-834 3743

ROBERT SENIOR
Restaurant 44
44 Bedford Street
Belfast Co Down BT2 7FF
(0232) 244844

127

Richard Sawyer was born in Suffolk, and his involvement with catering began at the age of six with a duster, a saucepan and a wooden spoon, when he was the only boy in the Domestic Science class at his local school! In 1977 he apprenticed at the Brampton Hotel in Cambridge and later at County Catering in Croydon. He joined The Connaught in 1980 as second commis, becoming one of Michel Bourdin's protégés. He moved through the kitchen's stations to third sous chef in 1985 – the youngest of this rank at the time – taking off what little time was needed to make his mark at Hotelympia, winning medals in 1980 and 1982. He then left London and headed back to the country as head chef of Le Talbooth in Dedham, Essex, 'to run the kitchen with a frenzied discipline', as a local paper put it.

On leaving Le Talbooth, he joined his friend from The Connaught days, John Elliott, as premier sous chef at The Capital Hotel in Knightsbridge, before collaborating with yet another friend from The Connaught, Bourdin protégé Herbert Berger, in their own restaurant, Keats, in an enviable position among the stylish houses of Hampstead's Downshire Hill.

A typical dish of Richard's would be a plump, baked wing of skate with morels and pleurotte mushrooms served in a very rich and very garlicky red wine sauce. More than likely it would be accompanied by an exquisite salad of rare leaves and herbs, which he fondly nurtures himself in his Kingston garden.

RICHARD SAWYER
Keats Restaurant
3A Downshire Hill
London NW3 1NR
01-435 3544

Gunther Schlender

After serving his apprenticeship at the Hotel Kaiserhof in Wuppertal, and then at the Palast Hotel in Mannheim, German-born Gunther Schlender concocted a plan to embark upon a world tour, but got no further than London where, in 1964, he came to learn English. Later, he applied to Claridges Hotel and was accepted as a commis chef. This was followed by a spell at the Café Royal in 1965 where he was chef gardemanger in Henri Lullier's brigade. From 1966 until 1984 he worked for Robert Carrier first at Carrier's in North London, becoming head chef after a few months, and then as head chef at Hintlesham Hall in Suffolk, which was awarded a Michelin Star.

In 1984, Gunther joined London's Rue St Jacques as head chef, deliberately modifying his cuisine to avoid the Carrier 'stamp'. Using a combination of traditional German and classical French, Gunther's cooking began to emerge as 'modern French with modern presentation', which could appear on his menu as noix de ris de veau rôti aux champignons sauvage et pin noix. In 1985, the *Caterer and Hotelkeeper* awarded it their Catey and it was the Decanter/Badoit Restaurant of the Year. The following year Rue St Jacques won a star from Michelin and Gunther became chef/director.

Gunther is enthusiastic about his love of cooking, and like so many chefs finds his rewards in the enjoyment of his customers. When he is away from Rue St Jacques, he will invariably choose to eat Chinese with his family.

GUNTHER SCHLENDER
Rue St Jacques
5 Charlotte Street
London W1P 1HD
01-637 0222

Richard Shepherd

'A man of exuberance, irrepressible energy and an incorrigible sense of humour – I can never get enough of him!' That's a description of Richard Shepherd from a close friend and fellow chef. Born in Weston-super-Mare and driven by an innate love of food and flair for cooking, Richard spent most of his school holidays working in hotels and restaurants for pocket money. In 1960 he became an apprentice at the Mount Pleasant Hotel, Great Malvern, moving as commis chef to The Savoy in 1963. It was while working at The Savoy that he was influenced by two great and legendary chefs: Silvano Trompetto and Louis Virot. Both played vital roles in the development of his style – Trompetto for his public image and Virot for his culinary skills. In 1967 Richard left The Savoy to become chef de partie at La Réserve in Beaulieu, France.

Returning to London in 1969 he continued his training as chef de partie at The Dorchester until 1971 when he joined The Capital Hotel as chef de cuisine. Both he and the restaurant were awarded a Michelin star in 1974 – he was the first Englishman to achieve this distinction in London.

In 1977 Richard joined Langan's Brasserie in Stratton Street, as chef de cuisine in partnership with Peter Langan and Michael Caine. Using his classical training, love of French cooking and wealth of experience assembled and drawn from many different restaurants and hotels over the years, he has developed an individual style which he calls 'basically English, respecting French tradition'. It is best described as a combination of classical, brasserie and straightforward food, where taste is the vital component. The 'Shepherd School of Cooking' has become Langan's hallmark and some dishes, such as spinach soufflé and crème brûlée, are legendary. With his perception of what the customer wants and a nose for success, Richard has propelled Langan's to the height of the London scene. Along with the floor to ceiling Hockneys, Gladwells and Procktors, the walls of books, and the collection of 'odd' lights, he has helped to create London's most fashionable restaurant of the decade and the gossip columnist's favourite. It is not uncommon for the restaurant to serve 600 covers a day.

Richard demands and receives a great deal of loyalty from his staff, many of whom have been with him for over a decade. He was honoured with the Catey award as Restaurateur of the Year by the *Caterer & Hotelkeeper* in 1984. He spends less time in the kitchen now in order to cope with his expanding business interests, which span Langan's Brasserie, Odin's Restaurant in London, Langan's Bistros in London and Brighton, and Shepherd's in Quinta do Lago in Portugal. Furthermore, as one of the industry's most charismatic and articulate personalities, Richard is increasingly busy on radio and television, and never afraid to voice his opinions. He starred in the first series of Thames Television's *Take Six Cooks*, appeared several times on BBC's *Food and Drink Programme*, *Breakfast Time*, ITV's *TV AM*, and featured in Roy Ackerman's *The Chef's Apprentice* (August 1989).

Although Richard is no longer an examiner for City & Guilds, having resigned owing to his many other commitments, he regularly judges competitions at colleges and national events. His concern for recruitment and education – essentially the future of his profession – motivates his tireless efforts to encourage aspiring young chefs. He is a member of the original Club Nine, a fellow of the HCIMA, and having been an active member of the British branch of the Académie Culinaire de France since 1980, he was made its chairman in 1986.

Apart from his passion for good wine, and friends, and the satisfaction he derives from happy customers, Richard enjoys a round or two of golf, skiing, and a Saturday afternoon of rugby with his son.

RICHARD SHEPHERD
Langan's Brasserie
Stratton Street
London W1X 5FD
01-493 8822

Anna Smith was born in Naples, and was therefore steeped in a love of food from a very early age, and indeed she attributes her entry into the hotel business to this love of cooking.

She started off the hard way – in at the deep end – by buying the Danescombe Valley Hotel with her husband Martin in 1985, and her confidence and style have grown together ever since. The beautiful Georgian building with a balconied first floor is idyllically situated, with steep thick woodlands behind and a view to the River Tamar. Anna describes her style now as an extension of home cooking, and like any good cook, loves seeing empty plates back from the dining room. She prefers to offer a set meal of four courses.

She most enjoys eating out at her local highly rated restaurants, such as The Seafood Restaurant at Padstow, The Carved Angel in Dartmouth, Gidleigh Park at Chagford, or Chez Nous in Plymouth. That said, Anna also admits to enjoying any food that has not been, as she puts it, 'tricked up'.

ANNA SMITH
Danescombe Valley Hotel
Calstock
Cornwall PL18 9RY
(0822) 832414

Donald Smith served a three-year apprenticeship at The Ritz hotel before doing his National Service. He then returned to The Ritz as first commis in the Larder. From there he moved to the pastry kitchen in Harrods and in 1958 went to Le Caprice as chef saucier. He was head chef at Annabel's club when it opened in 1963, and left in 1974 to be head chef at the Grosvenor House Hotel. He was made executive chef of the London Division of Trusthouse Forte and was guest chef at the Georges V Hotel in Paris.

A natural curiosity led him into a career in catering; his parents were very keen theatre goers, and as a small boy he would be taken along for a meal after a performance. He says he was always intrigued to know what went on behind the swing doors to the kitchen.

He describes his style of cooking as classic French and says that his own experience of ethnic foods has prompted his use of exotic spices and unusual vegetables in combination with the classic ingredients which remain the foundation of his cuisine.

DONALD SMITH
Le Muscadet
25 Paddington Street
London W1M 3RF
01-935 2883

A pub in the heart of one of the most English villages in the country, with soft pink weathered brickwork and a wisteria winding round the windows, is the dream of a good many city folk. For Richard and Kate Smith, the dream is a reality in the shape of a charming inn-cum-restaurant-cum-so-much-more, called The Royal Oak. They also own the Beetle and Wedge at Moulsford-on-Thames, and seem determined to re-establish English inn and pub food at the heart of English life.

Richard Smith grew up in South London and freely admits that his mother's cooking had a profound and lasting influence upon him. Like his own style was to be, hers was cooking without pretension, but with a desire to preserve and enhance natural flavours. Richard particularly remembers his mother's baking and her beautifully light, lovely cakes. Growing up with the thought that everyone ate as well as they did at home, it was only later he discovered to the contrary.

The family moved to Ilfracombe in Devon in 1969, and Richard's parents decided to run a small guest house. He attended the local technical college, then headed off to work in France and Switzerland. There followed a period of flitting from job to job, Richard always assuming that eventually he would take over from his parents and expand the business. However, they thought otherwise, so Richard and Kate decided to head out on their own. A decisive moment came when Kate applied for a job at Langan's Brasserie in London; a quirky turn of events meant that she actually managed to talk Richard Shepherd into hiring her husband instead!

Richard was senior sous chef at Langan's for almost five years and felt very much in sympathy with Shepherd. A shared liking for honest, genuine food prevailed, free from glib garnishing. But Richard also

learned how to manage people and organise a busy kitchen, pretty important when you're serving up to 500 meals a day. Even today, he puts on the menu only those dishes that he would like to eat himself, as opposed to more flamboyant dishes that might simply attract the food critics. 'Cooking needs a heart and a soul,' he says. This feeling for food is central to Richard Smith's attitude to the way he runs his establishments, and as far as he is concerned it is more important than technical expertise for its own sake.

After Langan's and a brief spell at the Greenhouse in Mayfair, Richard and Kate bought The Royal Oak. Like many people he always felt the middle ground of British catering was a disaster and, in part, his tactic has been to remedy this by serving freshly prepared bar food using top quality ingredients. Smith's is food for a hearty appetite. Among his favourite restaurants he lists Le Suquet (he calls the dish of scallops bordelaise there 'stunning'). More suprisingly perhaps is his choice of L'Ortolan, where the cuisine is virtually opposite in style to his own, but interestingly, Richard maintains that John Burton-Race's cooking possesses some of the same values as his own, albeit with a different emphasis.

RICHARD SMITH
Royal Oak Hotel
The Square
Yattendon
Nr Newbury
Berkshire RG16 0UF
(0635) 201325

133

Stephen Smith

Keith Stanley

After a college education at Manchester Polytechnic, Stephen Smith decided on a career in industry, eventually becoming a group catering manager for Ferranti with a large financial budget. Then came a short but interesting spell in the school meals service. However, like most college students, he had always nursed a desire to own and work in his own restaurant. So he started off with his business partner, Robert Barbour, when the latter's parents sold Restaurant Nineteen to them.

Although it had formerly been a guest house, their interests lay in the production and service of food, with bedrooms a second priority. Stephen now thinks it would have made more economic sense to have upgraded the bedrooms first, rather than later, which is what they actually did. Nevertheless, their arrival on the restaurant scene was quickly noticed and the glowing reports continue.

Because of Stephen's lack of prior experience in kitchens, his style of cooking showed no particular influence – and he feels that is still the case. Essentially, his style has developed along with his knowledge of food and cooking. It is definite, positive, with strong flavours and colours, but balanced by delicate and subtle flavours in other dishes. He always avoids complication at the expense of flavour. While an early tendency was towards the French style, he soon discovered that it was not what he wanted.

Perhaps Stephen's greatest satisfaction is gained when a dish leaves his kitchen and he knows without doubt that it is good. That said, food and drink is both hobby and way of life to him, so he eats out whenever possible. As he himself admits, his desire to be a chef came from his enjoyment of eating in restaurants. He entered the business by the front door, rather than the more traditional route! His preference is for places of similar standard to his own, but he also enjoys Chinese restaurants or wine bars, where good quality food is served, matched by interesting or unusual wines.

Stephen's advice for youngsters entering the industry is to eat out at every opportunity, and to learn and to work with food as often as possible. You also need to be prepared for long exhausting hours. Concerning the industry, he thinks there is a great future for the more casual restaurant which offers excellent quality and good value for money.

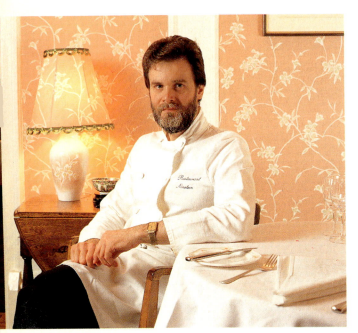

Stephen Smith
Restaurant Nineteen
19 North Park Road
Heaton
Bradford
West Yorkshire BD9 4NT

Keith Stanley's parents were involved in the restaurant business, and as a boy Keith would help them out by washing pots, pans and plates for extra pocket money. He did a two-year course at Birmingham College of Food, and then went to London for an extended apprenticeship at the Savoy Hotel. He was there for a total of twelve years, finally as maître chef des cuisines, and in December 1987 he moved across to the Ritz Hotel as head chef.

Keith describes his original style as classical, but the major turning point came during 1984–86 when he did a 'stage' in Paris and found lighter food for the new market. Similarly, in 1983 when in charge of the Grill Room at The Savoy, he had had to re-educate the established clientele towards a slightly lighter approach.

A very unselfish chef, Keith lists as one of his pleasures seeing someone who is working with him produce a better product than his own. For relaxation he enjoys simple, regional food. Good Chinese restaurants also fit the bill.

Keith Stanley
The Ritz Hotel
Piccadilly
London W1V 9DG
01-493 8181

A chef's curriculum vitae tends usually to be a lengthy list of work experience. Not so for Rick Stein – his is short and sweet. He worked for six months for British Transport Hotels as a management trainee at the Great Western Hotel, Paddington, and then went on to obtain a degree in English at Oxford University. And that's that.

Rick's charming restaurant with rooms, The Seafood at Padstow, was, in a sense, prompted by childhood memories. His parents had a holiday home in Cornwall and his father was part-owner of a fishing boat. At home there was always a plentiful supply of fresh fish, cooked simply and effectively by his mother, a completely natural cook. Thirteen years ago, Rick bought an old granary on the quayside at Padstow, which was operating as a night club for over-indulgent local fishermen. Gradually, the transition to restaurant took place and resulted in the spacious, airy room we find today, pepped up with art posters and plants which lend a contemporary feel to an otherwise cobbled and cottagey Cornish port.

Rick reckoned that serving fresh fish at the seaside would hold a romantic appeal if the surroundings were right and the quality of the produce assured. Among the original dishes still offered today are his own version of fish and chips using sea-bass, and plain grilled lobster. Since the early days, Rick has noticed a distinct improvement in the quality of his fish supply and in the imaginative response of his clientele which allows him, increasingly to make use of the more unusual finds in the nets.

Over the years Rick has evolved an individual style and has even ventured into the world of books by writing his *English Seafood Cookery*. This was intended to chart the development of a seafood culinary tradition in the UK, but in the final analysis only served to point out the distinct lack of one.

He finds it sad to admit that even with such marvellous resources right on their own quaysides, the Cornish have never fully exploited their gleaming, slippery treasure in this way.

Location and background have given Rick Stein a certain isolated resilience to the faddish aspects of cooking. Nevertheless, he counts Mosimann and Blanc among his peers – the latter he thinks is a true original, and a great source of inspiration. However, Rick's ultimate satisfaction is nearer to home. Developing a new recipe and seeing it work gives him the greatest pleasure. He's just acquired a new charcoal grill and was thrilled at having devised a blend of fresh herbs, lime juice and anchovy into a Thai-style sauce to accompany grilled Dover sole. The thrill he claims, is in working things out for yourself.

RICHARD STEIN
The Seafood Restaurant
Riverside
Padstow
Cornwall PL28 8BY
(0841) 532485

135

Sonia *Stevenson*

Sonia Stevenson went into the restaurant business 'out of sheer necessity', and if that quality is the mother of invention then Sonia has certainly invented some stunning meals at The Horn of Plenty. She had no formal training, and started off by doing exactly what she is doing now, but with the addition of twenty years' experience of the job plus the discovery of many new tastes along the way. Sonia is particularly proud that, despite the absence of formal training, she is a Master Chef of Great Britain. She stresses that she has never followed fashion, and nouvelle cuisine, for example, never had a chance at the Horn. Now it has passed by and no-one in Gulworthy has missed it. Her cooking encompasses both delicate haute cuisine dishes and the splendidly robust country and family-style dishes.

Patrick and Sonia Stevenson were both professional musicians when they met – she a violinist, he a singer – and she sees a lot of similarities between the art forms of music and food – they are ephemeral, you create them once and then they are gone leaving only memories. It was Patrick who encouraged her early experiments with cooking, eating out at top London restaurants in the '50s and '60s, patiently waiting whilst Sonia determinedly asked chefs – at Boulestin, and La Réserve, for instance – for the innermost secrets of their recipes. It was Patrick who found The Horn of Plenty in 1967 and persuaded Sonia that she was good enough to cook for it. He was absolutely right, and public and press acclaim followed. In the 1980s, the restaurant added rooms and thus even more comforts to be enjoyed under the Stevenson roof. Sonia says, 'we feel the peace and comfort of our rooms, enhanced by the glorious views from our situation high up above the Tamar valley, are unsurpassed.' Yet she sometimes still feels that the kitchen life is a hard one for women – not just from the point of view of strength.

There is still a slight tendency to see women's cooking in the traditional, domestic role; and most of the top professionals are men. Happily, Sonia Stevenson is one of a few exceptions to that rule.

SONIA STEVENSON
The Horn of Plenty
Gulworthy
Tavistock
Devon PL19 8JD
(0822) 832528

Chris Suter

A career in catering was the obvious choice for a publican's son whose hopes of playing professional football were not to be realised. From 1981 to 1983 Chris was an apprentice at the Beeton Restaurant in Cheshire and attended a local college on day release.

In 1984 he went to The Cumberland hotel as commis tournent. He then worked under Louis Outhier as first commis chef at 90 Park Lane, specialising in the preparation of fish dishes. He then went as demi chef and later chef de partie at Ettington Park, under Barry Forster and Michael Quinn. Prior to his present position at Bishopstow House, he spent seventeen months as sous chef and then head chef at Ménage à Trois, where he worked with Antony Worrall-Thompson. It was this experience that he found most inspiring and his starters and puddings owe a great deal to this period. He says he particularly admires the unfussy style of Nico Ladenis's main courses. As he is still so young he feels his style is still progressing and changing continually, so much so that he neither can nor would wish to categorise it.

CHRIS SUTER
Bishopstrow House
Warminster
Wiltshire BA12 9HH
(0985) 212312

DONATO SEPE
Ville Estense
642 King's Road
London SW6 2DU
01-731 4247

RAYMOND SHARP
Kirkby Fleetham Hall
Kirkby Fleetham
Northallerton
North Yorkshire DL7 OSU
(0609) 748226

DAVID SHEPHERD
Lewtrenchard Manor
Lewtrenchard
Lewdown
Near Okehampton
Devon EX20 4PN
(056 683) 256

ADAM SHERIF
Simpson's-in-the-Strand
100 The Strand
London WC2R OEW
01-836 9112

DAVID SHUTTLEWORTH
Corney & Barrow
109 Old Broad Street
London EC2N 1AP
01-638 9308

JOE SILK
The English House Restaurant
3 Milner Street
London SW3 1QA
01-584 3002

FRANCESCO SIMAO
The Butcher's Arms
Prior's Hardwick
Near Rugby
Warwickshire CV23 8SN
(0327) 60504

GUY SIMONITSCH
Number Ten
10 Pembridge Road
London W11 3HL
01-727 0320

WILLIAM ALEXANDER SIMPSON
The Rogano
11 Exchange Place
Glasgow
Strathclyde G1 3AN
041-248 4055

JAMES SINES
High Moor Restaurant
High Moor Lane
Wrightington Near Wigan
Lancashire WN6 9QA
(025 75) 2364

DICK SMITH
The White House Hotel & Restaurant
Williton
Somerset TA4 4QW
(0984) 32306

CLIVE SOUTHGATE
Moore Place
The Square
Aspley Guise Near Woburn
Bedfordshire MK17 8DW
(0908) 282000

SHIRLEY SPEAR
Three Chimneys
Colbost
Dunvegan Isle of Skye
Highland IV51 9SY
(047 081) 258

IAN STABLER
RSJ Restaurant
13a Coin Street
London SE1 8YQ
01-928 4554

EDWARD STEPHENS
The Greenway
Shurdington
Cheltenham
Gloucestershire GL51 5UG
(0242) 862352

ROBIN STEWART
Corney & Barrow
118 Moorgate
London EC2M 6UR
01-628 2898

NEIL STOTT
Otters
271 New King's Road
London SW6 4RD
01-371 0434

PETER SULLIVAN
The Opera Terrace
45 East Terrace
Central Avenue
Covent Garden
London WC2 8RS
01-379 0666

FREDA SUNLEY
Mustards Smithfield Brasserie
60 Long Lane
London EC1A 9EJ
01-796 4920

Bob Tansley

Bob Tansley is one of those gifted amateur cooks with no professional training, who burst onto the scene in the late '60s and have survived all the trends and vagaries of fashion since then. He says he just loves restaurants, so it was natural for him to work in one. He held two other establishments as tenancies, both in Worcestershire, before finally becoming owner and chef/patron at Brown's in 1980.

Bob describes his early style as 'casseroles and garlic bread', but his current style is lighter and fresher. He gains most pleasure from cooking fish, and aims simply to give his customers what they want.

His favourite restaurant in Britain is La Tante Claire in London, and after that he loves the restaurants of Paris. A man of simple tastes!

BOB TANSLEY
Brown's Restaurant
The Old Cornmill
South Quay
Worcester
Hereford & Worcester WR1 2JJ
(0905) 26263

Franco Taruschio

Franco Taruschio was born in Montefano, Italy, and went into the restaurant business because the catering industry was one of the few in Italy in 1958 that offered the opportunity of proper training with only a grammar school education. Following hotel school in Bellagio, Lake Como, he was sent as a commis to various establishments in Italy, Switzerland and France for experience.

He came to England in 1961, full of ambition and energy and spent two years as restaurant manager at the Three Horseshoes Hotel in Rugby before buying the Walnut Tree Inn, in the process spending all his money bar 3/9d! With his young wife Ann, Franco struggled very hard in the early days to carve out a living. But gradually, word spread and Franco was lucky to benefit from an influx of Italians into South Wales which meant a ready-made clientele, and secondly from a new awareness of Mediterranean cuisine thanks to Elizabeth David. He began by cooking French as well as Italian food, but is now happy to be styled modern European, adapted to the rural area in which he lives and making as much use as possible of local produce.

He still gets a tremendous buzz from the adrenalin running just before service. Otherwise, for his own pleasure he favours eating Oriental foods, particularly Thai.

FRANCO TARUSCHIO
Walnut Tree Inn
Llandewi Skirrid
Abergavenny
Gwent NP7 8AW
(0873) 2797

Paul Teal

Paul Teal went into catering in order to travel and experience a variety of ways of life. And he has certainly done that!

In preparation for his odyssey he did all the usual training, starting with domestic science at school and weekend work in local hotels, butcher's and nightclubs. He is certain that college does not prepare a student for what life in the catering trade is really like – that can only be discovered by living it.

After college Paul worked at two hotels in London – The Inn on the Park and The Berkeley – before setting off on his travels, which to date have taken him to Denmark, Sweden, Australia, New Zealand, Scotland, Bermuda and New York. He returned to London in 1984, and before his feet were firmly on dry land, he took a job aboard RS Hispaniola, moored by Victoria Embankment. He then spent two years at Inigo Jones in Covent Garden, a period of great influence on his otherwise cosmopolitan repertoire. Since 1987 he has been head chef at Dan's in Sydney Street.

Paul loves cooking at home for small numbers of friends, and meeting the almost endless array of characters within the trade.

PAUL TEAL
Dan's Restaurant & Garden
119 Sydney Street
London SW3 6NR
01-352 2718

Robert Thornton

After attending Hollings College Manchester for a two-year course, Robert Thornton served an apprenticeship at The Grosvenor House Hotel and did a day-release course at Westminster College. In 1971 he went to Germany as saucier at the Bayerischer Hof in München. The following winter he spent in Switzerland as gardemanger at the Darvos Schweizerhof.

In 1974 he returned to Manchester to help open the family restaurant and after one more tour of Switzerland and a brief sojourn in Berlin, Robert settled back into Manchester.

His experiences in Europe, particularly Switzerland, have been very influential on his style of cookery, which he describes as French. He particularly enjoys using fish, for its versatility.

ROBERT THORNTON
The Moss Nook Restaurant
Ringway Road
Moss Nook
Manchester M22 5NH
01-437 4778

Carla Tomasi

Ken Toye

Michael Truelove

Carla Tomasi describes herself as self-taught apart from a short course at Leith's School of Food and Wine. But the lack of formal training does not seem to have held her back at all, from her beginnings as a free-lance cook in her native Italy, to her present restaurant in Soho.

Carla says it was a challenge to come to a foreign country and establish herself here. Cooking was the best way she knew to make a living, and she wanted to see if there was a market for her ideas and abilities. She started at the Neal Street Restaurant, moving to Frith's in 1984, where she worked as a pastry chef for just three months before taking over the kitchens and, in 1987, buying the restaurant.

Carla's basic style has not really changed since she started out –her approach is to keep it simple, and to achieve an intensity of flavour by using good quality ingredients. She likes to serve very light food, and the menu changes constantly, offering a wide variety of dishes.

Carla loves to see people coming back into her restaurant time after time. When she isn't there on duty herself (which isn't often) she either eats at restaurants with a style similar to her own, or at Thai or Vietnamese restaurants.

CARLA TOMASI
Frith's
14 Frith Street
London W1V 5TS
01-439 3370

As the name of his restaurant in St Helen's Street, Ipswich, clearly implies, Ken Toye offers his customers a little more than the French regional cuisine in which he specialises as chef – he sings to them, too.

The Toyes started The Singing Chef nearly thirty years ago in Connaught Street as a small family concern with Ken in the kitchen and Cynthia front-of-house. Ken's philosophy is that it is the simplest dishes, that rely upon absolutely fresh, quality produce, which are the hardest to achieve yet the most enjoyable to eat. His menus take a new French region each month – no nouvelle cuisine, just honest, regional French food and good wines. Among his favourite dishes are bouillabaisse pêcheur (from fresh North Sea fish), carré d'agneau aux aromâtes, cassoulet de Castelnaundry, and his speciality omelette soufflée flambée.

The Singing Chef owes its success as much to the personality of the Toyes as to the unpretentious excellence of Ken's cuisine. 'We like our customers and many of them become friends,' he says. It is the sort of place you might choose for a fun evening with friends, and come away with equal praise for the food and the atmosphere that owners and customers create together.

KENNETH TOYE
The Singing Chef
200 St Helen's Street
Ipswich
Suffolk IP4 2RH
(0473) 55236

Michael Truelove was attracted by the whole lifestyle of the catering trade, and thrives on the unconventional hours and routines. His first job was as a humble kitchen porter, but he gained a transfer to a post as trainee chef – at the Post House Hotel just outside Leeds in his native Yorkshire. He was impressed by the pride taken in all jobs by all departments of the hotel, and this set him firmly on his future path.

Michael did most of his training on day release to the Thomas Danby College, followed by health and hygiene courses at Leeds Polytechnic. He then worked for seven years in one of the best restaurants in the county, the Box Tree at Ilkley, during which time it maintained all its Guide

ratings. Moving on to the Gleneagles Hotel in Scotland, he was well placed in the Prix Pierre Taittinger competition. Since 1987 he has been head chef at Crabwall Manor.

Originally his style was classical French. However, when modern trends came over from France, Michael followed suit. He most enjoys teaching others what he has learned himself, particularly in the fields of pastrywork and bakery. For him, France offers the best establishments for eating out.

MICHAEL TRUELOVE
Crabwall Manor
Mollington
Chester
Cheshire CH1 6NE
(0244) 851666

IVAN TANNIAN
Café St Pierre
29 Clerkenwell Green
London EC1R ODU
01-251 6606

MICHAEL TAYLOR
Bath Lodge
Norton St Phillip
Near Bath
Somerset BA3 6NH
(022 122) 3737

SIMON TENNET
Fisherman's Wharf
15 The Side
Newcastle-upon-Tyne
Tyne & Wear
091-232 1057

RICHARD THIEL
Steph's
39 Dean Street
London W1V 5AP
01-734 5976

KIRK THOMAS
The Copperfield Restaurant
49 Buxton Old Road
Disley
Near Stockport
Cheshire
(0663) 64333

PHILIPPE THYS
Luc's Restaurant & Brasserie
17-22 Leadenhall Market
London EC3V 1LR
01-621 0666

F TOMASSI
Poissonerie de l'Avenue
82 Sloane Avenue
London SW3 3DZ
01-589 2457

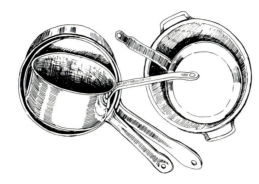

J'EAMTARVORN TONGCHAI
Deals
Harbour Yard
Chelsea Harbour
London SW10 OXD
01-376 3232

CHERYL TONKS
**Aval Du Creux Hotel
& Restaurant**
Sark
Channel Islands
(0481) 832036

JANET TOWER
The Twenty One
21 Charlotte Street
Brighton
East Sussex BN2 1AG
(0273) 686450

BRIAN TURNER
**The English Garden
Restaurant**
10 Lincoln Street
London SW3 2TS
01-584 7272

SUE TYAS
Over the Bridge Restaurant
Millfold
Ripponden
Near Halifax
West Yorkshire HX6 4DL
(0422) 823722

ANN TYNAN
Number Three
3 Magdelene Street
Glastonbury
Somerset BA6 9EW
(0458) 32129

RICHARD UTIN
Colleys Supper Rooms
High Street
Lechlade
Gloucestershire GL7 3AZ
(0367) 52218

MARGARET VAN VEELEN
Fifehead Manor
Middle Walop
Near Stockbridge
Hampshire SO20 8EG
(0264) 781565

PHILIPPE VANDEWALLE
Le Poulbot
45 Cheapside
London EC2V 6AR
01-236 4379

MARCO VESSALIO
Marco's Restaurant
17 Pottergate
Norwich
Norfolk NR2 1DS
(0508) 4424

Brian Turner

Brian Turner was born in Halifax. His father, who owned a transport cafe in Leeds, was a tremendous influence. Most of his school holidays and Saturday mornings were spent helping out. He attended Morley Grammar School where he was taught by the same domestic science teacher as a famous predecessor: Michael Smith, the late doyen of the English food scene. Encouraged by his teacher and by Michael, Brian took a general cookery course at Leeds Technical College (1962-1964), which was a combination of cooking and service. He left with a City & Guilds qualification, and a College Diploma in Waiting, and a college reference to the effect that he was a good manager, but not a good cook!

Determined to prove the College wrong, he applied to The Savoy, but had to wait two years for an appointment. In the meantime, he worked at Simpson's-in-the-Strand, and remembers well, on his first day, bumping into a young man who was to become one of his closest friends, Richard Shepherd. Richard was transferred to The Savoy in 1965 and Brian was relentless in his requests to follow suit. The move came early in 1967, and he spent the following two years working in the Grill kitchens under Louis Virot, of whom he has fond and grateful memories. He managed to combine his work at The Savoy with part-time study for the HCIMA examination.

In 1969 he spent four months with Dieter Sondermann at St Ermin's Hotel. In 1970 he joined Claridge's as chef tournant, and from there Richard Shepherd asked him to join The Capital Hotel as his sous chef. After a year, Brian decided that the teaching life was for him and spent the next twelve months as a lecturer at South East London Technical College. Meanwhile, Richard's department at The Capital was missing him, and as Brian was also missing the 'smell of the greasepaint', he was more than happy to return. Subsequently, Richard left for Langan's, and Brian took over at The Capital. In 1983 he opened the Metro Bar for David Levin, adjacent to The Capital and under its umbrella. It instantly won the AA's Wine Bar of the Year Award and the following year the London Section of the same competition.

In August 1986 he left The Capital, and in the October of that year he opened Turner's in Walton Street. As chef/patron he and his restaurant have won the acclaim of customers and critics alike, serving the finest ingredients in his own personalised and skilful recipes.

On his menu you might expect to find a starter of brandade of sole – two quenelle-shaped spoonfuls of light mousse of puréed Dover sole, potatoes, garlic and cream – served on a salad of haricots verts, followed by a main course of traditional French-style rack of lamb, roasted in a herb and breadcrumb crust.

In Autumn 1989, while remaining at Turner's, Brian opened Café Sud-Ouest and Restaurant Sud-Ouest at the south-west corner of Harrods.

Brian holds strong views about the state of education in catering, saying that there is more education in the kitchen than in colleges, possibly because there are more people in kitchens with a vested interest in propagating and perpetuating their skills and tradition. Consequently, he is active in his resolve to recruit school leavers into the profession. He is called upon regularly to judge college examinations and national events. He has been invited to join the panels of judges for the British Chef's Scholarship (1989/90) which is jointly sponsored by the Roux Brothers and Diner's Club, as well as the Académie Culinaire's Annual Awards of Excellence. In addition, he is a member of the Restaurateurs' Association of Great Britain and a Fellow of the HCIMA.

Brian is a no-nonsense Yorkshireman who likes all types of food but chooses according to his mood, and with a well-timed sense of humour to complement his extrovert tendencies, is a popular figure. As he says, 'What I like best is what I do best.' He also claims a broad taste in music, from brass to classical.

BRIAN TURNER
Turner's
87 Walton Street
London SW3 2HP
01-584 6711

143

Alan Vickops   Karl Wadsack

Alan Vickops was born in Kent. He completed a two-year full-time City & Guilds course at Thanet Technical College, and in 1974 he was employed as commis chef in Eugene Kaufeler's 135-strong brigade at The Dorchester. Alan stayed until 1981, rising to senior chef de partie, before moving on to The Ritz as Michael Quinn's second sous chef. In 1983 he joined the County Hotel in Canterbury as head chef, where he stayed until 1986 when he went to his present post at Alverton Manor.

Alan says that his style runs the whole gamut of classical to modern, and that it developed during his time with Anton Mosimann at The Dorchester. Canon of West Country lamb, deep-fried in a thin veil of strudel pastry with madeira sauce and nests of raspberries is one dish which reflects his style.

Alan tries to eat out at most of the good restaurants of the country house, or at the very best Asian establishments. He is mad about golf, but when not playing or cooking he simply enjoys the countryside.

ALAN VICKOPS
Alverton Manor
Tregolls Road
Truro
Cornwall TR1 1XQ
(0872) 76633

Karl Wadsack was born in Hanover, and trained there at the Hotel Regina. However, work was hard to find after the war and he wanted to see the world, so spent his first two cooking years on luxury liners, cruising the Americas, the Atlantic and the Caribbean, and sometimes staying ashore for a while to gain more culinary experience. It was during a sojourn in Sweden that he met his wife, June.

In 1966 he came to England, to the Lake District, where he worked at the Wild Boar Hotel, a 16th-century coaching inn, primarily to learn English. He was head chef there for three years. In 1969 he joined Trusthouse Forte, and for them he opened the St George's Hotel in Liverpool. In 1973 he moved on, to Quaglino's for three years, then two more at Chewton Glen. Finally, in 1978, he and June bought the Three Lions and opened their own business.

His style was originally classical but is now eclectic, lighter and more healthy. For instance, he does not have a frier, but makes great use of his steamer. He believes in decent-sized portions – as do his customers! He obtains good fresh fish from Poole and Brixham, and this is always a popular feature on his extensive, but freshly cooked menu.

He pays tribute to June's role in the team, working at front of house, training staff and buying the wine; and when they eat out, he likes to try something that he does not himself cook.

KARL WADSACK
The Three Lions
Stuckton Road
Stuckton
Fordingbridge
Hampshire SP6 2HF
(0425) 52489

ALAN WADE
MacDuff's
112 Killeague Road
Blackhill
Coleraine Co Londonderry BT51 4HH
(0265) 868433

NIGEL WALLIS
The Old Beams Restaurant
Leek Road
Waterhouses Staffordshire ST10 3HW
(0538) 308254

BERNARD WARNE
The Wordsworth Hotel
Grasmere
Near Ambleside Cumbria LA22 9SW
(096 65) 592

DENIS WATKINS
Angel Inn
Hetton
Near Skipton North Yorkshire BD23 6LT
(075 673) 263

CHRIS WELLINGTON
L'Hérisson
8a The High Street London SW19
01-947 6477

ELSIE WENLOCK
Weston Park
Shifnal Shropshire TF11 8LE
(095 276) 201

Richard Walton

Bruce Wass

David Watson

Richard Walton originally wanted to be manager of The Savoy Hotel and actually spent five years training to do so. But then he was packed off, as he puts it, into the kitchens of Beau Rivage in north west London, and found happiness there. Next he spent about a year at Robert Carrier's restaurant in Islington, before branching out and buying Chez Moi, with the then manager of Carrier's. He begged, borrowed and even sold his beloved sportscar to raise the money. It is this kind of tenacity that has held him there after twenty-three years!

Richard learned with Robert Carrier that it is not a sin to be adventurous in cooking, that inventiveness was a positive asset. He says he is still learning all the time, as new ingredient, and new trends appear on the scene. He loves introducing new dishes acquired during travels round the world, and when eating out he prefers Japanese and Chinese cuisines.

Richard's tips for anyone entering the industry would be that they should try to convert an interest and understanding into a personal 'philosophy' of taste and presentation. He also recommends that you realise that cooking will be a time-consuming occupation, possibly to the exclusion of everything else. Should you want to open your own restaurant, be prepared to be chef, psychologist, plumber, electrician, decorator, gas fitter and general dogsbody! But most of all, you must enjoy it!

Richard Walton
Chez Moi
1 Addison Avenue
London W11 4QS
01-603 8267

Cooking is clearly a reciprocal pleasure. People love to eat, and good chefs derive consummate pleasure from providing the wherewithal. Certainly this is the case for Bruce Wass, who has been running his own restaurant, Thackeray's House, for the last five years or so. Set back from the main road, this attractive green-painted clapboard building was once home to William Makepeace Thackeray. Nowadays, the interior is wonderfully elegant with its mix of polished silver, gilt mirrors, fresh flowers and a delightfully catholic selection of old prints and pictures. It comes as no surprise to learn that Wass previously worked as head chef at Odin's in London, where Peter Langan's wildly diverse tastes in art lined every available inch of wall space.

But this is all a far cry from Bruce Wass's humble start, an apprenticeship at London's Hyde Park Hotel. Spells in other West End bastions of classical cookery followed: Quaglino's, the Mirabelle, Claridge's and The Savoy, to name but a few. At Thackeray's, Bruce now reckons to be far more in tune with his customers' wishes. He's allied his classical background to a lighter, more contemporary style that's less formulaic.

So what does Bruce look for when he goes out to eat? Unfussy food with good flavours in a relaxed environment. Apparently, a visit earlier this year to the Walnut Tree at Abergavenny fitted the bill perfectly. He only wishes he lived nearer. However, the citizens of Tunbridge Wells will be glad that he does not!

Bruce Wass
Thackeray's House Restaurant
85 London Road
Tunbridge Wells
Kent TN11 1EA
(0892) 511921

A young Yorkshireman, David Watson couldn't make it as a professional footballer, and wasn't mechanically minded, but found cooking to be the answer to his problems. He began as a waiter in a pub near Thirsk, and progressed to the kitchens, working there all the time he was at Technical College in Scarborough doing his City & Guilds.

David rounded his training off with some work experience in Frankfurt before going to London, where he worked at The Hyatt Carlton Tower, Rue St Jacques and Waltons Restaurant. He returned to Yorkshire in 1989 as head chef at Pool Court.

David describes his cooking as international, based on classical French but with modern overtones. He loves seeing happy customers as well as a happy brigade. He enjoys eating any food, at any establishment, provided it's good, from the local chip shop to a Michelin-starred restaurant.

David Watson
Pool Court Restaurant
Pool-in-Wharfedale
Otley
West Yorkshire LS21 1EH
(0532) 842288

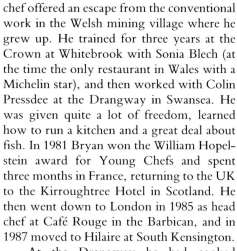
Bryan had always wanted to cook – being a chef offered an escape from the conventional work in the Welsh mining village where he grew up. He trained for three years at the Crown at Whitebrook with Sonia Blech (at the time the only restaurant in Wales with a Michelin star), and then worked with Colin Pressdee at the Drangway in Swansea. He was given quite a lot of freedom, learned how to run a kitchen and a great deal about fish. In 1981 Bryan won the William Hopelstein award for Young Chefs and spent three months in France, returning to the UK to the Kirroughtree Hotel in Scotland. He then went down to London in 1985 as head chef at Café Rouge in the Barbican, and in 1987 moved to Hilaire at South Kensington.

At the Drangway he had cooked nouvelle cuisine using lots of fish, especially with beurre blanc and sauce vierge, his two favourite sauces, But at lunchtime there was always a demand for roasts and pies, so he kept his hand in on these substantial standbys which are of use to him now at Hilaire, where he cooks simple, good tasting food without too much garnishing.

Bryan is content if he has served fifty dinners smoothly, with every dish that leaves the kitchen meeting his standards. He also enjoys eating out at any of the top restaurants in London, or the chef's old faithful, ethnic restaurants. In France, his favourite is the Bonne Auberge at Clisson – because it is simple, not too expensive, and the food is excellent. The criteria he applies at Hilaire.

BRYAN WEBB
Hilaire
68 Old Brompton Road
London SW7 3LQ
01-584 8993

PAULINE WEST
Bark House Hotel
Oakfordbridge
Bampton Near Tiverton
Devon EX16 9HZ
(039 85) 236

ALAN WHITE
**City Limits Restaurant
& Wine Bar**
16-18 Brushfield Street
London E1 6AN
01-377 9877

DAVID WHITFIELD
The Lake Isle
16 High Street East
Uppingham
Leicestershire LE15 9PL
(0572) 822951

KENNY WHYTE
Kildrummy Castle Hotel
Kildrummy
Alford
Aberdeenshire AB3 8RA
(097 55) 71288

GERD WIFFEMAN
La Brasserie Highgate
1 Hampstead Lane
London N6 4RS
01-341 9736

DAVID WILKINSON
Arisaig House
Beasdale
Arisaig
Inverness-shire PH39 4NR
(068 75) 622

WILLIAM WILLCROFT
Brasserie St Pierre
53-57 Princes Street
Manchester
Greater Manchester M2 4EQ
061-491 3609

DAVID WILLIAMS
La Belle Epoque
60 King Street
Knutsford
Cheshire WA16 2DT
(0565) 3060

JOHN WILLIAMS
Beechfield House
Beanacre
Near Melksham
Wiltshire SN12 7PU
(0225) 703700

MARTIN WILSON
The Old Inn
15 Main Street
Crawfordsburn
Co Down BT19 1JH
(0247) 853255

MARTIN WILSON
Orso Restaurant
27 Wellington Street
London WC2E 7DA
01-240 5269

PETER WILSON
**Langley House Hotel
& Restaurant**
Langley Marsh
Wiveliscombe
Near Taunton
Somerset TA4 2UF
(0984) 23318

JIM WINDLE
**The Bear Hotel
& Restaurant**
Park Street
Woodstock
Oxfordshire OX7 1SZ
(0993) 811511

ALLAN WITHERICK
Feldon House
Lower Brailes
Nr Banbury
Oxfordshire OX15 5HW
(060 885) 580

PETER WOOD
Solberge Hall
Newby Wiske
Northallerton
North Yorkshire DL7 9ER
(0609) 779191

DAVID WOOLFALL
Teignworthy
Frenchbeer
Chagford
Devon TQ13 8EX
(064 73) 3355

HEINZ WORZ
Rossetti
23 Queen's Grove
London NW8 6PR
01-722 7141

We cannot improve on Colin White's own letter to us, so here it is in full:

'I almost fell into this industry, having left school at fifteen with no regrets but no qualifications either. As an apprentice diet cook at a local hospital, I had good training in butchery, bakery, dietetics – not so today, I fear! – plus day release to take the City & Guilds exams. Best of all, it gave me civilised working hours and the free time in which to indulge my hobbies of climbing, photography and music.

'At the age of twenty-one I applied to Sharrow Bay for the post of "perfectionist young chef", and hotel work under Francis Coulson changed my life irrevocably. The satisfaction was enormous, but the hobbies soon fell by the wayside. And to think I chose Sharrow Bay partly for its location in the fells!

'I really started to learn when I ventured out on my own in the early 1970s, and many painful lessons there were on the business side. But my cooking got better and better, because it mattered so much to the success of the venture. My philosophy on food has always been to buy the best, prepare it meticulously and not muck about with it. I want harmony in my life and harmony in my food. As for the increasing insistence on certificates to prove a youngster's worth . . . if the college days of today's

youth equate with my hospital days, then they serve a purpose, but don't let's kid ourselves that the vast majority of colleges will teach anything meaningful at a practical level. Colleges need to place much greater emphasis on practical experience in the top echelons of the industry. If all youngsters could experience at first-hand the stimulation of working with the best materials, under the best chefs, perhaps fewer of them would settle for second best, swelling the drop-out rate.

'On current trends, I abhor the media hype which has encouraged . . . over-elaborate food, arrogant proprietors and staff, and bills that border on sharp practice. . . Is it no longer enough to sell good honest food, at sensible prices, in pleasant surroundings?'

COLIN WHITE
White's Restaurant
93 High Street
Cricklade
Nr Swindon
Wiltshire SN6 6DF
(0793) 751110

David Wilson is a member of the Scottish Olympic Cookery Team. He has already won seventeen awards for his confectionery works. He particularly enjoys working with sugar and says that party making is his forté. However, running a very successful hotel kitchen doesn't permit him the opportunity for the creativity he would enjoy.

As an advocate of the service industry as a whole, and the 'up-market' sector in particular, and with his artistic talent, he decided upon a career in quality catering.

He attended college on day release from a Scottish hotel, his first place of work, and then in 1982 went to The Inn on the Park in London for two years. He joined Blake's Hotel in 1984 as sous chef and was pastry chef there before becoming head chef in 1988.

DAVID WILSON
Blake's Hotel
33 Roland Gardens
London SW7 3PF
01-370 6701

SAMI YOUSSEF
L'Auberge
44 Forest Hill Road London SE22 0RR
01-299 2211

UWE ZANDER
Sheraton Skyline Hotel
Heathrow Airport Middlesex
01-759 2535

RAYMOND ZARB
Le Cèdre Restaurant
Walford House Hotel
Walford
Ross-on-Wye
Hereford & Worcester HR6 5RY
(0989) 63829

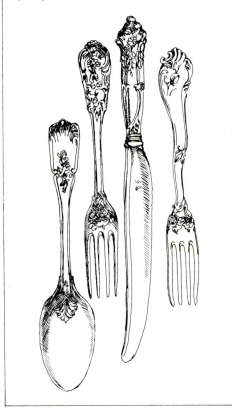

A background in marketing at Rio Tinto Zinc might not seem an ideal basis from which to start a restaurant, but a mixture of that, Patricia Wilson's textile design degree from Glasgow School of Art, a love of food and a general disappointment in standards of eating out, is the fount of David Wilson's success at the Peat Inn.

At the age of thirty he took the plunge, and started as a commis in the kitchen of Somerset Moore at The Pheasant, at Keystone in Huntingdon. This was doubly brave, as his wife had just given up work to have their first child! Not only did David learn about the basics of cooking but Moore gave him a complete grounding in the whole trade, from doing the books to working front of house. Two years later, in 1972, the Wilsons moved back up to Scotland, to The Peat Inn.

David Wilson has created a culinary mecca in this apparent backwater. The first Scot for a decade to gain a Michelin rosette, David is the man responsible for the renaissance in awareness of the quality of home-produced materials – white truffles, fresh herbs, fine delicate vegetables and the turning of the humble pigeon into a gastronomic treat. Over the years his style has changed from 'good British cooking', to what he now describes as 'modern French cooking'. Regular trips to France - eating in three-star places and sometimes working in them too – have been an important influence. Vergé and Guérard are well-known mentors, but today David also rates very highly a young chef working in Cannes called Jacques Chibois. Other influences come from books, and a small band of like-minded chefs and restaurateurs in Scotland. As for his own tastes when eating out? 'Every good restaurant in or near our base, and planned trips to the best. Japanese and any other cuisine, if it is well done.'

DAVID WILSON
The Peat Inn
Cupar
Fife KY15 5LH
(033 484) 206

THE·PEAT·INN

149

Antony Worrall-Thompson

Antony Worrall-Thompson was born to 'theatrical' parents in Stratford-upon-Avon. He boasts a public school education, with eleven 'O' levels and four 'A' levels to his credit. In 1969 he enrolled at Westminster College, leaving in 1971 with an HND in Hotel and Catering Management. Shortly afterwards, he left for Kenya and six months' VSO, returning in 1972 to Coombe Lodge Hotel in Essex as Food and Beverage Manager, and then later in the same year moving to the Golden Fleece Restaurant, Brentwood, as head chef/ manager. It was probably at about this time that he realised that cooking was his true vocation. In 1974 he became head chef at Ye Olde Logge in Brentwood; then in 1976 at the Adriatico Restaurant in Woodland Green; and in 1977 at Hedges Restaurant in South Woodford.

Disenchanted with rural life, Tony moved to London in September 1978 to become sous chef at Brinkley's Restaurant, just off Fulham Road, and head chef one month later. He took himself off on six months' 'educational sabbatical' in 1979, touring France, eating and working in three-star establishments with the likes of Bocuse, Troisgros, Pic, et al.

Then Antony returned to Brinkley's, resuming his position as head chef, and changing the menus according to his experience gained in France. Next stop was Dan's Restaurant in Chelsea where, as head chef in 1980, he changed its character from café to haute cuisine, propelling its image into the pages of glossy magazines and Sunday supplements.

In 1981 he was presented with a challenging financial partnership in Ménage à Trois in Knightsbridge, which he opened to 'abundant publicity and reviews: it was the only restaurant in London to serve only starters and puddings'.

He and Ménage have been profusely

written about. Antony claims that he and his restaurant, which appeared to cater solely for the rich, thin and precious (at least according to the media) became something of a culinary joke to his peers. He is virtually self-taught (not a worthy quality in his colleagues' estimation) and his cooking is eclectic to the point of eccentricity. He is an enthusiastic and colourful exponent of the filo pastry parcel, which might contain anything – goat's cheese, a spicy duck mixture, caviar, or something *very* chocolatey, and are always served in trios.

Since 1981, Antony has spread his wings beyond Ménage à Trois to take on consultancies in restaurants in Bombay, with the Taj Hotel Group; in Melbourne, Australia, with a private backer; and in New York again with the Taj Group. In addition, he is now consultant and director of food and wine for Ménage.

As if all this was not enough to prove himself in the eyes of his culinary critics, he 'hit the culinary jackpot' in 1987, winning the Mouton Rothschild Menu Competition,

followed by a most prestigious accolade: the Meilleur Ouvrier de Grande Bretagne – the chef's Oscar – which is the Académie Culinaire's competition, held every four years, to find the most talented chefs in the country. In 1989, he represented Great Britain in the Bocuse d'Or, which is a bi-annual competition launched by Paul Bocuse, and fêted by the culinary soul of France itself, attracting not only extensive media coverage but millions of French francs.

In January 1986, Antony opened Mise-en-Place Limited, a factory kitchen to supply his outside catering operation and high quality food shops, such as Harrods and his own KWT Foodshow – an inspired food 'bazaar', which he bought in October 1988. He was also the first chef/patron to be chosen to open and operate the restaurant at One Ninety Queen's Gate, a unique club with an abundance of style, designed exclusively for the restaurant industry.

Nor are Antony's talents restricted to cooking and eating. His powerful imagination and flair for interior design are additional factors contributing to the success of his ventures. He has made several appearances on television, appearing on Breakfast Television and the BBC's *Food and Drink* programme, among others. His book, *The Small and Beautiful Cookbook*, was published by Weidenfeld and Nicholson in 1984, and he is currently writing a second on entertaining, which is due for publication in 1990.

Antony is one of the judges for the Académie Culinaire's 1989/90 Annual Awards of Excellence. He is also a member of the Restaurateurs' Association of Great Britain. Antony feels genuine concern over the problems of recruitment and training. He speaks to students at colleges around the country and offers opportunities to apprentices to work for him.

Despite an extraordinary and energetic professional lifestyle, he does find time for art, antiques and swimming (incidentally, he swam the Channel when he was sixteen), and for his herb garden at his country cottage retreat by the banks of the Thames.

Antony Worrall-Thompson
One Ninety Queen's Gate
190 Queen's Gate
London SW7 5EU
01-581 5666

151

Index

152

D

153

154

T

U

V

ALFRESCO
LEISURE PUBLICATIONS PLC

Alfresco Leisure Publications PLC
35 Tadema Road, London SW10 0PZ

First Published 1990
Copyright © Alfresco Leisure Publications PLC, 1990

Produced and edited by
Alfresco Leisure Publications PLC *with*
Pilot Productions Ltd

Illustrated by Chris Ackerman-Eveleigh
Cover design by Chris Ackerman-Eveleigh
Designed by Malcolm Smythe
Studio work by Keith Shannon
Typeset by Dorchester Typesetting, Dorchester, Dorset
Printed and bound in Hong Kong

Edited by
Roy Ackerman
with contributions from Juliet Fussell, Sara Jayne, Angela Nicholson, Simon Parkes, and Christopher Trotter

Photography by: Leigh Simpson *(except where otherwise stated)*

Sonia Blech   *Picture by* Michael Joseph
Michel Bourdin   *Picture by* Zeno Sbernardori, courtesy of *Caterer & Hotelkeeper*
Philip Britten © Anthony Blake
Beth Coventry   *Picture by* Andrew Whittuck, courtesy of *Good Housekeeping Magazine.*
Gunn Eriksen © Express Newspapers plc
Patricia Hegarty *Picture by* James Merrell, *The Sunday Times Magazine,* © Times Newspapers Limited 1985.

Jim Kerr   *Picture by* Dougie McBride
Nico Ladenis © Anthony Blake
Michel Roux © Martin Brigdale
Michel & Albert Roux © Martin Brigdale
Richard Smith © *Caterer & Hotelkeeper*